Camping Virginia and West Virginia

Help Us Keep This Guide Up to Date

Every effort has been made by the author and editors to make this guide as accurate and useful as possible. However, many things can change after a guide is published—campgrounds open and close, grow and contract; regulations change; techniques evolve; facilities come under new management, and so on.

We appreciate hearing from you concerning your experiences with this guide and how you feel it could be improved and kept up to date. While we may not be able to respond to all comments and suggestions, we'll take them to heart and we'll also make certain to share them with the author. Please send your comments and suggestions to the following address:

FalconGuides
Reader Response/Editorial Department
246 Goose Lane, Suite 200
Guilford, CT 06437

Thanks for your input, and happy travels!

Camping Virginia and West Virginia

A Comprehensive Guide to Public Tent and RV Campgrounds

Second Edition

Desiree Smith-Daughety

FALCONGUIDES

GUILFORD, CONNECTICUT

FALCONGUIDES®

An imprint of Globe Pequot, the trade division of
The Rowman & Littlefield Publishing Group, Inc.
4501 Forbes Blvd., Ste. 200
Lanham, MD 20706
www.rowman.com

Falcon and FalconGuides are registered trademarks and Make Adventure Your Story is a trademark of The Rowman & Littlefield Publishing Group, Inc.

Distributed by NATIONAL BOOK NETWORK

Copyright © 2022 by The Rowman & Littlefield Publishing Group, Inc.

Photos by Desiree Smith-Daughety unless otherwise noted.
Maps by The Rowman & Littlefield Publishing Group, Inc.

British Library Cataloguing-in-Publication Information available

Library of Congress Cataloging-in-Publication Data

Names: Smith-Daughety, Desiree, 1968–, author.
Title: Camping Virginia and West Virginia : a comprehensive guide to public tent and RV campgrounds / Desiree Smith-Daughety.
Description: Second edition. | Lanham : Globe Pequot, [2022] | Series: State camping series | Includes index. | Summary: "A fully updated and revised guide to more than 100 public campgrounds in Virginia and West Virginia for tent and RV campers"—Provided by publisher.
Identifiers: LCCN 2021036228 (print) | LCCN 2021036229 (ebook) | ISBN 9781493043187 (paperback) | ISBN 9781493043194 (epub)
Subjects: LCSH: Camping—Virginia—Guidebooks. | Camping—West Virginia—Guidebooks. | Camp sites, facilities, etc.—Virginia—Guidebooks. | Camp sites, facilities, etc.—West Virginia—Guidebooks. | Recreational vehicle camping—Virginia—Guidebooks. | Recreational vehicle camping—West Virginia—Guidebooks. | Virginia—Guidebooks. | West Virginia—Guidebooks.
Classification: LCC GV191.42.V8 S55 2013 (print) | LCC GV191.42.V8 (ebook) | DDC 917.5068—dc23
LC record available at https://lccn.loc.gov/2021036228
LC ebook record available at https://lccn.loc.gov/2021036229

This book is dedicated to my parents, Robert and Susan, who took me and my sisters, Rachel and Debbie, on Sunday "day" trips and camping trips. They helped create my love for the outdoors and the desire to get outside and "go somewhere." And also, to my grandmother Dorothy, born and raised a Mountaineer. When we traveled together and crossed state lines, we had a tradition of honking the horn and singing "Roll Out the Barrel." To this day I carry on the tradition of honking, despite the puzzled looks of my fellow travelers. Last, but not least, my son, Cameron—the best traveling companion. He has grown to enjoy camping after years of being a youngster with no choice.

Contents

Acknowledgments xiv
How to Use This Guide xv
    Selecting a Campground xvi
Wildlife Encounters xxvi
Map Legend xxix

Introduction to Virginia 1
Heart of Appalachia / Southwest Blue Ridge Highlands Area 12
    Heart of Appalachia Area 13
 1 Breaks Interstate Park 15
 2 Cane Patch Campground 15
 3 Cave Springs Recreation Area 16
 4 High Knob Recreation Area 16
 5 Bark Camp Recreation Area 17
 6 Natural Tunnel State Park 17
 7 Cumberland Gap National Historic Park / Wilderness Road Campground ... 19

    Southwest Blue Ridge Highlands Area 21
 8 White Rocks Campground 23
 9 Walnut Flats Campground 24
10 Claytor Lake State Park 24
11 Beartree Campground 25
12 Hurricane Campground 26
13 Grindstone Recreation Area Campground 26
14 Washington County Park Camping 27
15 Grayson Highlands State Park 27
16 Fox Creek Horse Campground 29
17 Raccoon Branch Campground 29
18 Comers Rock Recreation Area 30
19 Raven Cliff Recreation Area Campground 30
20 Stony Fork Campground 31
21 Hungry Mother State Park 31

Shenandoah Valley / Northern Virginia Area 33
    Shenandoah Valley Area 35
22 Hidden Valley Recreation Area 38
23 Blowing Springs Campground 39
24 Bolar Mountain Recreation Area 39
25 McClintic Point Campgrounds 40
26 Douthat State Park 40
27 Morris Hill Campgrounds 42

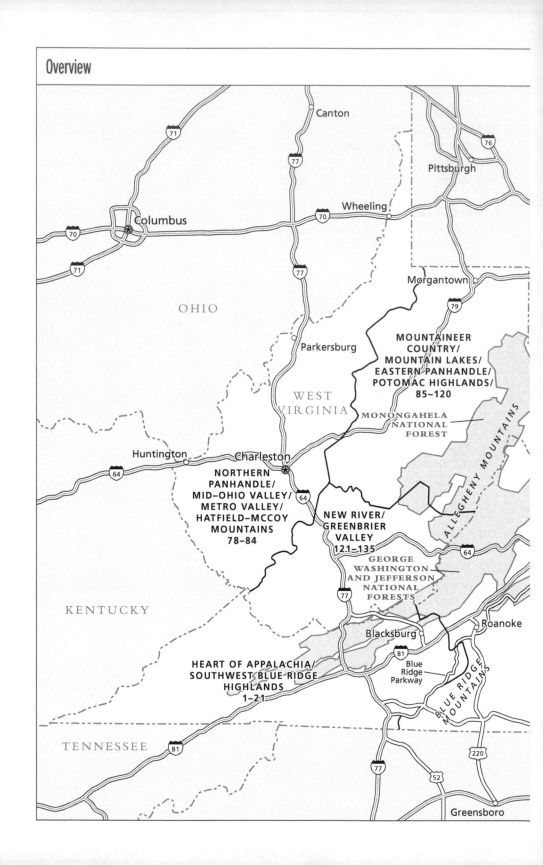

Canton

71

77

76

Pittsburgh

70

Wheeling

Columbus

70

71

77

Morgantown

79

OHIO

Parkersburg

MOUNTAINEER
COUNTRY/
MOUNTAIN LAKES/
EASTERN PANHANDLE/
POTOMAC HIGHLANDS/
85–120

WEST
VIRGINIA

MONONGAHELA
NATIONAL
FOREST

Huntington   Charleston

64

NORTHERN
PANHANDLE/
MID-OHIO VALLEY/
METRO VALLEY/
HATFIELD–MCCOY
MOUNTAINS
78–84

64

NEW RIVER/
GREENBRIER
VALLEY
121–135

64

GEORGE
WASHINGTON
AND JEFFERSON
NATIONAL
FORESTS

77

KENTUCKY

Roanoke

Blacksburg

81

HEART OF APPALACHIA/
SOUTHWEST BLUE RIDGE
HIGHLANDS
1–21

Blue
Ridge
Parkway

TENNESSEE

81

220

77

52

Greensboro

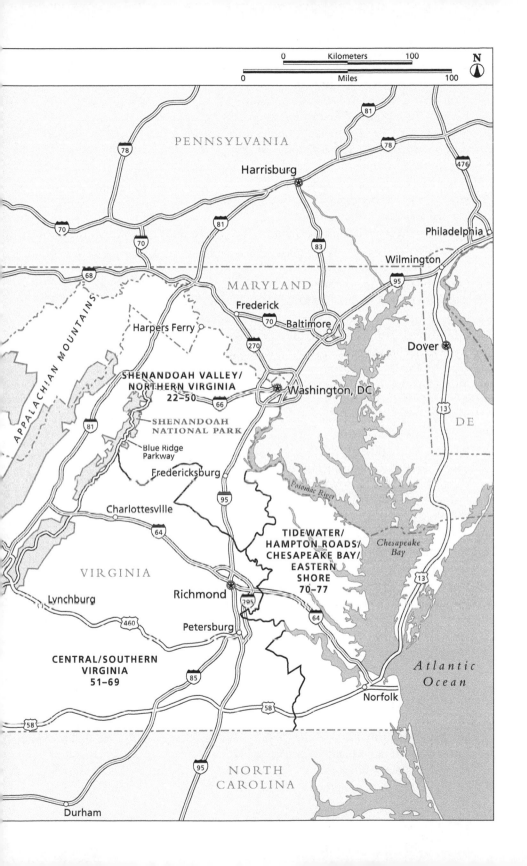

28 Wolf Gap Recreation Area 43
29 Elizabeth Furnace Campground.. 43
30 Little Fort Campground... 44
31 Raymond R. "Andy" Guest Jr. Shenandoah River State Park...................... 45
32 Mathews Arm Campground.. 46
33 Camp Roosevelt Recreation Area Campground........................ 47
34 Big Meadows Campground 47
35 Lewis Mountain Campground 48
36 Hone Quarry Campground 49
37 Natural Chimneys Campground 49
38 Shaws Fork Equestrian Campground... 50
39 Todd Lake Recreation Area 51
40 North River Campground 51
41 Loft Mountain Campground... 52
42 Sherando Lake Recreation Area 53
43 Otter Creek Campground... 53
44 Steel Bridge Campground.. 54
45 The Pines Campground.. 54
46 Cave Mountain Lake Campground 55
47 North Creek Recreation Area Campground............................... 55

Northern Virginia Area.. 57
48 Bull Run Regional Park 59
49 Pohick Bay Regional Park 59
50 Lake Fairfax Park Campground 60
51 Burke Lake Park Campground 60
52 Prince William Forest Park, Oak Ridge Campground................ 61
53 Lake Anna State Park 62

Central / Southern Virginia Area.. 64
Central Virginia Area 65
54 Bear Creek Lake State Park.. 67
55 Powhatan State Park.. 68
56 James River State Park 68
57 Holliday Lake State Park 70
58 Twin Lakes State Park 71
59 Pocahontas State Park 74
60 Peaks of Otter Campground 76
61 Smith Mountain Lake State Park... 76

Southern Virginia Area.. 78
62 Goose Point Campground 80
63 Horseshoe Point Campground 80
64 Salthouse Branch Campground.. 81

65 Fairy Stone State Park.. 81
66 Roanoke Mountain Campground.. 83
67 Rocky Knob Campground... 83
68 Staunton River State Park... 84
69 Longwood Park Campground... 85
70 Occoneechee State Park... 86
71 Rudds Creek Campground.. 87
72 Buffalo Park Campground.. 88
73 North Bend Park Campground.. 88

Tidewater / Hampton Roads / Chesapeake Bay / Eastern Shore Area 89
   Tidewater / Hampton Roads Area... 90
74 Chickahominy Riverfront Park... 92
75 Chippokes Plantation State Park... 93
76 Newport News Park Campsites.. 94
77 First Landing State Park... 95
78 Northwest River Park Campground 97

   Chesapeake Bay / Eastern Shore Area 99
79 Westmoreland State Park...101
80 Belle Isle State Park...102
81 Kiptopeke State Park..104

Introduction to West Virginia...106
Northern Panhandle / Mid-Ohio Valley / Metro Valley /
  Hatfield-McCoy Mountains Area...119
   Northern Panhandle / Mid-Ohio Valley Area.............................121
82 Tomlinson Run State Park..121
83 North Bend State Park..122

   Metro Valley / Hatfield-McCoy Mountains Area..........................125
84 Beech Fork State Park...125
85 East Fork Campground..127
86 Cabwaylingo State Forest...127
87 Chief Logan State Park...129
88 Kanawha State Forest..129

Mountaineer Country / Mountain Lakes / Eastern Panhandle /
  Potomac Highlands Area...132
   Mountaineer Country Area..133
89 Chestnut Ridge Regional Park 135
90 Coopers Rock State Forest 135
91 Tygart Lake State Park..137

Mountain Lakes Area...139
92 Cedar Creek State Park..142
93 Stonewall Resort State Park / Briar Point Campground 144
94 Bulltown Campground 144
95 Audra State Park 146
96 Gerald Freeman Campground at Sutton Lake...............................147
97 Bakers Run–Mill Creek Campground at Sutton Lake 148
98 Bee Run Campground at Sutton Lake 148
99 Holly River State Park 149
100 Kumbrabow State Forest / Mill Creek Campground 150
101 Battle Run Campground 150

Eastern Panhandle / Potomac Highlands Area.............................152
102 Robert W. Craig Campground 156
103 Hawk Recreation Area..157
104 Horseshoe Recreation Area and Campground..............................158
105 Blackwater Falls State Park 158
106 Canaan Valley Resort State Park 160
107 Red Creek Campground 162
108 Trout Pond Recreation Area 162
109 Big Bend Campground 164
110 Seneca Shadows Campground..165
111 Bear Heaven Recreation Area Campground 166
112 Stuart Recreation Area and Campground.....................................166
113 Laurel Fork Campground..167
114 Spruce Knob Lake Campground..168
115 Brandywine Recreation Area 168
116 Seneca State Forest..169
117 Tea Creek Campground..170
118 Cranberry Campground 170
119 Bishop Knob Campground 171
120 Big Rock Campground 172
121 Summit Lake Campground...172
122 Day Run Campground 173
123 Watoga State Park 173
124 Pocahontas Campground 175

New River / Greenbrier Valley Area...176
125 Plum Orchard Lake Wildlife Management Area...........................178
126 Babcock State Park 179
127 Little Beaver State Park 179
128 Lake Stephens Campground..181
129 Twin Falls Resort State Park 181
130 Camp Creek State Park and State Forest.....................................182

131 Panther State Forest/Wildlife Management Area 183
132 Berwind Lake Wildlife Management Area...184
133 Pipestem Resort State Park 185
134 Bluestone State Park 186
135 Bluestone Wildlife Management Area (WMA)...187
136 Moncove Lake State Park..188
137 Greenbrier State Forest 189
138 Blue Bend Recreation Area and Campground...189
139 Lake Sherwood Recreation Area and Campground 190

Camping Etiquette 191
About the Author...197

At press time all campgrounds in this book are open for camping. However, most public campgrounds are subject to changing governmental budgets, so please call the contact number given to be sure the campground you choose will be available when you're in the area.

Acknowledgments

I want to thank my driver, best helper, camping buddy, and wonderful son, Cameron. He handled a good majority of the driving because, as a new driver, he needed the practice. This enabled me to sit in the passenger seat, keep an eye on him, and also make notes and write. After his experience with driving in sections of road in each state that were switchbacks unfolding back and forth ahead of us for many miles, he earned the moniker "The Switchback King." Being a new driver and unfamiliar with many roads, he had to take his time, never knowing what came around the next bend. He was quite incensed when little old ladies in West Virginia passed him on narrow, windy roads. I explained that these ladies no doubt had been driving those roads a long time and were quite familiar with every curve—but for him to just concentrate on the road. He also exercised wonderful patience in answering my sudden calls to "stop here, no—here," and of "our exit is right there, turn now!"

In addition, when I did give him a break from driving, he took over as note-taker, writing down the random snippets that would come to me as I drove—one of the best places to do your heavy thinking. He also helped log the different photos that were taken and took detailed dictation on my captions for many. Having a second set of hands is ever so useful.

I also want to thank the many rangers and tourism representatives who spoke with me and helped me with various pieces of information, whether it was confirmation of park amenities, or directions, or some other detail. In particular, I want to thank the following for assistance in getting photos to supplement mine: Karen Beck-Herzog, Public Affairs Officer and Special Park Uses Coordinator for Shenandoah National Park; Jim Meisner Jr., Public Relations Specialist for Virginia Department of Conservation and Recreation; Sissie Summers, Chief Naturalist and wearer of multiple hats for West Virginia State Parks & Forests; Ron Snow, photographer for West Virginia Department of Commerce; Steve Shaluta Jr., photographer for West Virginia Department of Commerce; and Kimberly D. McHenry, Marketing and Communications for West Virginia Department of Commerce.

Also, I can't forget the various Good Samaritans in Virginia and West Virginia who were always helpful to a traveler asking for directions—or direction clarification. Some of the nicest people you would ever want to meet live in these two states, always ready to help.

How to Use This Guide

There are two major sections to this book: The first section is devoted to the Commonwealth of Virginia, and the second section is devoted to the State of West Virginia. Between them, you could spend decades exploring all these states have to offer, from rich history to outdoor recreation to simply relaxing before a beautiful view. Both states offer richly diverse regions within their borders, so that visiting just one area of the state will give you but a fraction of the state's total flavor and offerings.

This book focuses exclusively on public campgrounds—and because there are so many from which to choose, you potentially could be kept busy for a lifetime of getaways, if you choose. Private campgrounds and RV-only campgrounds are beyond the scope of this book, though I do offer information on whether or not a campground is RV friendly. In general, most campgrounds are: The only thing that makes them

Shenandoah National Park Courtesy National Park Service, Shenandoah National Park

Fields in Appomattox Court House region, Central Virginia

"unfriendly" is the size of your vehicle compared to the size of the campsites or even the challenge of the roads leading to the campground. These are duly noted. I recommend, should you have any questions, to contact the campground directly to ensure that your vehicle can be accommodated, both by the local road conditions and the sites themselves. I did car camping, and there were some switchback roads that I had doubts my car would make, so better to be prepared.

Selecting a Campground

West Virginia and Virginia offer amazing diversity, from unique landscapes to a wide selection of campgrounds tucked into forests, along waterways, and near major state attractions.

All public campgrounds are managed by a selection of agencies, and within these management types, you will tend to find similar amenities. Even so, campgrounds can range from recreation meccas to primitive-style campsites. However, the camping experience is what you make of it, and a lot depends on knowing where you want to go, what you want to do, and what types of amenities you would like to find once you get there. Even if you choose a more basic campground, you can combine activities

Modern amenities at Lake Anna State Park

that are available within the campground or in the vicinity of the campground to create a one-of-a-kind camping experience. Or maybe you would like to just get away from it all and avoid crowds, so you will want to locate an out-of-the-way spot. It is what you want out of your camping experience that will most dictate your selection from one of the great campgrounds listed in this guide. Your considerations in selecting a campground will be as unique and individual as you are. For example, if you want to fish, you will want to be near water. If you have kids, you will want to make sure you have access to amenities that will keep them happy and occupied. If you absolutely want to be able to shower every day, you will want a campground that offers hot shower facilities. This guide will help you to winnow down your choices until you find the campground that works best for you, your family, and/or friends.

The public campgrounds within this guide will fit into one of the categories in the following section.

Types of Campgrounds

Federal: You will find that campgrounds located in one of the national forests or parks fall under the USDA Forest Service, the Bureau of Land Management, or the US Army Corps of Engineers. Amenities can run the gamut. For example,

A rocky stream in West Virginia's Mountain Lakes Region

they could be primitive-type campgrounds, where you may find pit or vault toilets and no running water, to somewhat developed campgrounds, where you will find hand pumps and spigots for drinking water, to very developed campgrounds that offer full running water that allows for hot showers, drinking water, and flush toilets. It just depends on how developed the campground is by that particular agency—and that will be reflected in the cost to camp there. There are also other considerations you may have that you value over the development level of a campground. For example, while many may see it as a negative that there is no running water, others will see the pros of the local recreational offerings, such as proximity to popular rock-climbing sites, historic battlefields, or fishing spots. Again, the less developed the campground, the lower the price—with some campgrounds charging absolutely nothing for travelers to camp there. I have included these, because sometimes you just cannot beat the price of "free," especially when you still have access to gorgeous trees and scenery, local offerings, and simply the opportunity to get away. Either the agency itself manages the campground area, or it is run by concessionaires.

A red barn in western West Virginia

As for the US Army Corps of Engineers, they are found next to their waterworks projects, so you will find these next to most lakes that they have created through the building of dams. There are seven US Army Corps of Engineers campgrounds in Virginia, and seven in West Virginia.

In West Virginia and Virginia, the USDA Forest Service manages the national forests, which are further subdivided into local districts, each individually managing their own section. West Virginia has more than thirty campgrounds managed by the Forest Service, spread across the Monongahela National Forest and George Washington and Jefferson National Forests, both located in the eastern section of the state. In Virginia there are twenty campgrounds found in the GWJ.

In addition, the National Park Service manages campgrounds in Shenandoah National Park in Virginia. These areas are located in the western portion of the state.

State: The bulk of public campgrounds in both Virginia and West Virginia are operated by each state's Park Service. In addition, the state parks manage recreation areas and historic sites that include battlefields. Also, the state park campgrounds are pretty consistent in basic amenities, and some are highly developed to the point where you will feel you are away at a resort. In West Virginia there are about thirty state parks from which to choose, managed by West Virginia State Parks & Forests, and in Virginia you will have more than twenty state parks that are managed by the Virginia Department of Conservation and Recreation.

County/Local: There are some county and local campgrounds sprinkled throughout these states, and they are well developed and offer a variety of recreation activities. Because they are tucked into regions and do not have the same marketing capacity as the federal or state parks, you could consider these a best-kept secret to all but the locals.

Finding a Campground

Virginia and West Virginia are separated into two sections in this guide. The states are further broken down into regions, following some of the major region groups that each state's Bureau of Tourism uses. In both states the way the major interstates and highways have been developed create nice sections within each state, making it convenient to travel a main road to get to a particular region. Further, each region shares more similarities than not, usually in landscape features. Maps throughout this guide show the location of the campgrounds that fall within each region.

Fee Structure

Here are the guidelines I have set up so you will understand the fee structure into which each campground falls. There are some campgrounds that are free. Yes, you read that right: You pay absolutely nothing to stay overnight. Of course, it will not be fancy. The amenities will match that great deal, also falling under the adage "you get what you pay for," as these campsites will be quite primitive. But in the majority of those cases, at the very minimum, you will have access to drinking water and a pit or vault toilet. It is nice to know that even those on the tightest of budgets can manage a trip outdoors with this type of offering.

Good family times when camping COURTESY NATIONAL PARK SERVICE, SHENANDOAH NATIONAL PARK

Some sites can be reserved online, and the information is noted within that campground's listing. Others offer a mix of reservable sites and first come, first served and you check in when you get to the location. Still others may operate on an honor system, so you will want to have exact cash on you.

If you are a senior citizen, ask about a senior discount (if I have not noted one under the listing). Also, rates drop in the off-season for many of the parks that are still open. The off season is anything that falls outside of the summer rush.

All prices are set annually by the various parks and are therefore subject to change. I recommend that if you have any concerns, go ahead and contact the campground to confirm the rates. Rates can vary depending on the type of site you select within a campground, such as primitive versus full hookups of electricity, water, and sewer. However, the listing for each campground will provide either one of these symbols, or two, depending on the range of pricing for that particular location.

$ = $0 to $5
$$ = $6 to $10
$$$ = $11 to $20
$$$$ = $21 to $30+

About the Campground Listings

Each campground listing is set up in the same format, making it easy to quickly home in on the information you need, as well as compare campground amenities. Each listing is formatted as follows:

Location: This will provide a way for you to help find the campground on a larger map, giving you a larger city or town nearby and the average distance and direction from that town, so you can pinpoint the destination.

Sites: Here you will find the number of sites available within the campground and the type of campsite (i.e., it has electric and/or water hookup). The more sites a campground has, the larger the camping area, though it is not necessarily a larger campground. It could be a tiny campground in the middle of the forest or tucked in among multiple campground offerings in the area. Generally, campgrounds have guidelines about how many tents, vehicles, and people are allowed per site, though most accommodate as much as space will allow. So, if you have more than a few people and more than one tent, you may fall outside of what is permitted within one site and will need to get two. Often, campgrounds need to make sure that the campsites do not experience overuse that would result from large groups in one site, which can cause erosion and degrading. If you have any situation that you think might be out of the norm, I recommend you contact the campground directly. You may need to locate group camping, which many campgrounds offer in conjunction with their regular sites but that I do not cover within this guidebook.

Facilities: This section gives you the key amenities that the campground offers, from the type of toilet facilities to whether or not the campground provides shower facilities, laundry facilities, or any of an array of other offerings, including swimming beaches and fishing piers. The vast majority of campgrounds offer drinking water. However, there are a few instances in the primitive campgrounds where there is no drinking water or it is very limited, or it is turned off during the winter months. I do make a note in the "About the campground" section. If you are traveling in the off-season, such as late fall, winter, or very early spring, I recommend you double-check to make sure the water is on and running if you are counting on the campground to provide it. Otherwise, pack your own water. It is not a bad idea to have a few gallon jugs of water stashed in the trunk, anyway—just in case. Picnic areas are different from picnic shelters; the former are picnic tables in separate sections from the campsites and available for anyone to utilize. Often these areas are shared with the day-use visitors to the park. Picnic shelters are those larger structures that are generally reservable for big groups.

Fee per night: This provides the fee range for the campground, as given in the fee structure key noted earlier. The price to camp should fall within the fee range, barring a price increase that places it in a different fee bracket.

Management: The management agency the campground falls under, whether it is the state park service, forest service, etc., that maintains the grounds.

A trailhead in West Virginia

Prickett's Fort State Park in West Virginia

Contact: Here you will find at least one phone number, which will belong to the campground or the district managing that campground. Additional phone numbers may be for reservations. In addition, the website is given, as many campground websites will lead you to a reservation site, which is typically www.recreationpa.gov or www.reserveamerica.com. It just depends on who is managing the location, whether or not reservations are accepted, or if they use one of these central sites. For example, in West Virginia, mail-in reservations are accepted for many locations under some strict guidelines (this is discussed further on page 127 in the section on West Virginia). If a campground is first come, first served, I note it in the section About the campground, which gives you a broader picture of the site.

Activities: In this section you will find activities that you can do in or close to the campground. I do not list basic activities such as "scenic drive" or "nature watching" because these are available everywhere. I think any place outside is scenic and offers nature viewing! And since none of these campgrounds is located next to landfills, then they qualify as scenic. *A note of caution:* If you are basing your campground selection on an amenity such as a swimming pool being available, always double-check to make sure it is open. Some quirky things can happen. For example, one campground was doing construction, so its swimming pool was not available. In other cases, if it is late in the season, such as late August when students go back to school, a swimming pool may not be open because there are no lifeguards available. If you are traveling with kids and you have promised a swimming pool, the last thing you want is some unexpected surprise that results in your having to explain that there's no swimming pool after all to disappointed little faces.

Season: This gives the approximate range for when a campground is open. However, *please note:* I recommend always calling in advance, especially if you are traveling out of season or going to a campground that has a river running through it. For example, while I was researching this book, one campground was closed in the middle of its "in" season due to flooding.

Finding the campground: I provide directions that start from the closest main highway or nearest main city or town and lead you into the campground. You may be coming from a different direction, but at least you will know the closest main roads to get to from your destination so you can plan accordingly.

GPS coordinates: If you travel with a GPS system, plug in these coordinates to help you get to the campground. I am a firm believer in having more than one system to rely on in finding something—especially in more remote areas. I like to have directions that are done by one of the online mapping systems, as well as a map. There are some remote areas where I also feel a compass and bread crumbs would be helpful, because it is relatively easy to do enough twists and turns in the road until you are no longer sure in which direction you are pointing. In short, it never hurts to have backup.

About the campground: In this section you will learn all you need to know about what you will find in the campground and in the vicinity. It is an expansion on, and elaboration of the activities listed earlier, as well as special notes so that you have a good idea of what to expect if you choose this campground. I have also tried to list anything that is accessible to people with disabilities, whether it is the toilet, campsite, or other amenities such as a fishing pier or picnic area.

Wildlife Encounters

Let me tell you about the wildlife you may encounter in Virginia and West Virginia—and how to avoid potentially negative encounters.

In both states, for example, squirrels, chipmunks, a variety of birds, and deer can be easily spotted. In addition, black bears can be seen, and they seem to be especially immune to shyness in Shenandoah National Park in Virginia. They walk right across Skyline Drive and mosey along their way, exercising their right to be there. But just because they are not always shy does not mean they are tame or eager for an encounter. Most animals run off at the sight of humans. I don't know if it's our hair, the clothes we choose to wear, or our smell that offends them, but by and large, they are not interested in getting to know us better. However, we share something in common with them: We all like food. For this reason, when camping here or in any of the campgrounds, practice good food storage and trash disposal habits. It isn't just

Miles of mountain views

Swan on a Virginia waterway

bears that are drawn to the smell of food: Raccoons are quite adept at using their little paws to open things and help themselves. Do not store food or toiletries in your tent or sitting out on the picnic table at your site. Keep everything stored tightly in your vehicle. And if you encounter a black bear while hiking, for example, it will probably be just as startled as you, but do not run. Stand tall and back away slowly. Some people will carry a bell from their backpack that makes noise, which lets animals know you are coming (if your heavy tread and breaking sticks underfoot don't do it first). If you have any questions or concerns about bears, ask the campground ranger for advice and tips, and do a little research before you head out on your trip.

Snakes are common, but that doesn't mean you will commonly see one. The best way to avoid encounters with snakes is to be aware of your surroundings: where you place your feet while hiking, and where you sit on rocks or place your hands while climbing. I must confess that I struggle to follow my own advice and on the couple of occasions when I have come across a snake, I all but stepped on it because I was too distracted. Luckily, I walked away without a bite, which goes to show that snakes are not out to "get you" and are just living their lives. Snakes may cross your path as you are walking, simply trying to get from here to there. Basically, they are taking care of their business and really have no interest in you. One time I was hiking and did not notice a snake coiled up next to the trail, sunning itself on a warm rock that was situated just right for catching one of the sunbeams through a break in the trees. Being cold-blooded creatures, they seek the heat of the sun. Being always cold myself, I can relate. However, your takeaway lesson here is to expect the unexpected and live and let live. Venomous snakes include rattlesnakes and copperheads in both states, and cottonmouths in Virginia in the southeastern section of the state. Harmless varieties include the northern black racer, worm snakes, scarlet snakes, water snakes, garter snakes, king snakes, and many more; the varieties of harmless species far outnumber the venomous ones. So, if you do see a snake, do not panic: The odds are that it is harmless and would kindly like to keep living and not get confused with a venomous cousin. Just stop and let it make its way, as it will surely do—in the opposite direction. Sadly, many snakes get caught up in a case of mistaken identity, and just because you see a venomous snake does not mean it wants or is going to harm you.

Animals of all kind attack when they feel threatened for whatever reason, and occasionally that may be because a boot just landed next to their head or in the case of female bears, they were cut off from a cub. I know this does not make it any less

Heron PHOTO COURTESY OF THE VIRGINIA DEPARTMENT OF CONSERVATION AND RECREATION

A deer crossing

nerve shattering, but again, by and large you could camp all year long, hike for miles and miles and still never have an encounter with anything bigger than a salamander or something as benign as a deer.

I recommend you steer clear of any furry animal that seems overly friendly and comes near you, such as raccoons, foxes, or other mammals. Rabies make animals behave out of character, so anytime an animal is behaving more like something out of a Walt Disney film than like its true self, wanting to avoid humans, you would do best to avoid it.

At most campgrounds, there will be billboards posted with notices of what type of wildlife you may encounter during your stay and additional tips to help you get along in their natural habitat. I do not want to scare anyone off: Awareness is simply the key to avoiding any possible negative encounters and also increases your appreciation for the area you are staying in. As my dad always told me when I was little about anything I was scared of, whether it was bug, reptile, or amphibian: "It's more scared of you than you are of it."

There are dozens of species of birds, and some of the best places for viewing them are in designated wildlife regions. Virginia has fifteen national wildlife refuges and thirty-nine wildlife management areas. West Virginia has two wildlife refuges and

Pleasant Creek Wildlife Management Area

seventy-eight wildlife management areas, accounting for approximately 8 percent of the land area within the state. These areas protect critical wildlife habitat and provide incredible recreation opportunities for visitors.

Do not feed or otherwise try to engage wildlife you come across. Feeding them makes them dependent on humans for food. Also, it can make them sick, because it is not their natural diet and they may not be able to digest it well. Trying to pet animals is not safe for you because animals have a healthy instinct for self-defense, and it is not good for the animals because it makes them feel unsafe in their environment.

Map Legend

Transportation

≡⟨81⟩≡ Interstate Highway

≡⟨15⟩≡ US Highway

—⟨402⟩≡ State Highway

Land Management

National Park/Forest

— — — — State Line

———— Regional Boundary

Symbols

 ❶ Campground

✪ Capital

○ City/Town

Water Features

Body of Water

James River

Welcome to the Commonwealth of Virginia, one of the original thirteen colonies, which has a rich history. It is nicknamed the "Old Dominion" state and is the birthplace of many famous people in history such as Pocahontas, George Washington, Thomas Jefferson, James Madison, Patrick Henry, Booker T. Washington, Robert E. Lee, Stonewall Jackson, and Ella Fitzgerald. Its capital is Richmond, located in the east central area of the state. Its slogan is "Virginia is for Lovers," and you will no doubt love the varied offerings that range from seashore to mountain range across this gorgeous state.

Climate

Being situated below the Mason–Dixon Line qualifies Virginia as a Southern state, which would ideally make it a relatively temperate state for the overall region, but because of its geography, there is marked diversity in what you will find from one end to the other. A lot depends on which region you are in, whether the mountains in the west, which can see cold winters, with some areas receiving a lot of annual rain and others very little, or the coast, where you will see weather affected by coastal conditions and humidity typical of the south.

Geography

From mountains to piedmont to shoreline, Virginia offers some diverse geography. There are four major rivers in the state: the James River, the York River, the Potomac River (which runs along the line between Virginia and Washington, DC), and the Rappahannock River. Regions vary in landscape. There are the coastal plains found in what is known as the "Tidewater" region in the east. It is flat, sitting amid major rivers that flow into the Chesapeake Bay and along the Atlantic Ocean. Down in the southeastern section of the state, you will find Dismal Swamp—an anomaly this far north, but typical of marshy, swamp areas found farther south. As you travel farther west, you will note the rolling nature of the landscape, known as the "Piedmont" region. This covers a very large area of the state, from outside of the Tidewater area, down to the North Carolina border and north. You will notice more agricultural

Central Virginia trailhead COURTESY VIRGINIA DEPARTMENT OF CONSERVATION AND RECREATION

endeavors here, including tobacco fields, soybean, and corn crops. Continue toward the southwest to the Appalachian region, covered in forests and home to coal mines. Travel toward the northwest and you will be entering the Blue Ridge Mountains, which include Shenandoah National Park and the Shenandoah Valley region. This area is renowned for its fall foliage, a big draw to visitors from all over, especially the Washington metropolitan region. The Shenandoah region and areas farther south have caverns that you can visit for an admission fee. Luray Caverns are a National Landmark and are the biggest caverns located in the eastern section of the United States.

History

Virginia has a long and interesting history. The first permanent settlement of the English in America, Jamestown Colony, was founded in 1607. Pocahontas was born in the Tidewater region and had ties to Jamestown.

Tobacco became the principle export of Virginia, its cultivation taught by the Indians. Jamestown was the first capital of Virginia, and then Williamsburg, until the capital city was again relocated to Richmond. During the Colonial era, Virginia produced many great leaders who figured prominently in the struggle for independence from England, including George Washington, Thomas Jefferson, George Mason, and Patrick Henry. Today, you can travel the Road to Revolution Heritage Trail, located in Central Virginia, which follows the life of Patrick Henry, who became the first governor of Virginia. The trail links various sites important in his life, including the place where he was born; Hampden-Sydney College, which he helped found; a tobacco farm he owned; and St. John's Church, where he delivered the speech that made him famous: "Give me liberty or give me death," which helped spark the fight for independence.

Appomattox Court House region

During the Civil War, Richmond became the capital not just of Virginia, but also of the seceded states. Many epic Civil War battles were fought on Virginia's land, making the state a history buff's delight, with battlefields and museums stretched from one end to the other. It is the home of Appomattox, where General Robert E. Lee surrendered to General Ulysses S. Grant, effectively ending the bloody war. Appomattox Court House National Historical Park, worth the drive, is near the campground at James River State Park and within easy driving distance of other local campgrounds. Today, Richmond continues to serve as the capital of the state. Pocahontas State Park has a large recreational campground located minutes away.

Major Tourist Attractions

Virginia is covered with major tourist attractions with something to delight every member of the family.

For history buffs, there are attractions that celebrate every step of Virginia's long history. At Historic Jamestown Settlement, ongoing archaeological digs continue to piece together the earliest American history of the area, with displays of artifacts that help bring the history alive.

Near Jamestown, you can enter the world of colonial life at historic Colonial Williamsburg, which offers garden, home, and even ghost tours. Also, visit Yorktown Victory Center and Yorktown Battlefield, where the last major battle was fought and won during the Revolutionary War and General Cornwallis surrendered to General Washington and the war came to an end. There are several campgrounds in the region, making it convenient to plan day trips. This area is often referred to as the "Historic Triangle" because of these three big history draws.

The Road to Revolution Heritage Trail, which follows the life of Patrick Henry, is found in the Richmond area. Stay at a local campground and save time for a driving tour. You can also tour the homes of George Washington, located in Mount Vernon in Alexandria, which is close to Washington, DC, and farther west, Monticello, the home of Thomas Jefferson.

Numerous Civil War battles were fought in Virginia, and there is a Civil War Trail that helps history buffs to navigate dozens of Civil War–related battlefield and historic sites. These include the battlefields of Fredericksburg and Spotsylvania, now preserved in the National Park Service's Fredericksburg and Spotsylvania National Military Park.

The pioneers followed one major route when headed west through Virginia: the Wilderness Road that led to the Cumberland Gap, which is now a National Historical Park. Daniel Boone and the exploration team of Lewis and Clark used it as well on their journeys across the Blue Ridge Mountains.

For nature lovers, in addition to all the wonderful campgrounds, there are natural wonders to enjoy across the commonwealth. Explore caverns around the Shenandoah region, including Luray, Endless, and Skyline Caverns. Travel to the east to visit the Chincoteague National Wildlife Refuge located on the eastern shore, a peninsula shared with Maryland that juts between the Chesapeake Bay to the west and the Atlantic Ocean to the east. And see what caught Thomas Jefferson's eye: the Natural Bridge, which he purchased from England. It is still considered a natural wonder, one that many have traveled to see.

Virginia has done a wonderful job of creating special Scenic Drives that really show off the natural beauty of some sections of the state. Here are just a couple: Skyline Drive travels 105 miles along the length of the ridge in Shenandoah National Park before joining up with the Blue Ridge Parkway farther south, which runs for more than 216 miles until it comes to the North Carolina border where it continues south. When planning your route to your campground, see if you can locate a scenic drive or byway to get there—it will enhance your appreciation of the state's offerings.

For the kids, if they can't expend enough of their energy at the campsite, you could plan day trips to one of several attractions that appeal to any age: Kings Dominion is a huge water and ride theme park located just off I-95, about 20 miles north of Richmond, and Busch Gardens Europe is located in Williamsburg. The Virginia Beach region has the Virginia Marine Science Museum, and nearby in Hampton, the Virginia Air and Space Museum. Near the Natural Bridge, travel way back in time at Dinosaur Kingdom and get a scare at Haunted Monster Museum.

Wine lovers rejoice: This is wine country with hundreds of vineyards scattered throughout the state and twenty-three wine trails to lead you through them. Wine production has a long history dating back to Jamestown, and Thomas Jefferson carried on the tradition at his home at Monticello. Today, the state is recognized for having quite the respectable winemaking capability and quality products.

These are just some of the attractions that are within driving distance of campgrounds listed in this guide.

Recreational Opportunities

When it comes to recreational opportunities in the state, you just might need a vacation after you take your camping vacation in Virginia. In fact, you may have to work hard at forcing yourself to sit still, because the state has so much to offer.

Rivers, mountains, lakes, ocean, swamp, forests . . . what more could you ask for in terms of outdoor recreation? I want to give you a quick taste of recreational opportunities that are available, depending on which section of the state you visit, along with some special considerations to know before you go. I could write a whole book on all there is to see and do in Virginia, but this will give you a jump-start for discovering all of the recreational opportunities on your own.

Horseback riding: Virginia has a long equestrian history, from horse country located around the Lexington region to the west to the annual July wild pony swim in Chincoteague. There are approximately 285 public access trails throughout Virginia, and several campgrounds listed in this guide are horse-lover friendly, providing camping facilities for both equestrians and their horses. For example, James River, Grayson Highlands, and Occoneechee State Parks are just a few that provide campsites for equestrians. In the state parks some trails will be designated as equestrians only, while others may be multiuse, which means sharing the trail with hikers and bikers. One of these is the Wilderness Road Trail, once a major pioneer migration route across the Blue Ridge Mountains. You can also find trails that go across battlefields, along the beach to the east, and throughout the mountains in the west. State law requires that visitors carry a copy of a negative Coggins report with each horse brought to a park. Make sure before you ride that you are familiar with the trail administrator's special requirements, which could potentially include a usage fee. For example, if you are horseback riding in a Virginia State Forest, you will need a Virginia State Forest Use Permit. If you don't own a horse, there are also rides and lessons available from private enterprises throughout the state.

Fishing: Rivers, creeks, lakes, bay, and ocean—if you are an avid fisherman, you may have a tough time choosing your favorite fishing spot. Many waterways are stocked with trout. Some of the best bass fishing anywhere can be found on the Upper James River. The North Fork Moormans near Skyline Drive in Shenandoah National Park is said to have the best native brook trout fishing, but this is a catch-and-release area. There are different regulations and fees, depending on where you are camping. And if you fish in a National Forest or State Forest, you will need a use permit, and some locations require a daily permit, such as Douthat State Park. Fishing licenses vary depending on whether you are a resident or nonresident and what type of fishing you are doing, fresh or salt water or fishing for trout. Before you pack your fishing rod and tackle box, first check the website www.HuntFishVa.com to do your due diligence in familiarizing yourself with regulations for where you're planning to fish. For example, your camping trip may be located near a dam or in a wildlife recreation area, so special requirements may need to be met. You can also obtain a license online at www.HuntFishVa.com, through a local sporting goods store, or call (866) 721-6911 to order a license by phone. Many campgrounds offer fishing piers and docks, and some even have boat rentals. To learn more about the best fishing spots closest to your camping destination, visit www.fishvirginiafirst.com.

Hiking: Shenandoah National Park alone has more than 500 miles of hiking trails. The Appalachian Trail cuts through the state for 544 miles, and Virginia holds the title of "state with the most miles of the AT," with more than 100 miles just in Shenandoah National Park. In addition, George Washington and Jefferson National Forests offer additional miles, accessible through many of the campgrounds listed in this guide. The Virginia Creeper Trail is located in the southwestern section of the state and is a multiuse trail of about 35 miles. It is a former railroad trail that has been thankfully repurposed for outdoors enthusiasts through a rails-to-trails program. Almost every park offers at least one trail for hiking and usually many more. In addition, most areas are also close to trailheads that are within driving distance of the campground, expanding your trail choices.

Biking: Some great mountain-biking trails exist in the mountains of George Washington and Jefferson National Forests. A location that offers 20 miles of single-track, dirt, and pavement is Sherando Lake Recreation Area. Farther down in Mount Rogers National Recreation Area, there are more than 400 miles of trails that range from moderate to very strenuous. Another popular attraction is the Virginia Creeper Trail, suitable for both biking and hiking and located in the southwestern region. For road cyclists Skyline Drive and Blue Ridge Parkway are very popular choices, as well as roads in the Shenandoah Valley just below. Most campgrounds offer something for cyclists, either within the campground area itself or nearby. If you mountain bike in a Virginia State Forest, you will need a use permit. Some jurisdictions have bicycle helmet laws for kids under a certain age, so know before you go.

Water sports: Whether you enjoy swimming, waterskiing, or boating, there are plenty of water opportunities from which to choose that include ocean, bay, rivers, lakes, and swimming pools. From motor boating to kayaking, there is something for everyone to enjoy in the water. Surprisingly, there is white-water kayaking available on a section of the James River around the capital city of Richmond and also in the Shenandoah region. In addition, you can kayak in the ocean around Kiptopeke State Park. Kayak or canoe on one of the many rivers and lakes throughout the state or go rafting or tubing on one of the rivers. There are designated water trails throughout the state, including on the Upper James River northeast of Roanoke in the Allegheny and Blue Ridge Mountains region. You can find outfitters that offer guided day trips. Motorboat enthusiasts, *please note:* Motorboats must be registered and titled if your camping trip includes a boat ride on public waters in the state. Many campgrounds provide boat launches, and some have access to marinas, either within the campground or nearby. You can also rent boats at some of the parks from concessionaires that operate there. Also, many campgrounds offer swimming facilities—some almost resort-like with waterslides and other areas providing swimming beaches—which are sure to be a big hit with kids. You are allowed to swim in the streams in Shenandoah National Park, but swim at your own risk and know that the rocks can be very slippery when wet.

Snow sports: Virginia offers some skiing opportunities in the Blue Ridge Mountains, with downhill skiing, tubing, and snowboarding available at Wintergreen Resort in Charlottesville and, in the same area, cross-country skiing available on a section of the Blue Ridge Parkway between miles 12 and 14 at Reed's Gap. Over in the Allegheny Mountains on the western side of the state, you will find enough snow to snowshoe and cross-country ski. The mid-Atlantic does see some big snowstorms on occasion, so depending on your ability to withstand the cold while camping, you may be able to find a campground open in the vicinity of good skiing at just the right time.

Rock climbing: One of the biggest rock-climbing draws in the state is in the northern section at Carderock in Great Falls. This would be an easy day trip from one of the northern Virginia campgrounds. Rappahannock Rocks near Fredericksburg is another section that offers some potential for rock climbers.

Caving: If you enjoy spelunking, check with a local spelunking organization in Virginia for directions to the best caves in the state. The majority of caves are located in the Shenandoah Valley region. There are also multiple commercial caverns in this area where you can pay for a tour of the underworld, such as at Luray Caverns, Shenandoah Caverns, and several more. If you are not a spelunking hobbyist, this is the best (and safest) way to visit caves and learn more about what made them and the unique ecological environment inside.

ATV: There are some trail systems located in the state. One is in the Edinburg region in the Lee Ranger District of George Washington and Jefferson National Forests. There is a per rider and a general permit fee, and there are two trails featured: Peters Mill Run and Taskers Gap ATV / OHV trails. There is also one in Harrisonburg in the North River District of the forest, called Rocky Run ATV trail. Another is the South Pedlar ATV Trail System, which requires a fee and the purchase of a Special Recreation Permit. There are also privately owned, commercial trails. I recommend checking first before making plans to make sure trails are not closed for any reason.

Geocaching: Virginia's state parks participate in geocaching, with most of the parks having at least one "treasure" to be found. If you do not own a GPS, most parks also have rental units you can use. There are also cities and counties that participate in the fun, so you may be able to find a treasure trail close to your campground, even if you are not staying over in a state park. One such trail is located near the Blue Ridge Parkway in the Lexington area and is called the Gems of Rockbridge Geocaching Trail.

Golf: Golf courses abound in the state, so no matter where you go to camp, you are more than likely going to be within a stone's throw of one. Your chances of that improve the closer you get to the main population areas in the north, central, and eastern regions. The Eastern Shore, however, lists only one, and you can play looking out over the Chesapeake Bay.

Overview of Camping in the State

When you visit the state parks listed in this guide, you will see signs everywhere proclaiming "Virginia State Parks Voted America's Best." You may soon share that view of all of Virginia's campgrounds as you make the difficult selection between parks tucked into forested mountain areas, in the Piedmont Region near major rivers and lakes, or those located over on the eastern shore near the Bay and the Atlantic Ocean.

Shenandoah National Park and the Shenandoah Valley region are renowned for their fall foliage, a big draw to visitors from all over, especially the Washington metropolitan region. *Please note:* There is an entrance fee to get into Shenandoah National Park that is valid from the date you buy it through the next six days. Campgrounds can fill very quickly—and quite early—as everyone tries to guess when the colors will be at their peak.

Central Virginia, Pocahontas State Park outside Richmond

Farther west and down into the southwest are more rugged mountainous regions, providing many recreational opportunities.

In the center of the state, you have the perfect launching spot for exploring the outdoors as well as historical landmarks.

The eastern shore region provides its own unique camping experience, close to many major cities and yet a world away once you enter your campground area.

Most campsites can accommodate six people per site and larger group camping areas are available, too. Developed campsites have water, picnic tables, and grills, and they provide marked paths to bathhouses and toilets. Most Virginia state parks offer hiking trails, fishing, playgrounds, and picnic facilities. Some have bike and equestrian trails, in addition to swimming facilities. Many even provide sports equipment rentals to enjoy the amenities of that particular park, including boats, bikes, and horses.

You will find that no fewer than six of the Virginia state parks were part of the Depression-era public works project that employed thousands, and there will be some mention of the "Civilian Conservation Corps" at those parks and other historic sites. A museum located in Pocahontas State Park near Richmond is dedicated to their efforts.

I recommend camping during the weekdays if you want to escape the crowds. In many of the parks, there are much smaller numbers of people and you will almost have the area to yourself. The more off the beaten path a campground is, the better your chances for finding fewer people. The closer to main highways and cities, the busier the parks seem to be.

Special note on firewood: The overwhelming majority of campgrounds have a firewood quarantine in effect, which means you cannot bring firewood from outside of the campground into the campground where you are staying. You must purchase your firewood from the place you camp, because it is sourced locally. The reason is the potential for transporting into the state some very destructive insects and diseases that can be in the wood and that will kill native trees. This is one way to be a nice guest and not bring the equivalent of bed bugs with you to your temporary camping home.

Travel Tips

Navigation

The majority of campgrounds are very easy to locate, as they are near main interstates and marked well with clear signage. Even so, I recommend having a backup plan for your preferred method of navigating, whether it is GPS, folding maps, an atlas, or directions you downloaded from the internet.

Traffic considerations

If you are not familiar with I-95, it is a main thoroughfare going north and south. The traffic can back up considerably the closer you get to Richmond and points north, especially during rush hour on weekdays, and of course, during peak travel times on the weekend. Bumper-to-bumper traffic is what they call it and for good reason. So if you see signs for a rest area, I recommend getting off while you can and not waiting to get a little farther up the road, especially if you are traveling with kids or anyone who needs frequent bathroom breaks! There may not be another one for many miles, other than food service chains and gas stations, and you may get caught in traffic that you were not counting on (or could even conceive of, the volume being so thick in some areas).

Traveling north, the area outside of Richmond can be very confusing, especially if you are trying to reach points farther north, and the closer you get to the Capital Beltway (I-495).

So, the more populated the area, of course, the more traffic. However, here is something else to consider: Shenandoah National Park is not populated in terms of development, but it is a tourist magnet, especially during the fall season when everyone in the area would like to take a nice Sunday drive and see the leaves with their fiercest color changes. Then Skyline Drive can be very busy. Weekdays are always best for scenic drives, so if your object is to relax, see if you can plan your camping trip so that you alleviate some of the potential traffic headaches.

Driving considerations

Most areas of the state have great roads. The areas to the west are more mountainous and where you will find more switchbacks. Signs will be posted to warn of upcoming sharp turns.

Keep your speed within the range posted and make sure you have plenty of gas and inflated tires. It is not desolate, but it can be some distance between towns and you do not want to be on the side of the road if you can help it, simply because your camping trip should include much better adventures than car trouble.

Brief Description of the Regions

The regions are broken down as follows:

Heart of Appalachia / Southwest Blue Ridge Highlands Area: This region is in the southwest section of the state.

Shenandoah Valley / Northern Virginia Area: This region is in the north and northwest region of the state.

Central / Southern Virginia Area: This region covers the vast spread of flatter plains in the middle and bottom section of the state.

Tidewater / Hampton Roads / Chesapeake Bay / Eastern Shore Area: This area hugs the main bodies of water in the eastern section of the state, where the Chesapeake Bay meets the Atlantic Ocean.

These different areas match the state's tourism department designations and they make perfect sense in terms of what is close to what when it comes to driving and geography. Within each section you will be provided with more in-depth information about that particular area.

Heart of Appalachia / Southwest Blue Ridge Highlands Area

This region forms the southwest toe of Virginia, stretching to meet the state lines of three states: West Virginia and Kentucky to the north and west, and North Carolina along its southern border. This region offers what was Jefferson National Forest (and is now part of George Washington and Jefferson National Forests [GWJ]), which features Mount Rogers National Recreation area in the southern portion and covers more than 120,000 acres. It is Appalachian country and coal country and offers gorgeous campgrounds with great recreational opportunities, including more than 400 miles of trails just in the Mount Rogers portion. There are big rocky outcroppings and grasslands in this area, and Mount Rogers is the highest mountain in the state at more than 5,700 feet.

Heart of Appalachia Area

This area hugs the Kentucky state line to its north and part of the North Carolina state line to its south, featuring the stunning and rugged Blue Ridge Mountains for which the state is renowned. Campgrounds in this region include two State Parks, one National Park, and four parks run by the Forest Service.

Area attractions include the Wilderness Road, the migration route for pioneers dating back to Daniel Boone and Lewis and Clark, a major thoroughfare across the Blue Ridge Mountains. One trail for hikers is the Pine Mountain Trail, accessible from Breaks Interstate Park and a strenuous trek along the border with Kentucky. This region offers many festivals, including a bluegrass festival in May.

	Total Sites	Max. RV Length	Hookups	Fire Ring/Grill	Toilets	Showers	Drinking Water	Dump Station	Recreation	Fee ($)	Reservable
1 **Breaks Interstate Park**	124	40	E, W, S	Y	F	Y	Y	Y	H, F, B, L, C, HB	$$$-$$$$	Y
2 **Cane Patch Campground**	35	32	E	Y	F	Y	Y	Y	H, S, F, B	$$$	N
3 **Cave Springs Recreation Area**	37	22	E	N	F	Y	Y	Y	H, S	$$$	N
4 **High Knob Recreation Area**	13	16		N	F	Y	Y	N	H, S, F	$$	N
5 **Bark Camp Recreation Area**	34		E	Y	F	Y	Y	Y	H, S, F, B	$$$	N
6 **Natural Tunnel State Park**	34	38	E, W	Y	F	Y	Y	Y	H, S, F, B, C	$$$$	Y
7 **Cumberland Gap National Historic Park / Wilderness Road State Park**	160	50	E	Y	F	Y	Y	Y	H, C, HB	$$$	N

Max. RV Length: Measured in feet
Hookups: W = Water, E = Electricity, S = Sewer
Fire Ring/Grill: Y = Yes, N = None
Toilets: F = Flush, P = Pit, V = Vault
Showers: Y = Yes, N = None
Drinking Water: Y = Yes, N = None
Dump Station: Y = Yes, N = None
Recreation: H = Hiking, S = Swimming, F = Fishing, B = Boating, L = Boat Launch, C = Cycling, HB = Horseback Riding, OHV = Off Highway Vehicles
Fee: $ = 0–$5, $$ = $6–$10, $$$ = $11–$20, $$$$ = $21–$30+
Reservable: Y = Yes, N = No

Heart of Appalachia Area

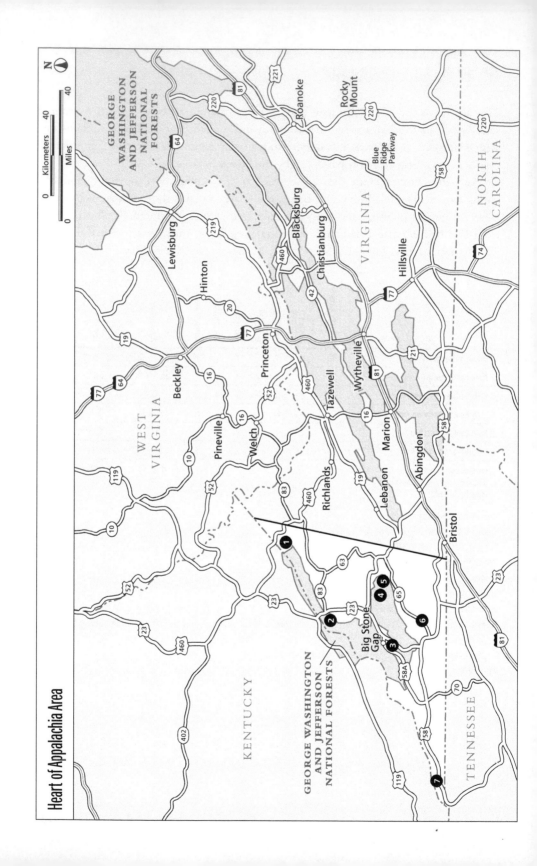

1 Breaks Interstate Park

Location: Located on the Virginia–Kentucky state line, SR 80, 8 miles north of Haysi
Sites: 9 standard, 115 standard electric
Facilities: Flush toilets, fire ring, showers, playgrounds, basketball court, gift shop, boat launch, boat rental, water park, camp store, dump station, visitor center, laundry facility, amphitheater, restaurant
Fee per night: $$$–$$$$
Management: Breaks Interstate Park Commission
Contact: (276) 865-4413; (800) 933-7275; www.breakspark.com/lodging-accommodations/campground.html
Activities: Basketball, hiking, fishing, biking, horseback riding, boating, geocaching, birding, golf
Season: Open end of March to end of October
Finding the campground: Take Virginia SR 80. Follow it to the campground entrance.
GPS coordinates: 37.286299 / -82.293528
About the campground: This campground is located in an area called "The Grand Canyon of the South," named for its deep river gorge created by the Russell Fork of Big Sandy River. The gorge is 5 miles long and about 0.25 mile deep. The Russell Fork provides very challenging white-water rafting, with one of the drops called El Horrendo, if that gives you any indication. It is called an "Interstate" park because It Is situated across the state lines of both Virginia and Kentucky, so you get two states for the price of one. It sits on more than 4,500 acres of woodland, so campsites are mostly wooded sites, with a selection of grassy sites available as well. The park is home to Laurel Lake, where boating and fishing are popular options. There is a boat launch and you can also rent a pedal boat or canoe to explore the lake. Mountain bike rentals are also offered for riding on roads and designated bike trails. In addition, there are playgrounds for the kids and interpretive programs provided by park rangers, as well as a restaurant and a visitor center with museum. Access the Pine Mountain Trail from here and hike along the border with Kentucky, which offers dozens of miles of hiking in the Cumberland Mountain range. It is strenuous going and not to be taken lightly: You are advised to carry a map with you. Horseback riding can also be done along the trail. There are numerous scenic overlooks, giving you a good view of the region and lots of photographic opportunities. Full RV hookups are available.

2 Cane Patch Campground

Location: Located near Virginia–Kentucky state line, 7 miles southwest of Pound
Sites: 28 standard, 7 standard electric
Facilities: Flush toilets, showers, fireplace, fire grill, playground, basketball court, volleyball court, amphitheater, dump station
Fee per night: $$$
Management: USDA Forest Service, Clinch Ranger District
Contact: (276) 328-2931; www.fs.usda.gov
Activities: Boating, swimming, fishing, hiking, volleyball, basketball

Season: Open mid-May to mid-September

Finding the campground: Take US 23 North toward Pound, VA. Take a left turn onto SR 671 West. Follow it to the campground entrance on the right.

GPS coordinates: 37.102889 / -82.678429

About the campground: This campground is located in George Washington and Jefferson National Forests at North Fork of Pound Lake Recreation area. Within walking distance is Phillips Creek Day Use Area, where you may swim at the swimming area located at Phillips Creek. If you like to fish, there is river and stream fishing available, but you do need a Virginia state fishing license. Campsites are first come, first served. Water available. RV friendly up to 32 feet.

3 Cave Springs Recreation Area

Location: 11 miles southwest of Big Stone Gap

Sites: 28 standard, 9 standard electric

Facilities: Flush toilets, showers, dump station, picnic tables, picnic area, swimming beach

Fee per night: $$$

Management: USDA Forest Service, Clinch Ranger District

Contact: (276) 546-4297; www.fs.usda.gov

Activities: Hiking, swimming

Season: Open mid-May to mid-September

Finding the campground: From Big Stone Gap take US 58 Alternate. Take a right onto SR 621 and follow it to the Cave Springs Recreation Area entrance, which will be on the right.

GPS coordinates: 36.800311 / -82.923860

About the campground: Located in GWJ National Forests, this park has a one-acre lake that is mountain spring fed. There's a beach area that features white sand. One hiking trail goes to the cave, from which the mountain spring originates and where the campground got its name. Another trail goes to an overlook. Close to Stone Mountain Trail and Wilderness Area. RV friendly up to 22 feet.

4 High Knob Recreation Area

Location: 10 miles south of Wise

Sites: 13 standard

Facilities: Flush toilets, showers, picnic tables, picnic area, swimming beach, amphitheater

Fee per night: $$

Management: USDA Forest Service, Clinch Ranger District

Contact: (276) 679-1754; www.fs.usda.gov

Activities: Hiking, swimming, fishing

Season: Open mid-May to mid-September

Finding the campground: Take US 58 Alternate and head west. When you reach Norton, take SR 619 headed south. Take Forest Service Route 238. Follow it to the campground entrance.

GPS coordinates: 36.887613 / -82.614014

About the campground: Located in GWJ National Forests, this park offers High Knob Lake, a cold water, spring-fed lake covering four acres and stocked with a variety of fish. A sandy beach area is available for swimmers. The campground sits at a high elevation (the highest in the Clinch Ranger District), making it an ideal location to escape the heat and humidity of summer. There is a trail that wraps around the lake. RV friendly up to 16 feet.

5 Bark Camp Recreation Area

Location: 21 miles southwest of Coeburn
Sites: 25 standard, 9 standard electric
Facilities: Flush toilets, showers, fire grills, picnic tables, boat launch, fishing pier, picnic area, amphitheater, dump station
Fee per night: $$$
Management: USDA Forest Service, Clinch Ranger District
Contact: (276) 328-2931; (276) 467-1209; www.fs.usda.gov
Activities: Hiking, fishing, boating, swimming
Season: Mid-May to mid-September
Finding the campground: From Coeburn, take US 58A west. At the "High Knob" sign, take a left onto SR 706 (Stone Mountain Road). Follow to the Bark Camp sign, where you will take a left. Next, take a right onto Bark Camp Road, where you will see a sign for Bark Camp Lake. Take a right at the sign for the campground and follow it to the entrance.
GPS coordinates: 36.869388 / -82.526290
About the campground: Located in GWJ National Forests, this park is run by the Forest Service. It features a warm water, man-made lake that covers more than 45 acres. The lake is stocked with rainbow trout, bluegill, catfish, crappie, bass, and northern pike. Electric boats are allowed, but no gas-powered boats are permitted. There are two fishing piers that are accessible to people with disabilities, as well as a trail that is accessible on the northern section of the shoreline. Take a brief hike to see Kitchen Rock, a unique geological formation. There are also 3 miles of trail that run along the shoreline available for hiking. The park is located next to High Knob Recreation Area. The campground is RV friendly.

6 Natural Tunnel State Park

Location: Located in Duffield, 13 miles north of Gate City
Sites: Cove View Campground, 16 electric and water sites, Lover's Leap Campground, 18 electric and water sites
Facilities: Flush toilets, fire ring, picnic table, showers, restrooms, laundry facility, campground store, dump station, playground, visitor center, swimming areas
Fee per night: $$$$
Management: Virginia Department of Conservation and Recreation

Natural Tunnel State Park COURTESY VIRGINIA DEPARTMENT OF CONSERVATION AND RECREATION

Contact: (276) 940-2674; (800) 933-7275; www.dcr.virginia.gov/state_parks/nat.shtml
Activities: Volleyball, horseshoes, fishing, boating, biking, swimming, playground, hiking
Season: Open late March to early December
Finding the campground: Take I-81 to US 23 North to Gate City, and then turn off at the park, which is located at mile marker 17.4. Drive about 1 mile on the Natural Tunnel Parkway to get to the park's entrance.
GPS coordinates: 36.702220 / -82.745634
About the campground: Two campgrounds, so amenities vary. Every site has electricity and water, and the campground can accommodate RVs up to 38 feet (20-, 30-, and 50-amp electrical service available). A wide range of amenities includes a volleyball court, an Olympic-size swimming pool, horseshoe pits, amphitheater, visitor center, gift shop, and nature and history programs, including guided canoe trips, cave tours, and guided walks. The park is convenient to the Daniel Boone Wilderness Trail driving tour. Daniel Boone is thought to be one of the first people of European descent to see the Natural Tunnel.

7 Cumberland Gap National Historic Park / Wilderness Road Campground

Location: 11 miles west of Ewing
Sites: 119 standard, 41 standard electric
Facilities: Flush toilets, showers, fire grills, picnic tables, dump station, visitor center, camp store
Fee per night: $$$
Management: National Park Service
Contact: (606) 248-2817; www.nps.gov
Activities: Hiking, horseback riding, biking
Season: Open year-round
Finding the campground: Take SR 58 west to its intersection with SR 25 east (located in Kentucky). Follow it to the park's entrance.
GPS coordinates: 36.602370 / -83.631003
About the campground: This region of the state was once used as the passageway to the West and is the southwesternmost campground in the state of Virginia. It sits along the border of Kentucky. It is estimated that more than 300,000 pioneers crossed through here around the time of the American Revolution and over the next 30 years. Here is where it gets a little confusing: There is a Wilderness Road State Park that is 5 miles away from the Cumberland Gap National Historic Park, which has the Wilderness Road Campground. The names are very close, but the amenities are different. Wilderness Road State Park offers primitive camping only, mostly for groups and equestrian campers. They do not have water, so they provide only pit and vault-type toilets. However, the National Park Service campground is what this listing is referencing, which has water and other amenities. The National Park is located in three states: Virginia, Kentucky, and Tennessee. Campsites are first come, first served. RVs up to 50 feet (20-, 30-, and 50-amp electrical service available). Bears love the region, too, so be sure to store your food in tight containers in your vehicle and put trash in bear-proof containers within the park. The camp store offers camping

Cumberland Gap National Historic Park/Wilderness Road State Park COURTESY VIRGINIA
DEPARTMENT OF CONSERVATION AND RECREATION

supplies. Campground programs available every Saturday night led by park rangers. There are 85 miles of hiking trails within the park, which also connects with the Wilderness Road Trail, 12 miles of trail within the Wilderness Road State Park that can be used by hikers, cyclists, and equestrians. Senior discounts available.

Southwest Blue Ridge Highlands Area

To the west of the Heart of Appalachia is the Southwest Blue Ridge Highlands area; its most prominent offering is the Mount Rogers National Recreation Area, named for the highest mountain peak in the state. The Appalachian Trail comes up from North Carolina and enters and traverses the recreation area before continuing north and then east. The Blue Ridge Parkway runs through the region to the east of the recreation area.

There are multiple parks here. The USDA Forest Service dominates the administration of campgrounds, overseeing ten in this region, while there are three state parks and one county park.

Biking is a popular activity, with the Blue Ridge Parkway for road cyclists (and scenic drive aficionados) and hundreds of miles of trails in Mount Rogers National Recreation Area for off-road enthusiasts and hikers. In addition, there are miles of equestrian trails, river trails, and a range of fishing spots in rivers, creeks, and lakes. The Virginia Creeper Trail starts in Damascus and runs near several campgrounds in the recreation area. Other popular hiking trails include Dragon's Tooth, Cascade Falls, and McAfee's Knob in the Blacksburg area. Steep and rocky Dragon's Tooth is challenging. McAfee Knob is considered the most photographed spot on the Appalachian Trail because of the way it juts out above an amazing view below and in the distance. An excellent multiuse trail is located in the New River Trail State Park, with 57 miles of multiuse trail running next to the river for many of those miles. While it does have a campground, it is primitive and you cannot get to the campsites with your vehicle, so it is not listed below. The park does provide a boat launch.

For fishermen, the New River also offers excellent fishing for smallmouth bass, trout, walleye, and muskie. Kayakers can go to the Russell Fork River and enjoy the scenery from a different vantage point.

The area is also well known for "The Crooked Road: Virginia's Heritage Music Trail," where you can locate plenty of places to hear bluegrass, folk, and country music. This music heritage trail covers 250 miles across the southwest and southern end of the state. Along its route you can see the Ralph Stanley Museum, the Carter Family Memorial Music Center, the Blue Ridge Music Center, and other venues.

Southwest Blue Ridge Highlands Area

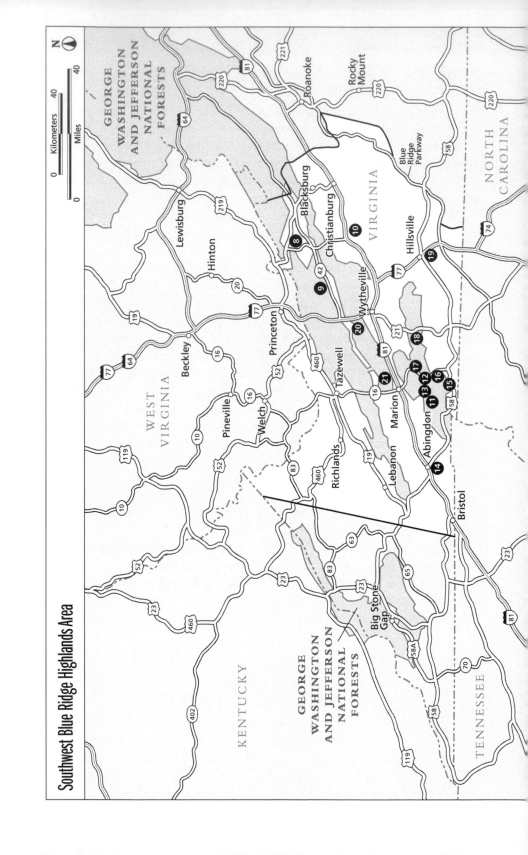

	Total Sites	Max. RV Length	Hookups	Fire Ring/Grill	Toilets	Showers	Drinking Water	Dump Station	Recreation	Fee ($)	Reservable
8 White Rocks Campground	28	65		Y	F, V	N	Y	Y	H	$$$	N
9 Walnut Flats Campground	8			Y	V	N	Y	N	H, F	$	N
10 Claytor Lake State Park	110	40	E, W	Y	F	Y	Y	Y	H, S, F, B, L	$$$$	Y
11 Beartree Campground	90			Y	F	Y	Y	Y	H, S, F, C	$$$$	N
12 Hurricane Campground	30			Y	F, V, P	Y	Y	N	H, F, C, HB	$$$	N
13 Grindstone Recreation Area Campground	108		E	Y	F	Y	Y	Y	H, S, C, HB	$$$$	N
14 Washington County Park Camping	142		E, W, S	Y	F	Y	Y	Y	H, F, B	$$$–$$$$	N
15 Grayson Highlands State Park	87		E, W	Y	F, V	Y	Y	Y	H, F, C, HB	$$$$	Y
16 Fox Creek Horse Campground	32			N	P	N	N	N	HB	$	N
17 Raccoon Branch Campground	20		E	Y	F	N	Y	Y	H, F, C	$$$–$$$$	N
18 Comers Rock Recreation Area	6			Y	V	N	Y	N	H, C	$	N
19 Raven Cliff Recreation Area Campground	20	32		Y	V, P	N	N	N	H, F, HB	$	N
20 Stony Fork Campground	50		E	Y	F	Y	Y	Y	H, F, C	$$$–$$$$	N
21 Hungry Mother State Park	81		E, W, S	Y	F	Y	Y	N	H, F, S, B, L, C	$$$$	Y

Max. RV Length: Measured in feet
Hookups: W = Water, E = Electricity, S = Sewer
Fire Ring/Grill: Y = Yes, N = None
Toilets: F = Flush, P = Pit, V = Vault
Showers: Y = Yes, N = None
Drinking Water: Y = Yes, N = None
Dump Station: Y = Yes, N = None
Recreation: H = Hiking, S = Swimming, F = Fishing, B = Boating, L = Boat Launch, C = Cycling, HB = Horseback Riding, OHV = Off-Highway Vehicles
Fee: $ = 0–$5, $$ = $6–$10, $$$ = $11–$20, $$$$ = $21–$30+
Reservable: Y = Yes, N = No

8 White Rocks Campground

Location: 35 miles west of Blacksburg
Sites: 28 standard
Facilities: Flush toilets, vault toilets, fire rings, picnic tables, dump station
Fee per night: $$$
Management: USDA Forest Service / Eastern Divide Ranger District
Contact: (540) 552-4641; www.fs.usda.gov
Activities: Hiking

Season: Open April to first week of December

Finding the campground: From Blacksburg take US 460 west. Turn right on SR 635. Turn right on SR 613. Take a left into the campground entrance and follow it for about a mile.

GPS coordinates: 37.428605 / -80.503078

About the campground: This is a "no frills" campground located in George Washington and Jefferson National Forests. Campsites are first come, first served. Flush toilets are available from May to the first of October; vault toilets are available in April and in November. Drinking water is only available May through October. There are multiple hiking trails from which to choose in the area. Some campsites are situated next to a creek that runs through the campground, and there are streams in the area that are good for trout fishing. RV friendly with some sites able to accommodate up to 65-foot vehicles.

9 Walnut Flats Campground

Location: 41 miles west of Blacksburg

Sites: 8 standard

Facilities: Vault toilets, fire grills

Fee per night: $

Management: USDA Forest Service / Eastern Divide Ranger District

Contact: (540) 552-4641; www.fs.usda.gov

Activities: Hiking, fishing

Season: Open April to first week of December

Finding the campground: From Blacksburg take US 460 west. Take the second exit for Pearisburg onto SR 100. Take SR 42, and then turn right onto SR 606. Turn right on SR 201. Follow it to the campground entrance on the left.

GPS coordinates: 37.198185 / -80.885876

About the campground: This is a no-fee, primitive campground. Campsites are first come, first served. It does offer drinking water and features a wildlife pond. Nearby Dismal Falls and Creek provide fishing, and the creek is stocked with trout. There are a few hiking trails in the area, such as the Appalachian Trail and the Flat Top Mountain Trail system. RV friendly for smaller vehicles.

10 Claytor Lake State Park

Location: Dublin, 28 miles southwest of Blacksburg

Sites: 70 standard sites, 40 with electric and water hookups

Facilities: Flush toilets, showers, fire rings, fire grills, dump station, boat launch, swimming beach, gift shop, picnic shelters, playground, snack bar, visitor center, fishing pier

Fee per night: $$$$

Management: Virginia Department of Conservation and Recreation

Contact: (540) 643-2500; (800) 933-7275; www.dcr.virginia.gov / state_parks/cla.shtml

Activities: Boating, swimming, hiking, fishing, horseshoes

Claytor Lake State Park COURTESY VIRGINIA DEPARTMENT OF CONSERVATION AND RECREATION

Season: Early March to early December
Finding the campground: Take I-81 to exit 101 toward Claytor Lake. From there take State Park Road (SR 660). Follow it to the park entrance.
GPS coordinates: 37.057553 / -80.628073
About the campground: Located along the beautiful Claytor Lake, which is 21 miles long so there is plenty of open space for boating. It was created by the dam built on the New River. There is a marina available here. Rent a motorized boat to explore the lake or bring your own and use the boat launch. There is excellent hiking and biking located nearby in the New River Trail State Park, offering 57 miles that parallel the New River for two-thirds of that distance. Some campsites are wooded. RVs welcome; the park can accommodate larger RVs up to 40 feet.

11 Beartree Campground

Location: 18 miles northeast of Damascus
Sites: 90 standard
Facilities: Flush toilets, showers, fire rings/grills, picnic tables, picnic shelters, beach area, playground, boat rental, dump station, visitor center
Fee per night: $$$$
Management: USDA Forest Service / Mount Rogers National Recreation Area District
Contact: (276) 388-3642; (877) 444-6777; www.fs.usda.gov
Activities: Hiking, swimming, fishing, canoeing, biking

Season: Open mid-April to end of October

Finding the campground: From I-81 take exit 19 in Abingdon. Take Route 58 east and follow it to the entrance for Beartree Recreation Area. Take a left and follow it to the campground entrance.

GPS coordinates: 36.655017 / -81.692978

About the campground: Located in the Mount Rogers National Recreation Area of the GWJ National Forests. A meandering creek winds through the campground, offering the opportunity for fishing or for kids to splash around. You will also have access to 14-acre Beartree Lake, where fishing and swimming are permitted. Fish for brown trout, rainbow trout, smallmouth bass, and sunfish, either from the shoreline or from one of the two fishing piers. There's a beach area for swimming, or you can rent a canoe to explore the lake. Beartree Lake Trail follows along the lake for a nice hike, with a portion of it paved. Nearby is the Virginia Creeper Trail, which is popular for hiking and biking. RV friendly.

12 Hurricane Campground

Location: 17 miles southeast of Marion

Sites: 30 standard

Facilities: Flush toilets, pit/vault toilets, showers, fire rings, picnic tables, picnic area, playground

Fee per night: $$$

Management: USDA Forest Service / Mount Rogers National Recreation Area District

Contact: (276) 783-5196; (877) 444-6777; www.fs.usda.gov

Activities: Hiking, biking, horseback riding, fishing

Season: Open mid-May to end of October

Finding the campground: From Marion take I-81 to exit 45 for SR 16 south toward Sugar Grove. Take a right on SR 650, which will be a gravel road. Follow it to the campground entrance (which is a paved road).

GPS coordinates: 36.722631 / -81.490916

About the campground: You are within steps of the Appalachian Trail at this campground, so make sure you do a little AT hiking before you leave. Within the campground, catch the Hurricane Knob Trail. It takes you up to Hurricane Knob, which sits at an elevation of 2,175 feet and is beautiful. The trail is a loop, so you will end up back where you started when you descend from the Knob. There are two creeks, Hurricane Branch and Comers Creek, both of which are stocked with trout and make for great fishing. Campsites are shaded. RV friendly, though large RVs are not recommended.

13 Grindstone Recreation Area Campground

Location: 23 miles west of Troutdale

Sites: 48 standard, 60 standard electric

Facilities: Flush toilets, showers, fire rings, fire grills, picnic tables, dump station, water play area, amphitheater, volleyball courts, playground

Fee per night: $$$$
Management: USDA Forest Service / Mount Rogers National Recreation Area District
Contact: (276) 388-3983; (877) 444-6777; www.fs.fed.us
Activities: Hiking, biking, horseback riding, volleyball, swimming
Season: Open end of April to end of November
Finding the campground: From Troutdale take exit 45 for SR 16 headed south. Take a right onto SR 603. Follow it to the campground entrance on the left.
GPS coordinates: 36.688344 / -81.539299
About the campground: Beautifully wooded, this campground sits within the Mount Rogers National Recreation Area and offers a lot of territory to explore. There are some first-come, first-served sites available during the busy season, and all sites become such in the off-season. There's a creek that runs through the campground, and this is where a water play area has been created that kids will enjoy. Ample hiking, biking, and horseback riding opportunities are also available with multiple trails from which to choose. The Virginia Creeper Trail is nearby, which is popular with cyclists. Due to the campground's high elevation, you can escape the heat and humidity of Virginia here during the height of summer. RV friendly.

14 Washington County Park Camping

Location: 10 miles south of Abingdon
Sites: 10 standard, 132 standard electric, water, and sewer
Facilities: Flush toilets, showers, fire grills, picnic tables, picnic shelters, playground, dump station, boat ramp, snack bar
Fee per night: $$$–$$$$
Management: Washington County Park Authority
Contact: (276) 628-9677; www.washcova.com/government
Activities: Fishing, boating, hiking
Season: Open April to end of October
Finding the campground: Take US 11 west / Main Street to SR 75. Take a left on County Park Road. Turn left onto Lake Road, then take your first right onto County Park Road once again. Follow it to the park entrance.
GPS coordinates: 36.599854 / -82.016443
About the campground: This park managed by Washington County is situated on South Holston Lake, providing multiple water recreation opportunities. There is a boat ramp and access points for launching a canoe or kayak. Campsites are first come, first served. RV friendly with sites that provide full hookups.

15 Grayson Highlands State Park

Location: 37 miles south of Marion
Sites: 28 standard, 36 with electric and water, 23 horse (stable, covered, and open stalls)

Grayson Highlands State Park Courtesy Virginia Department of Conservation and Recreation

Facilities: Flush and vault toilets, showers, fire rings, fire grills, picnic tables, picnic shelters, playground, dump station, gift shop, concessions, visitor center
Fee per night: $$$$
Management: Virginia Department of Conservation and Recreation
Contact: (276) 579-7092; (800) 933-7275; dcr.virginia.gov/state_parks/gra.shtml
Activities: Fishing, horseback riding, hiking, biking
Season: May to October
Finding the campground: From I-81 take exit 45 in Marion onto SR 16 south. Take a right on US 58. Follow it to the park entrance.
GPS coordinates: 36.639774 / -81.486207
About the campground: Located in the GWJ National Forests, in a gorgeous mountaintop setting that is close to the Appalachian Trail, within 10 miles of the Virginia Creeper Trail, and Virginia's two highest points, Mount Rogers and Whitetop Mountain. This park is an excellent launch point for activities in the Mount Rogers National Recreation Area. Scenic views are outstanding, with peaks more than 5,000 feet, waterfalls, and stunning overlooks. Nature and history programs, along with events and festivals throughout the year, both inside and outside of the park, provide plenty of entertainment opportunities. The park offers more than 67 miles of trails for horseback riding, with a special horse camping area. There are also 10 miles of cold streams for trout fishing. You may be treated to seeing one of the wild ponies that live in the area. Do not feed them per the request of park officials and with good reason: It can cause digestive issues for them. RV friendly.

16 Fox Creek Horse Campground

Location: 4 miles west of Troutdale
Sites: 32 standard
Facilities: Portable toilets, hitching posts
Fee per night: $
Management: USDA Forest Service / Mount Rogers National Recreation Area District
Contact: (540) 783-5196; (800) 628-7202; www.fs.usda.gov
Activities: Horseback riding
Season: Open April to end of November
Finding the campground: Take I-81 in Marion, then exit 45 to SR 16 headed south toward Troutdale. Turn right onto SR 603, which is also called Laurel Valley Road. Follow it to the campground entrance on the right.
GPS coordinates: 36.697868 / -81.503797
About the campground: A very primitive campground located in the Mount Rogers National Recreation Area, but the big draw here is for horse lovers: You have access to many well-groomed trails in the Mount Rogers High Country, the Virginia Highlands Horse Trail, and Iron Mountain Trail. Some of these trails, however, can get quite rocky. All of this is what makes the campground such an enticement to equestrians despite its primitive nature. This campground can serve as your launch point. No drinking water is available, so you will need to bring water. There is a creek that runs through, so this may be an option for watering horses. Nearby Grindstone Recreation Area Campground provides water, showers, and a dump station for a fee.

17 Raccoon Branch Campground

Location: Located in Sugar Grove, 11 miles south of Marion
Sites: 12 standard, 8 standard electric
Facilities: Flush toilets, fire grills, picnic tables, picnic area, dump station
Fee per night: $$$–$$$$
Management: USDA Forest Service / Mount Rogers National Recreation Area District
Contact: (276) 783-5196; (877) 444-6777; www.fs.usda.gov
Activities: Fishing, hiking, biking
Season: Open mid-April to end of October
Finding the campground: From I-81 take exit 45 in Marion onto SR 16 south. The campground entrance will be on the right.
GPS coordinates: 36.747078 / -81.425114
About the campground: Located next to the Raccoon Branch Wilderness and at the base of Dickey Knob in the Mount Rogers National Recreation Area, this park also offers streams running through it: Dickey Creek and Raccoon Branch. Fish for trout in the creek, but it will require a fishing license. To reach the top of Dickey Knob, follow along the Dickey Knob Trail either by foot or by bike. Once there, you will have a view of the valley. The park is close to the Appalachian Trail, so you can hike a section while you're here. Free Wi-Fi is available at campsites that have electric

hookups—a unique extra that you don't find many places, which is just as well if you're trying to take a relaxing break. RV friendly.

18 Comers Rock Recreation Area

Location: 13 miles southwest of Speedwell
Sites: 6 standard
Facilities: Vault toilets, fire grills, picnic tables, picnic area
Fee per night: $
Management: USDA Forest Service / Mount Rogers National Recreation Area District
Contact: (800) 628-7202; www.fs.usda.gov
Activities: Hiking, biking
Season: Open mid-April to end of October
Finding the campground: From I-81 take exit 73 in Wytheville to get on US 11 (also called Main Street). Stay on Main Street when it turns into SR 21 heading south. Turn right onto Forest Service Road 57. Follow it to campground entrance. The Forest Service Road is gravel, so use caution.
GPS coordinates: 36.763065 / -81.224910
About the campground: This is a very primitive campground located in the Mount Rogers National Recreation Area, but not without its draw. Here you will be on top of Iron Mountain and have access to a range of hiking trails, including those leading into Dry Run Wilderness, and a climb to the peak of Comers Rock, where there is an old fire tower. A section of the Iron Mountain Trail for mountain biking runs from the campground to Hale Lake. The lake is just 2 miles away, so you can break up your hikes and biking with a trip there for fishing or boating.

19 Raven Cliff Recreation Area Campground

Location: 15 miles west of Hillsville
Sites: 20 standard
Facilities: Portable toilets, vault toilet, fire grills, picnic tables, picnic area, picnic shelter
Fee per night: $
Management: USDA Forest Service / Mount Rogers National Recreation Area District
Contact: (276) 783-5196; (800) 628-7202; www.fs.usda.gov
Activities: Fishing, tubing, hiking, horseback riding
Season: Open mid-April to end of October
Finding the campground: From I-81 take exit 67 in Wytheville to US 11 / Main Street. Follow it until Main Street becomes US 21 south and stay straight to remain on it. Take SR 619 at Speedwell, then turn onto VA 619 headed east. Follow to the campground entrance.
GPS coordinates: 36.836279 / -81.066541
About the campground: Located in the eastern section of Mount Rogers National Recreation Area, this site is named for the 200-foot-tall sandstone cliff located here. This is a remote campground with a couple of nice draws: It is remote and you will probably not have to fight off any

crowds, and you can bring a tube and go tubing in Cripple Creek during the warmer summer months. A couple of large fields are great for a game of softball, kickball, or soccer. **Please note:** No drinking water is available, so be sure to pack plenty of potable water for drinking, cooking, and washing off. You can also fish for smallmouth bass, or trout, which are stocked in the spring in Cripple Creek. You will need a valid Virginia state fishing license. An old iron furnace dating from the early 1800s, and used during the Civil War, is located in the area and reachable by a creekside trail. Campsites are first come, first served. Horse trailers are allowed, and there is access to the Virginia Highland Horse Trail. RV friendly up to 32 feet.

20 Stony Fork Campground

Location: 9 miles northwest of Wytheville
Sites: 15 standard, 35 standard electric
Facilities: Flush toilets, showers, fire grills, dump station, picnic areas, horseshoe pit
Fee per night: $$$–$$$$
Management: USDA Forest Service / Mount Rogers National Recreation Area District
Contact: (276) 783-5196; (800) 628-7202; www.fs.usda.gov
Activities: Hiking, biking, fishing, horseshoes
Season: April to November
Finding the campground: From I-77 take exit 47. Turn left onto SR 717 to the park entrance.
GPS coordinates: 37.010236 / -81.181263
About the campground: Situated at the base of Big Walker Mountain and next to Big Walker Scenic Byway in GWJ National Forests. Close to the Appalachian Trail, Stony Fork provides a range of hiking trails from which to select. Stony Fork Nature Trail is 1 mile, or you can take the more strenuous Seven Sisters Trail that goes from the campground area up Little Walker Mountain. To extend the hike, you can continue on the Scenic Byway. Or you can do an out-and back hike of a section of the Appalachian Trail. Try north one day and south the next. The area makes for some good mountain biking as well. One fork of Stony Fork Creek goes through the campground and provides trout fishing. Some of the campsites are accessible to people with disabilities. If you time your visit right, you will be treated either to spring blooms of rhododendron and azaleas or stunning fall foliage when the forest turns golden, both occasions when you will want to take advantage of the Scenic Byway for optimum viewing. RV friendly.

21 Hungry Mother State Park

Location: In Marion off I-81
Sites: 11 standard, 40 with electric and water, 30 with electric, water, and sewer
Facilities: Flush toilets, showers, fire ring, basketball court, beach area, boat launch (non-gas powered only), boat rental, concession, store, gift shop, horseshoes, picnic shelters, playground, tennis court, laundry facility, restaurant
Fee per night: $$$$

Hungry Mother State Park COURTESY VIRGINIA DEPARTMENT OF CONSERVATION AND RECREATION

Management: Virginia Department of Conservation and Recreation
Contact: (276) 781-7400; (800) 933-7275; http://dcr.virginia.gov/state_parks/hun.shtml
Activities: Swimming, boating, canoeing, kayaking, hiking, biking
Season: Open year-round
Finding the campground: From I-81 take exit 47 onto Route 11 toward Marion. Turn right on Route 16 north. Follow it to the park entrance.
GPS coordinates: 36.877296 / -81.526408
About the campground: This was one of the state's first state parks. There are two campgrounds located at this site: One is in Hungry Mother State Park and the other is Camp Burson, located just before the entrance to Hungry Mother State Park, providing 52 of the total available campsites. Situated on Hungry Mother Lake, which covers 108 acres, the park offers a beach area for swimming, boat rentals that include canoes, kayaks, paddleboats, and jon boats, and a boat launch. No gas-powered boats are allowed on the lake. You can cool off there after you have explored the 12 miles of hiking and biking trails through the woodlands. Lake Loop is a trail that goes around the lake and is almost 6 miles in length. Molly's Knob Trail goes to the top of the park's highest point and is 1.5 miles long. There is a fishing pier for you to try your luck catching a range of fish, from bass to walleyes. RVs are welcome.

Shenandoah Valley / Northern Virginia Area

Northern Virginia and the Shenandoah Valley region have a unique mix of bustling city, mountain and forest areas, rolling farmlands, and fields. The diversity between the Beltway, which loops around the nation's capital, and the bucolic two-lane roads within just an hour's reach make Virginia a state that really does offer something for everyone, and all within driving distance of the Washington, DC, metropolitan area.

To the west lies Shenandoah National Park, located in the Blue Ridge Mountains. This national treasure offers expansive views from its ridged peaks down into the Shenandoah Valley region below, moderate to challenging hiking trails, multiple waterfalls, and various historic sites that give a glimpse into Appalachian history. In addition, the Appalachian Trail runs through the park for approximately 105 miles of its total 1,280-mile length. The park is a huge draw in the autumn for its stunning fall foliage display, and Skyline Drive becomes one of the most popular scenic drives in the region when fall colors are at their peak. Or rather, when people guess the peak will hit. Skyline Drive eventually connects with the Blue Ridge Parkway, considered "America's Favorite Scenic Drive," which takes you farther south down into Virginia and on into North Carolina and Great Smoky Mountains National Park.

Lying to the west of Shenandoah National Park is George Washington and Jefferson National Forests and the Allegheny Mountains, providing a perfect backdrop for the campgrounds in this region.

Many campgrounds are alongside creeks.

Shenandoah Valley Area

Pastures, woodlands, and pure, natural beauty capture what the Shenandoah Valley is all about. It is said that two-thirds of the US population lives within one day's drive of Shenandoah National Park. If you travel to this region, you will have plenty to do in terms of recreation and drinking in scenic beauty. We can thank the Civilian Conservation Corps for planting the park area where it had once been deforested to make way for farmland. You will still see some old structures here that date back hundreds of years to when this was a farming community.

To gain access to the beginning of Skyline Drive and Shenandoah National Park, start at the entrance located in Front Royal to the north. The National Park Service operates several campgrounds here, and the park covers 196,000 acres of forested land. During a good part of the year, nature programs and history/interpretive programs are offered that are enjoyable for kids and adults. There are more than 500 miles of hiking trails in the park from which to choose, including the Appalachian Trail. There are hiking trails appropriate for casual hikers, hiking with kids, and very strenuous options. One hike that is quite popular and strenuous is Old Rag Mountain, which is worth the sweat to crest it in order to enjoy the view. It takes about 1 mile of crawling uphill on rocks to get to its peak. Amazingly, that does not deter the crowds in the least. Another popular hike (also strenuous) is White Oak Canyon/Cedar Run Trail for a view of White Oak Canyon Falls and swimming holes. There are also equestrian trails in the park. Do not be surprised if you see a black bear. Sightings are not rare here. While sitting outside of a store, I saw one along with her cub crossing Skyline Drive in no particular hurry. With that in mind, you definitely want to store your food in bear-proof containers. (Refer to the "Wildlife Encounters" section for tips.) During your stay at one of the campgrounds here, be sure to hike to see one of the ten waterfalls in the park. Keep in mind that to get to them you may be hiking down, but there will still be the uphill return trip, and this can make it quite strenuous. For fishermen there are about thirty-six species of fish in the park's streams. Cyclists can challenge themselves to riding along Skyline Drive with its demanding ascents. Farther south on the Blue Ridge Parkway, road cycling is also popular. Skyline Drive ends in Waynesboro and the Blue Ridge Parkway picks up from there.

To the west of Shenandoah National Park is George Washington and Jefferson National Forests; campgrounds there are operated by the USDA Forest Service. It offers hundreds of miles of mountain biking, hiking, ATV/ORV and equestrian trails, and numerous fishing opportunities with dozens of species of fish. Great North Mountain is a ridge on the border between Virginia and West Virginia. Here you will find more than 80 miles of trails suitable for hiking and biking through the forest area. One trail leads to Big Schloss, a stone formation that offers a great view down into West Virginia and is a popular hike in this area. A section of the long-distance Tuscarora Trail goes over this mountain, starting from the Appalachian Trail to the east,

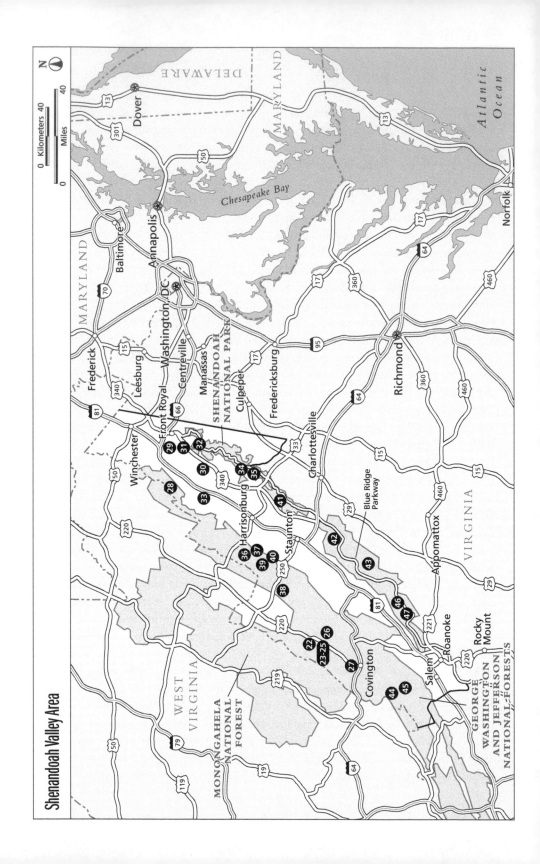

Shenandoah Valley Area

	Total Sites	Max. RV Length	Hookups	Fire Ring/Grill	Toilets	Showers	Drinking Water	Dump Station	Recreation	Fee ($)	Reservable
22 Hidden Valley Recreation Area	31			Y	V	N	Y	Y	H, S, F, B, C, HB	$$$	N
23 Blowing Springs Campground	22			Y	V	N	Y	Y	H, S, F	$$$	N
24 Bolar Mountain Recreation Area	123		E	Y	F	Y	Y	Y	H, S, F, B, L	$$$-$$$$	Y
25 McClintic Point Campgrounds	20			Y	V	Y	Y	Y	H, S, F, B	$$$	Y
26 Douthat State Park	87	50	E, W	Y	F	Y	Y	Y	H, S, F, B, L, HB	$$$$	Y
27 Morris Hill Campgrounds	52			Y	F	Y	Y	Y	H, S, F, B, L, C	$$$	N
28 Wolf Gap Recreation Area	9			N	V	N	Y	N	H, C	$	N
29 Elizabeth Furnace Campground	32			Y	F,V	Y	Y	Y	H, F, C	$$$	N
30 Little Fort Campground	11			Y	V	N	N	N	OHV, H, F, C	$	N
31 Raymond R. "Andy" Guest Jr. Shenandoah River State Park	42	60	E	Y	F	Y	Y	N	H, F, B, L, C, HB	$$$$	Y
32 Mathews Arm Campground	163			Y	F	N	Y	Y	H, F, C, HB	$$$	Y
33 Camp Roosevelt Recreation Area Campground	10			Y	F	N	Y	Y	H, C	$$	N
34 Big Meadows Campground	168			Y	F	Y	Y	Y	H, F, C, HB	$$$	Y
35 Lewis Mountain Campground	32			Y	F	Y	Y	N	H, F, C, HB	$$$	N
36 Hone Quarry Campground	26			Y	V	N	N	N	H, F, C	$	N
37 Natural Chimneys Campground	165		E, W, S	Y	F	Y	Y	Y	H, S, C	$$$$	Y
38 Shaws Fork Equestrian Campground	5			N	V	N	N	N	H, HB	$	N
39 Todd Lake Recreation Area	20			Y	F	Y	Y	Y	H, S, B, C	$$$	N
40 North River Campground	9			Y	V	N	N	N	H, F, C	$	N
41 Loft Mountain Campground	199			Y	F	Y	Y	Y	H, F, C, HB	$$$	Y
42 Sherando Lake Recreation Area	37		E	Y	F,V	Y	Y	Y	H, S, F, B	$$$$	N
43 Otter Creek Campground	69			Y	F	N	Y	Y	H, F	$$$	Y
44 Steel Bridge Campground	20			Y	P	N	N	N	F	$	N
45 The Pines Campground	10			Y	V	N	Y	N	H, F	$	N
46 Cave Mountain Lake Campground	27	30		Y	F	Y	Y	Y	H, S, F	$$$	N
47 North Creek Recreation Area Campground	16			Y	V	N	Y	N	H, F	$$$	N

Max. RV Length: Measured in feet

Hookups: W = Water, E = Electricity, S = Sewer

Fire Ring/Grill: Y = Yes, N = None

Toilets: F = Flush, P = Pit, V = Vault

Showers: Y = Yes, N = None

Drinking Water: Y = Yes, N = None

Dump Station: Y = Yes, N = None

Recreation: H = Hiking, S = Swimming, F = Fishing, B = Boating, L = Boat Launch, C = Cycling, HB = Horseback Riding, OHV = Off-Highway Vehicles

Fee: $ = 0-$5, $$ = $6-$10, $$$ = $11-$20, $$$$ = $21-$30+

Reservable: Y = Yes, N = No

where it splits off to head west before rejoining the trail in Pennsylvania after having first crossed into West Virginia and Maryland.

There are famous caverns to visit, including Luray Caverns, considered one of the largest caverns on the East Coast. It has one particularly unique geologic feature: The stone formations in one area can actually make musical sounds that resemble an organ. If it is a hot and humid summer day, this would make a perfect day trip close to the local campgrounds and would provide the opportunity to cool off naturally. There are also Skyline Caverns, Endless Caverns, and Shenandoah Caverns from which to choose.

The Shenandoah River flows through the valley area, offering a chance to raft, tube, canoe, or kayak. If you don't have your own equipment, there are outfitters in the area. Northeast of Roanoke, the Upper James River Water Trail begins with 14 miles designated a "Virginia Scenic River," which is also suitable for kayaking, canoeing, or tubing. Crabtree Falls is south of Shenandoah National Park and considered one of the most popular waterfall hikes in the state with five major cascades. It is close to the Blue Ridge Parkway, and there is a fee to park in the area.

The Shenandoah Valley is also where you will find some of Virginia's wineries, the rich soil of the valley region the perfect viniculture medium. If you are a wine aficionado, find a local Wine Trail and travel with care.

22 Hidden Valley Recreation Area

Location: 6 miles west of Warm Springs
Sites: 31 standard
Facilities: Vault toilets, fire grills, picnic tables, picnic areas, dump station
Fee per night: $$$
Management: USDA Forest Service / George Washington and Jefferson National Forests / Warm Springs Ranger District
Contact: (540) 839-2521; www.fs.usda.gov
Activities: Hiking, biking, fishing, swimming, horseback riding, canoeing, kayaking
Season: Open first week of March through early December
Finding the campground: From I-81 take SR 39 west. Turn right onto SR 621. Turn left onto FR 241 / Hidden Valley Road. Follow it to the campground entrance on the left.
GPS coordinates: 38.104432 / -79.812621
About the campground: This Forest Service campground is located in George Washington and Jefferson National Forests and is a historic Civil War site, featuring Warwick Plantation, which dates to the mid-1800s and is now a bed-and-breakfast inn. Situated in a valley (hence the name) and along Jackson River, it is a peaceful location with hay fields. Its claim to fame is that the location was featured in the movie *Sommersby,* which was filmed here. Jackson River is stocked with trout and popular with fly fishermen. The lower Jackson River is good for kayaking and canoeing. Fishing here requires a valid Virginia state fishing license. Altogether there are about 20 miles of mountain biking and hiking trails available, ranging from 1 mile to 7 miles in length. The Hidden Valley Trail is open to equestrians, too. Toilets are wheelchair accessible. Lake Moomaw is nearby. RV friendly.

23 Blowing Springs Campground

Location: 10 miles west of Warm Springs
Sites: 22 standard
Facilities: Vault toilets, fire grills, picnic tables, picnic areas, dump station
Fee per night: $$$
Management: USDA Forest Service / George Washington National Forest / Warm Springs Ranger District / American Land & Leisure
Contact: (800) 342-2267; www.fs.usda.gov
Activities: Hiking, fishing, swimming
Season: January through early December
Finding the campground: From I-81 take SR 39 west. Follow to the campground entrance on the left.
GPS coordinates: 38.069384 / -79.883658
About the campground: This Forest Service campground is located in George Washington National Forest and is a rustic location. The name "Blowing Springs" refers to an unusual geological occurrence: Air is blown out of the rocks through a duct that has formed, and it is always measured at 58 degrees. Water is available at this site, but you must pump it by hand, and no water is available from March to April. There is a hiking trail a little over 1 mile long, and fishing is available in Back Creek. It is stocked with trout, and you must have a valid state fishing license. In addition, you have access to trails that lead to swimming holes, a unique find in a campground. Choose between a shady or sunny campsite. Close to Lake Moomaw and Bolar Mountain National Forest Recreation Area for additional recreational opportunities. RV friendly, but driving up the hill may be challenging.

24 Bolar Mountain Recreation Area

Location: 10 miles west of Warm Springs
Sites: 2 tent only, 81 standard, 34 standard electric, 6 walk to
Facilities: Flush toilets, showers, fire grills, fire rings, picnic tables, picnic areas, picnic shelters, dump station, volleyball courts, horseshoe pit, swimming beach, boat ramp, boat rentals, educational programs, marina, playground
Fee per night: $$$-$$$$
Management: USDA Forest Service / George Washington and Jefferson National Forests / Warm Springs Ranger District / American Land & Leisure
Contact: (540) 839-2521; www.fs.usda.gov
Activities: Hiking, fishing, boating, volleyball, kayaking, canoeing, horseshoes, waterskiing, swimming
Season: Open late May through early September
Finding the campground: From I-81 take SR 39 west. Turn left on SR 600. At the intersection of SR 600 and Twin Ridge Drive, bear to the left. SR 600 will become SR 603. Follow it to the recreation area and campground entrance.

GPS coordinates: 37.984783 / -79.969636

About the campground: This Forest Service campground is located in George Washington and Jefferson National Forests on 2,500-acre Lake Moomaw and provides a lot of great amenities and recreational opportunities. Boats up to 25 feet in length permitted. Lake has an average 80-foot depth. Fish for bass, rainbow trout, brown trout, and crappie. You will need a valid Virginia state fishing license. For hikers there are 11 miles of trails available that lead to Grouse Point Overlook and Islands Overlook Spur. Make reservations at least two days before arriving. There are some waterfront sites. RV friendly, but driving up the hill may be challenging.

25 McClintic Point Campgrounds

Location: 10 miles west of Warm Springs
Sites: 20 standard
Facilities: Vault toilets, outdoor showers, fire grills, fire pits, picnic tables, dump station, fishing dock
Fee per night: $$$
Management: USDA Forest Service / George Washington and Jefferson National Forests / Warm Springs Ranger District / American Land & Leisure
Contact: (540) 839-2521; (800) 342-2267; (877) 444-6777; www.fs.usda.gov
Activities: Hiking, fishing, boating, kayaking, canoeing, waterskiing, swimming
Season: Open first week of March through early December
Finding the campground: From I-81 take SR 39 west. Turn left on SR 600. At the intersection of SR 600 and Twin Ridge Drive, bear to the left. SR 600 will become SR 603. Follow it to the campground entrance, McClintic Point, which will be on the right.
GPS coordinates: 38.014028 / -79.920055

About the campground: This Forest Service campground is located in George Washington and Jefferson National Forests. Situated at the northernmost section of 2,500-acre Lake Moomaw, campsites are reservable and also first come, first served. Some sites are waterfront. Fish for bass, rainbow trout, brown trout, and crappie in the lake. You will need a valid Virginia state fishing license. There is an accessible fishing dock available. For boating you will need to drive to ramps located outside of the campground and available at other recreation areas surrounding Lake Moomaw. For hikers and mountain bikers, the area has plenty of hiking trails from which to choose. There is no water available from March to the end of April. RV friendly.

26 Douthat State Park

Location: 35 miles west of Lexington, northeast of Clifton Forge
Sites: 73 with electric and water, 14 horse sites
Facilities: Flush toilets, showers, fire grills, picnic tables, dump station, boat launch and rental, camp store, snack bar/concession, gift shop, picnic areas/shelters, playgrounds, restaurant, amphitheater
Fee per night: $$$$
Management: Virginia Department of Conservation and Recreation

Douthat State Park Courtesy Virginia Department of Conservation and Recreation

Contact: (540) 862-8100; (800) 933-7275; http://dcr.virginia.gov/state_parks/dou.shtml
Activities: Hiking, swimming, boating, biking, fishing, horseback riding
Season: Open year-round
Finding the campground: Take I-64 west to exit 27, then turn right onto SR 629. Take a left onto US 220 / Douthat Road (which becomes Douthat State Park Road). Follow it to the park entrance.
GPS coordinates: 37.898931 / -79.807662
About the campground: Douthat State Park was a CCC project, one of the original six Virginia State Parks to be created, and it is listed on the National Register of Historic Places due to its influence as a model for park development across the nation. There are miles of outdoor adventure available at Douthat State Park with 2 miles of stream fishing available. The park is located in the cool, lush interior of George Washington and Jefferson National Forests, spread across almost 4,500 acres of greenery. The drive to the interior of the park is more than 7 miles long and ideal for road biking (making use of the road before the park entrance as well), while the trails are suited for mountain bikes. The Allegheny Highlands Trail System is a project of the forest service, which is connecting hiking trails between the park and Covington to develop more than 60 miles of looped trails suitable for equestrians and mountain bikers, too. See if you can fit in exploration of about 40 miles of hiking and biking trails, ranging in difficulty from flat to more strenuous, located within the park. All of these options combined will provide more than 100 miles of trail-exploration opportunities. There are four campgrounds ranging from standard to equestrian to RV, with sites available for up to 50-foot campers. Equestrian campground with horse trailer parking area. Some campsites offer views of 50-acre Douthat Lake. For the kids there is a fishing area just for them and a discovery center. The lake has a swimming beach area as well as a modern bathhouse where you can shower and change clothes. The lake itself is stocked with trout and also has largemouth bass, chain pickerel, and sunfish. Fishing licenses and permits are sold in the park store. Rent a paddleboat and explore the lake by water or bring your own boat (non-gasoline powered only) and use the boat launch.

27 Morris Hill Campgrounds

Location: 13 miles north of Covington
Sites: 52 standard
Facilities: Flush toilets, showers, fire grills, picnic tables, dump station, boat ramp, playground, swimming beach
Fee per night: $$$
Management: USDA Forest Service / George Washington and Jefferson National Forests / James River Ranger District / American Land & Leisure
Contact: (800) 342-2267; (877) 444-6777; www.fs.usda.gov
Activities: Hiking, swimming, boating, biking, fishing (including fly fishing), waterskiing
Season: Open first week of May to late October
Finding the campground: Take I-64 exit 16A to US 220 north. Turn left onto SR 687. Turn left on SR 641 / 666. Turn right onto SR 605. Follow it to the campground entrance on the left.
GPS coordinates: 37.932932 / -79.970026
About the campground: This Forest Service campground is located in George Washington and Jefferson National Forests on a ridge just south of Lake Moomaw, so there is access to the lake

for boating, swimming, and fishing. The lake covers more than 2,500 acres and has a beach and three boat ramps from which to launch a boat, none of which is located in the campground itself. The closest is 1.5 miles away, and there is one 35 miles to the north. Power boats are permitted on the lake. In addition, Jackson River is close by and excellent for canoeing or kayaking, and there are five access points available and open to the public for use. Jackson River and Back Creek are great for fly fishermen looking to cast a line and catch trout. Also available are bass and crappie. You must have a Virginia state license to fish in the lake, river, or creek. Choose from two trails, one for biking and the other with more than 3 miles of hiking. Drinking water is available at this location as are accessible toilets. RV friendly.

28 Wolf Gap Recreation Area

Location: 49 miles west of Front Royal
Sites: 9 standard
Facilities: Vault toilets
Fee per night: $
Management: USDA Forest Service / George Washington and Jefferson National Forests / Lee Ranger District
Contact: (540) 984 4101; www.fs.usda.gov
Activities: Hiking, biking
Season: Open year round
Finding the campground: From I-81 take exit 279 west onto SR 675. At the stop sign take a right onto SR 42, then turn left to get back on SR 675. When you come to a fork in the road, bear right to remain on SR 675. Follow it to the campground entrance on the right, located at the top of the mountain.
GPS coordinates: 38.924348 / -78.689022
About the campground: This Forest Service campground has no fee and is located in George Washington and Jefferson National Forests. It is a year-round, primitive campground, but drinking water is available. From the campground, you have access to mountain biking and hiking trails, including Big Schloss Overlook, which gives you a view of two states' worth of mountains for the price of one hike.

29 Elizabeth Furnace Campground

Location: 10 miles west of Front Royal
Sites: 32 standard
Facilities: Flush toilets, vault toilets, showers, fire grills, picnic tables, dump station, playground
Fee per night: $$$
Management: USDA Forest Service / George Washington and Jefferson National Forests / Lee Ranger District
Contact: (540) 984-4101; www.fs.usda.gov
Activities: Hiking, fishing, biking

Season: Open year-round

Finding the campground: From Front Royal at the intersection of US 340 (North Shenandoah Avenue) and SR 55 (Strasburg Road), take SR 55 headed west. Turn left onto CR 678 (Fort Valley Road). Follow it to the campground entrance on the left.

GPS coordinates: 38.924192 / -78.331483

About the campground: This Forest Service campground is located in George Washington and Jefferson National Forests. Campsites are wooded and have tent pads and some are situated next to a stream that runs through the campground. Open year-round. The flush toilets and the showers are closed during the off-season, winter months, and there is also no potable water during this time. However, you do have access to vault toilets. Elizabeth Furnace was once an area that produced "pig iron," and there are a couple of interpretive trails where you can learn how this iron was made. There's a swinging bridge that leads to an old cabin, so you can soak up some mountain history as well as enjoy beautiful scenery during your stay. In addition, there are a couple of hiking and biking trails. Signal Knob Trail is one that both hikers and mountain bikers use. It is more than 10 miles long and takes you to the top of Signal Knob. You also have access to the miles of trails that run through GWJ, though you may need to drive to whichever ones you select. You can fish for trout in the local streams, but it is required that you have a Virginia state fishing license. RV friendly, though the parking at sites can vary in size and shape, so be forewarned if you have a larger vehicle.

30 Little Fort Campground

Location: 3 miles east of Detrick

Sites: 11 standard

Facilities: Vault toilet, fire ring, picnic tables

Fee per night: $

Management: USDA Forest Service / George Washington and Jefferson National Forests / Lee Ranger District

Contact: (540) 984-4101; www.fs.usda.gov

Activities: OHV trail, hiking, fishing, biking

Season: Open year-round

Finding the campground: From I-81 take exit 279 for SR 675 headed east. When you come to a T intersection in Edinburg, turn left onto US 11. Turn right to get back on SR 675. When you come to the stop sign at Kings Crossing, turn left (headed north) to the town of Detrick. Turn left on SR 758. Follow it to the campground entrance.

GPS coordinates: 38.866956 / -78.44444

About the campground: This is a bare-bones but no-fee campground located in GWJ National Forests. Camp access to off-highway vehicles, but you must have a special recreation permit to use the OHV/ATV trail. It is the largest of this type of trail in the state. Trails for hiking and mountain biking nearby. Access to stream fishing. No running water.

31 Raymond R. "Andy" Guest Jr. Shenandoah River State Park

Location: Located 8 miles south of Front Royal, 15 miles north of Luray
Sites: 10 tent only, 32 standard electric
Facilities: Flush toilets, showers, fire rings, fire grills, picnic tables, picnic shelters, boat launch
Fee per night: $$$$
Management: Virginia Department of Conservation and Recreation
Contact: (540) 622-6840; (800) 933-7275; http://dcr.virginia.gov/state_parks/and.shtml
Activities: Canoeing, kayaking, fishing, hiking, biking, horseback riding
Season: Open year-round
Finding the campground: Take I-66 West to exit 13 and turn left off the ramp. Go one block and take a right at the light onto Route 55 West. Go five stoplights and turn left onto 340 South. Drive 8 miles; the park entrance is located on the right.
GPS coordinates: 38.849071 / -78.307408
About the campground: The park sits along 5.5 miles of Shenandoah River shoreline, with the 10 tent-only campsites nestled along the riverfront. A cartop boat launch is available for canoes and kayaks. The park is wheelchair accessible. It is considered a "trash free facility," which means campers must haul out their trash. There are 24 miles of trails, 7 of which are considered multi-use, to explore by foot, bike, or horseback. RVs are welcome up to 60 feet.

Raymond R. "Andy" Guest Jr. Shenandoah River State Park COURTESY VIRGINIA DEPART-MENT OF CONSERVATION AND RECREATION

32 Mathews Arm Campground

Location: In Shenandoah National Park at mile marker 22.1
Sites: 163 standard
Facilities: Flush toilets, fire grates, fire grills, picnic tables, drinking water, dump station
Fee per night: $$$
Management: National Park Service
Contact: (877) 444-6777; online reservations available at www.recreation.gov
Activities: Hiking, biking, fishing, horseback riding, interpretive programs, scenic driving
Season: Mid-May to late October
Finding the campground: Located off mile 22.1 on Skyline Drive. Take Highway 211 west for 28 miles to Shenandoah National Park and Skyline Drive Thornton Gap Entrance. Follow Skyline Drive north about 9 miles and turn left into the campground.
GPS coordinates: 38.760216 / -78.296530
About the campground: If you are entering Shenandoah National Park from the north, this is the first campground along Skyline Drive. It puts you next to the closest trail that leads to the tallest waterfall in the park: Overall Run Falls, which is 93 feet tall. Also, it is located 2 miles from Elkwallow Wayside, a convenience store offering outdoor supplies, a food concession counter, and gas. There are no showers at this location, but there are several bathrooms. This is a good-size campground that will accommodate large RVs, but no hookups are available.

Mathews Arm Campground COURTESY NATIONAL PARK SERVICE, SHENANDOAH NATIONAL PARK

33 Camp Roosevelt Recreation Area Campground

Location: 8 miles north of Luray
Sites: 10 standard
Facilities: Flush toilets, fire grills, picnic tables, dump station
Fee per night: $$
Management: USDA Forest Service / George Washington and Jefferson National Forests / Lee Ranger District
Contact: (540) 984-4101; www.fs.usda.gov
Activities: Hiking, biking
Season: Open first week of May to middle of October
Finding the campground: From Luray take SR 340 north. Take a left onto Mechanic Street, which will become Bixlers Ferry and SR 675. When you come to a fork in the road, bear left to remain on SR 675. When you reach the end, turn right to once again remain on SR 675 (also called Fort Valley Road). Follow it to the campground entrance on the right.
GPS coordinates: 38.733407 / -78.517365
About the campground: This Forest Service campground is located in the GWJ National Forests and holds the distinction of being the first Civilian Conservation Corps camp in the country; it was called Camp Roosevelt at the time. The foundations for the original buildings are still there. The Lions Tale Trail is unique in that the Forest Service and the local Lions Club joined forces to create this interpretive trail that is fun for both kids and adults. For hikers the 9-mile Massanutton Mountain Trail is available. This section of the GWJ is renowned for its numerous mountain-biking trails. Campsites are wooded and first come, first served. Camp Roosevelt Recreation Area is located near Shenandoah National Park and also Luray Caverns, which offers fee-based tours of some of the most beautiful underground geological foundations you will ever see. Learn the difference between a stalactite and a stalagmite. RV friendly.

34 Big Meadows Campground

Location: In Shenandoah National Park at mile marker 51.2
Sites: 168 standard
Facilities: Flush toilets, coin showers, fire pits, picnic tables, picnic area, dump stations, laundry facility, camp store
Fee per night: $$$
Management: National Park Service
Contact: (877) 444-6777; online reservations available at www.recreation.gov
Activities: Hiking, biking, fishing, horseback riding, interpretive programs, scenic driving
Season: May to November
Finding the campground: Take US 29 south to Warrenton, Virginia. Next, take US 211 west to Shenandoah National Park and Skyline Drive Thornton Gap Entrance. Go south on Skyline Drive for 19 miles, then turn right into the Big Meadows area, following the signs to the campground.
GPS coordinates: 38.528155 / -78.436597

Big Meadows Campground Courtesy National Park Service, Shenandoah National Park

About the campground: This campground provides the largest number of sites and greatest access to the outdoor playground that is Shenandoah National Park. Showers are coin operated. Use your site as a launch pad from which to hike the hundreds of miles of trails that vary in difficulty from easy to strenuous to see waterfalls or drive Skyline Drive to take in the scenic overlooks. The campground is centrally located and is near one of the biggest facilities in the park, the Harry F. Byrd Sr. Visitor Center. It is also near three waterfalls and one of the park's most popular, strenuous, and famous hikes—to the top of Old Rag Mountain—a peak that's more than 3,200 feet tall. Other popular hikes include Dark Hollow Falls Trail and Rose River Trail for views of the waterfalls with those names. RV friendly.

35 Lewis Mountain Campground

Location: In Shenandoah National Park at mile marker 57.5
Sites: 32 tent only
Facilities: Flush toilets, coin showers, fire grates, picnic tables, picnic areas, camp store, laundry facility
Fee per night: $$$
Management: National Park Service
Contact: (877) 444-6777; online reservations available at www.recreation.gov
Activities: Hiking, biking, fishing, horseback riding, interpretive programs, scenic driving
Season: Mid-May to late October

Finding the campground: Take US 33 west to Shenandoah National Park and Skyline Drive at the Swift Run Entrance. Follow Skyline Drive south to the campground entrance off milepost 57.5 on Skyline Drive.

GPS coordinates: 38.436708 / -78.478074

About the campground: This is the smallest campground in Shenandoah National Park. It is very quiet, and gives the feeling of being true backcountry in the midst of an otherwise busy park, while also offering amenities such as a camp store and a laundry facility. For showers bring a roll of coins because they are coin operated. Sites are first come, first served. No RVs are allowed in this campground.

36 Hone Quarry Campground

Location: 20 miles west of Harrisonburg

Sites: 26 standard

Facilities: Vault toilets, fire grills, picnic tables, picnic areas

Fee per night: $

Management: USDA Forest Service / George Washington and Jefferson National Forests / North River Ranger District

Contact: (540) 432-0187; www.fs.usda.gov

Activities: Hiking, fishing, biking, rock climbing

Season: Open year-round

Finding the campground: From Harrisonburg take US 42 south to a right turn onto SR 257 in Dayton headed west. When you reach a stop sign, turn left to remain on SR 257. Take a right onto Forest Service Road 62. Follow it to the campground entrance.

GPS coordinates: 38.462272 / -79.134960

About the campground: This Forest Service campground is located in GWJ National Forests. It is primitive, but beautiful, in the midst of pine trees and featuring a 15-foot-tall waterfall. There is no drinking water available, so you will need to pack your own for cooking, cleaning, and drinking. Toilets are vault style and wheelchair accessible. From this campground you have access to trails that lead to rock-climbing areas. For hikers there are two loop hikes available, both providing access to overlooks. There is a stream where you can fish for trout, in addition to the nearby Hone Quarry Reservoir, which is stocked with trout, sunfish, crappie, bass, and channel catfish. You must have a Virginia state fishing license. Nonmotorized boats are welcome. RV friendly, and though there is no dump station within the campground, there is one located about 1 mile away.

37 Natural Chimneys Campground

Location: 12 miles southwest of Bridgewater

Sites: 20 standard, 141 standard electric and water, 4 standard electric, water, and sewer

Facilities: Flush toilets, showers, fire rings, picnic tables, dump station, swimming pool, basketball court, volleyball court, horseshoe courts, playground, picnic shelters, nature center

Fee per night: $$$$

Management: Augusta County Parks and Recreation
Contact: (540) 245-5727; you can e-mail reservation requests to camping@co.augusta.va.us
Activities: Hiking, biking, swimming, basketball, volleyball, horseshoes, performances
Season: May to end of October
Finding the campground: From Bridgewater take SR 42 south. Take a right onto Moscow Loop Road, which will turn into Natural Chimneys Road (stay straight). Turn right onto Natural Chimneys Lane. Follow it to the campground entrance.
GPS coordinates: 38.357581 / -79.083678
About the campground: This park is near Natural Chimneys, seven unique geologic limestone formations that look like the majestic chimneys of a medieval-era giant's house, reaching from the lowest at 65 feet to as high as 120 feet. You will also find a swimming pool along with a kiddie pool for a small entrance fee. The River Trail is suitable for both hiking and biking use, with a section running alongside the North River that is an easier, flat trail for about 1 mile. Other trails are in the strenuous range for both hikers and mountain bikers. One such trail goes to the top of the Chimneys and you can see down over the valley. The North River provides excellent trout fishing when it is stocked during the fall, winter, and spring seasons. It is usually dry in July, going back underground (there are a lot of cave formations below ground in this region). You will need a Virginia state license to fish at any of the fishing holes. Campsites are reservable or first come, first served and offer plenty of room. An amphitheater in the park is the venue for performances, especially on weekends. Such performances include concerts and a Renaissance Fair. There's also a playground and nature center. Regulations specify up to eight people and two cars maximum. RV friendly.

38 Shaws Fork Equestrian Campground

Location: 32 miles northwest of Staunton
Sites: 5 standard
Facilities: Vault toilets, corral
Fee per night: $
Management: USDA Forest Service / George Washington and Jefferson National Forests / North River Ranger District
Contact: (540) 432-0187; www.fs.usda.gov
Activities: Hiking, horseback riding
Season: April to mid-December
Finding the campground: From Staunton take US 250 headed west past Churchville. Turn left on SR 616. Follow it to the campground entrance on the left.
GPS coordinates: 38.320617 / -79.416338
About the campground: This Forest Service campground is located in GWJ National Forests and caters to equestrians. It is a very small, primitive campground, and there is no fee to camp. For your horse(s) there is a corral available and access to horse trails right from the campground. There is no drinking water available, so pack enough for both you and your horses. Horses must be in alignment with the state's Coggins Test requirements. Located near the town of McDowell, which features a Civil War battlefield. RV friendly.

39 Todd Lake Recreation Area

Location: 18 miles southwest of Bridgewater
Sites: 20 standard
Facilities: Flush toilets, showers, fire grills, picnic tables, picnic areas, swimming beach, volleyball court, horseshoe pits, playground, dump station
Fee per night: $$$
Management: USDA Forest Service / George Washington and Jefferson National Forests / North River Ranger District
Contact: (540) 432-0187; www.fs.usda.gov
Activities: Hiking, biking, swimming, boating, canoeing, kayaking, volleyball
Season: Open mid-May to mid-October
Finding the campground: From Harrisonburg take SR 42 south. Turn right on SR 747. Turn left on SR 730. Turn right onto SR 718, and then take a left on Forest Development Route 95. Follow it to the recreation and campground entrance.
GPS coordinates: 38.365871 / -79.209490
About the campground: This Forest Service campground is located in the GWJ. Todd Lake is stream-fed and covers 7.5 acres. Two campsites and toilets and the beach are accessible to people with disabilities. Nonmotorized boats only, so bring a canoe or kayak. You can also swim and lounge on the sandy beach. Fish for sunfish, though you will need a valid Virginia state fishing license. Access to hiking and mountain-biking trails, including the Trimble Mountain Trail and a lake-circling trail. RV friendly for smaller vehicles only, and there is a dump station located about 1 mile away on FR 95.

40 North River Campground

Location: 27 miles northwest of Staunton
Sites: 9 standard
Facilities: Vault toilets, fire grills, picnic tables, picnic areas
Fee per night: $
Management: USDA Forest Service / George Washington and Jefferson National Forests / North River Ranger District
Contact: (540) 432-0187; www.fs.usda.gov
Activities: Hiking, biking, fishing
Season: Open year-round
Finding the campground: From Staunton take US 250 headed west toward Churchville. Turn right onto SR 715, which will turn into Forest Development Road 96. Follow FDR 96, and then take a right on FDR 95. At the intersection with FDR 958, take a right turn. Follow it to the campground entrance on the left.
GPS coordinates: 38.339587 / -79.207261
About the campground: This Forest Service campground is located in GWJ National Forests. It is a remote campground featuring two creeks and no designated sites, so you can set up camp wherever you like in one of the inner or outer loops that make up the campground area. There is access

to North River Gorge, where you will find hiking and biking trails. Fishing for trout is available in the stream, but you will need a valid Virginia state fishing license. There is no drinking water, so pack enough to cover cleaning, cooking, and drinking. Located in proximity to Wild Oak National Recreation Trail, Elkhorn Lake, and Stanton Dam, which will further expand your recreation options. RV friendly.

41 Loft Mountain Campground

Location: In Shenandoah National Park at mile marker 79.5
Sites: 155 standard nonelectric, 44 tent only
Facilities: Flush toilets, coin showers, fire grills, picnic tables, drinking water, dump station, camp store
Fee per night: $$$
Management: National Park Service
Contact: (877) 444-6777; online reservations available at www.recreation.gov

Loft Mountain Campground Courtesy National Park Service, Shenandoah National Park

Activities: Hiking, biking, fishing, horseback riding, interpretive programs, scenic driving

Season: Open mid-May to late October

Finding the campground: Take US 33 west to Shenandoah National Park and Skyline Drive at the Swift Run Entrance. Follow Skyline Drive south approximately 15 miles and turn left into the Loft Mountain area, following the signs to the campground. Located off milepost 80 on Skyline Drive.

GPS coordinates: 38.254069 / -78.664792

About the campground: This is the largest campground in Shenandoah National Park, offering spectacular scenic views due to its positioning atop Big Flat Mountain. Two waterfalls are nearby as well as other hiking trails.

42 Sherando Lake Recreation Area

Location: 12 miles south of Waynesboro

Sites: 18 standard, 19 standard electric

Facilities: Flush/vault toilets, showers, fire ring, picnic tables, picnic shelters, dump station, beach area, fishing dock, vending machines, visitor center, gift shop/store, playground

Fee per night: $$$$

Management: USDA Forest Service / George Washington and Jefferson National Forests / Glenwood-Pedlar Ranger District

Contact: (540) 291-2188; www.fs.usda.gov

Activities: Hiking, swimming, fishing, boating

Season: Early April to late October

Finding the campground: From I-64 take exit 96, then go south on SR 624. This will turn into SR 665 at Lyndhurst. Continue to the park entrance on the right.

GPS coordinates: 37.919477 / -79.007304

About the campground: This campground, built as a CCC project, is situated in the GWJ National Forests and is managed by the USDA Forest Service. Gas-powered boats are not permitted on the lake. Choose from several hiking trails, some leading to Bald Knob, and others leading around the lake and branching out into the forest area and up to the Blue Ridge Parkway. There are two sections to the lake: The upper section offers 25 acres of water for fishing but no swimming. If you want to swim, head to the lower section of the lake, where you can also boat and fish. RV friendly up to medium length.

43 Otter Creek Campground

Location: Near Lynchburg

Sites: 45 tent only, 24 RV

Facilities: Flush toilets, fire rings, fire grills, picnic tables, lantern posts, drinking water, dump station

Fee per night: $$$

Management: National Park Service

Contact: (828) 298-0398; online reservations available at www.recreation.gov

Activities: Fishing, hiking
Season: Mid-May to end of October
Finding the campground: Take the Blue Ridge Parkway to milepost 60.8.
GPS coordinates: 37.575935 / -79.337785
About the campground: This campground sits along Otter Creek at the lowest elevation of the Blue Ridge Parkway, near the James River. Some campsites are set next to the creek, and some are available first come, first served. Otter Lake provides the opportunity to fish, and there are four hiking trails of varying lengths. The Otter Creek Trail leads to the James River Visitor Center. No hookups.

44 Steel Bridge Campground

Location: Near Paint Bank, 45 miles northwest of Roanoke
Sites: 20 standard
Facilities: Pit toilets, fire rings, fire grills, picnic tables
Fee per night: $
Management: USDA Forest Service / George Washington and Jefferson National Forests / Eastern Divide Ranger District
Contact: (540) 552-4641; www.fs.usda.gov
Activities: Fishing
Season: Open April to first week of December
Finding the campground: From I-81 northbound take exit 141 onto SR 419 headed north. Take SR 311 to Paint Bank. Turn right onto SR 18. Follow it to the campground entrance. The road is unpaved with a dirt road leading to the sites.
GPS coordinates: 37.601120 /-80.218992
About the campground: This is a no-fee, primitive campground located in GWJ National Forests. There is no drinking water, so bring plenty of your own. The campsites are set up next to Potts Creek, which runs through the campground and is stocked with trout for fishing. Sites are wooded with no tent pads.

45 The Pines Campground

Location: 15 miles north of New Castle, 29 miles northwest of Roanoke
Sites: 10 standard
Facilities: Vault toilets, fire grills, picnic tables
Fee per night: $
Management: USDA Forest Service / George Washington and Jefferson National Forests / Eastern Divide Ranger District
Contact: (540) 552-4641; www.fs.usda.gov
Activities: Hiking, fishing
Season: Open April to first week of December

Finding the campground: From New Castle take SR 311 north. Turn right onto SR 611. Turn left on SR 617. Follow it to the campground entrance on the left.

GPS coordinates: 37.605011 /-80.076158

About the campground: This is a more primitive campground located in GWJ National Forests. There is no fee to camp here. It is first come, first served. Located next to Barbours Creek, which offers trout fishing. It is ideal if you have a jeep, because Potts Mountain Jeep Road is located nearby, which offers some exciting and challenging four-wheeling, if that interests you. RV friendly for smaller vehicles.

46 Cave Mountain Lake Campground

Location: 22 miles south of Lexington

Sites: 27 standard

Facilities: Flush toilets, showers, fire ring/grill, picnic tables, beach area, dump station

Fee per night: $$$

Management: USDA Forest Service / George Washington and Jefferson National Forests / Glenwood-Pedlar Ranger Districts

Contact: (540) 291-2188; www.fs.usda.gov

Activities: Hiking, swimming, fishing

Season: Open early April to late October

Finding the campground: From I-81 take exit 175 to US 11. Take a right onto VA 130 East, then turn right onto SR 759. Take a right onto SR 781. Follow it to the park entrance on the left.

GPS coordinates: 37.565921 / -79.540074

About the campground: This campground is managed by the USDA Forest Service and located in the GWJ. No boats of any kind are permitted on the lake. The lake covers seven acres and has a sandy beach from which you can swim. There are hiking trails ranging from a walk around the lake to more strenuous hiking nearby along the ridgetops. RV friendly up to 30 feet at some sites.

47 North Creek Recreation Area Campground

Location: 7 miles northeast of Buchanan

Sites: 16 standard

Facilities: Vault toilets, fire rings, fire grills, picnic tables

Fee per night: $$$

Management: USDA Forest Service / George Washington and Jefferson National Forests / Glenwood-Pedlar Ranger Districts

Contact: (540) 291-2188; www.fs.usda.gov

Activities: Hiking, fishing

Season: Open year-round

Finding the campground: From I-81 take exit 168 toward Arcadia onto SR 614 (Jennings Creek Road). Take a left onto Forest Service Route 59, which is North Creek Road. Follow it to the campground entrance on the right.

GPS coordinates: 37.541870 / -79.583444

About the campground: This campground is managed by the USDA Forest Service, with some sites situated alongside North Creek. There are tent pads, and drinking water is available. There is one loop hiking trail that is 2.5 miles long. You can fish in North Creek for native and rainbow trout. You must have a valid Virginia state fishing license per regulations. The campground has been closed for flooding before, so you may want to call in advance if there have been heavy rains. RV friendly and there is a dump station located west of the campground on FR 59.

Northern Virginia Area

Even though the northern section of Virginia is a sprawling urban center within commuting distance of Washington, DC, you will find some amazing pockets of green space. While there is only a smattering of campgrounds in this area, you will find them well-developed with great offerings in terms of recreation and convenience, if you want to reach the urban centers or are traveling from one. They include two run by Fairfax County, one by the National Park Service, and one state park that is located a bit farther south from all of the development. I-95, a major highway, runs through this area, making it convenient to zip north and south. However, traffic does get heavy, especially on weekends, since it is a main thoroughfare. The best times to travel are before sunup and well after sundown, as morning and late afternoon into evening rush hour traffic on weekdays and travelers on weekends can make for a lot of stop-and-go traveling. Dulles International Airport is also located in the far northern section of the area.

This area has a lot to offer history buffs in the form of several famous Civil War battlefields. Manassas National Battlefield Park is just to the west of the urban area off I-66. Preservationists and history lovers had to fight off the threat of encroaching development here at one point: Developers were intent on altering the battlefields of the First and Second Battles of Manassas that are honored here. Fortunately, the

	Total Sites	Max. RV Length	Hookups	Fire Ring/Grill	Toilets	Showers	Drinking Water	Dump Station	Recreation	Fee ($)	Reservable
48 **Bull Run Regional Park**	132		E, W, S	Y	F	Y	Y	Y	H	$$$$	Y
49 **Pohick Bay Regional Park**	150		E	Y	F	Y	Y	Y	H, F, B, L, C	$$$$	Y
50 **Lake Fairfax Park Campground**	136	31	E	Y	F	Y	Y	Y	H, S, F, B, C	$$$$	Y
51 **Burke Lake Park Campground**	100	25		Y	F	Y	Y	Y	H, F, B, C	$$$$	N
52 **Prince William Forest Park, Oak Ridge Campground**	100	32		Y	F	Y	Y	N	H, F, C	$$$$	Y
53 **Lake Anna State Park**	46	60	E	Y	F	Y	Y	N	H, S, F, B, L, C, HB	$$$$	Y

Max. RV Length: Measured in feet
Hookups: W = Water, E = Electricity, S = Sewer
Fire Ring/Grill: Y = Yes, N = None
Toilets: F = Flush, P = Pit, V = Vault
Showers: Y = Yes, N = None
Drinking Water: Y = Yes, N = None
Dump Station: Y = Yes, N = None
Recreation: H = Hiking, S = Swimming, F = Fishing, B = Boating, L = Boat Launch, C = Cycling, HB = Horseback Riding, OHV = Off-Highway Vehicles
Fee: $ = 0-$5, $$ = $6-$10, $$$ = $11-$20, $$$$ = $21-$30+
Reservable: Y = Yes, N = No

Northern Virginia Area

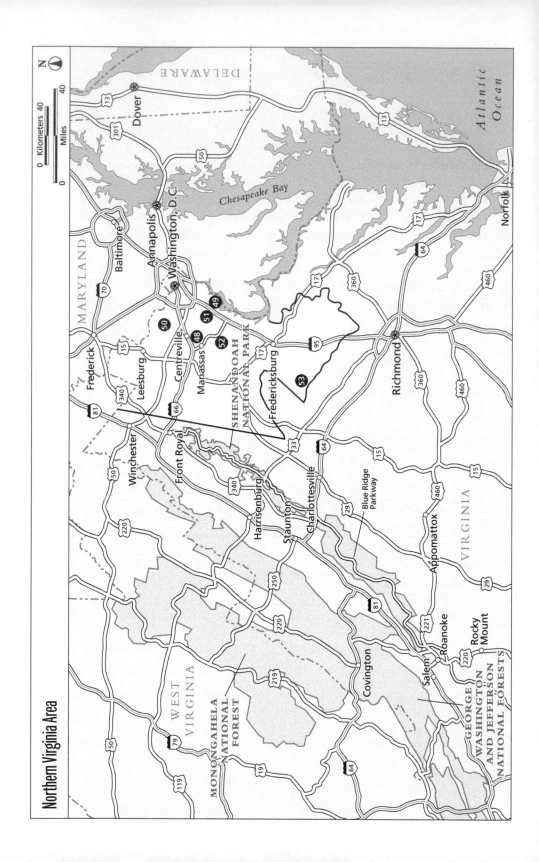

resulting public outcry ensured their plans were thwarted. Farther south, just off I-95, you will find the sites of more significant battlefields: Fredericksburg and Spotsylvania National Military Park has four Civil War battlefields contained within.

These historic sites and plenty of shopping are within easy driving distance of campgrounds in this area. You could even use your campsite as a convenient launch point to venture north into Washington, DC, and Old Town Alexandria for a nice day trip or two.

48 Bull Run Regional Park

Location: In Centreville
Sites: 83 standard electric, 18 standard electric and water, 31 standard electric, water, and sewer
Facilities: Bathhouses, showers, flush toilets, laundry facilities, fire rings, fire grills, picnic tables, camp store, playground, outdoor water park, dump station
Fee per night: $$$$
Management: NOVA Parks
Contact: (703) 631-0550; www.novaparks.com/parks/bull-run-regional-park
Activities: Hiking, disc golf
Season: Open year-round
Finding the campground: From I-66 take the Route 29 exit. Turn onto Bull Run Post Office Road to Bull Run Drive. Follow it to the campground entrance. Check in at the camp store.
GPS coordinates: 38.803953 / -77.477097
About the campground: This campground is located in Fairfax County, just 27 miles outside of Washington, DC, and its variety of tourist offerings. There's a park entrance fee for visitors who aren't residents of a local jurisdiction. Some sites are back in, while others are pull through for RVs, so state your preference when reserving. For disc golf, there's a small fee per person and disc rentals are available at the camp store. An outdoor waterpark is within walking distance.

49 Pohick Bay Regional Park

Location: In Lorton
Sites: 50 standard, 100 standard electric
Facilities: Flush toilets, showers, fire rings, fire grills, picnic tables, camp store, laundry facility, boat launch, dump station
Fee per night: $$$$
Management: NOVA Parks
Contact: (703) 339-6104; www.novaparks.com/parks/pohick-bay-regional-park
Activities: Hiking, fishing, biking, disc golf, boating
Season: Open year-round
Finding the campground: From I-95 northbound take exit 161 toward Lorton (Route 1 North). At first stop light, turn right onto Gunston Road. Follow it for 4 miles to the campground entrance.

GPS coordinates: 38.671842 / -77.169093

About the campground: This waterfront campground is located in Fairfax County, just 22 miles outside of Washington, DC, alongside Pohick Bay on the Mason Neck Peninsula. Activities include access to miniature golf and disc golf. You may rent a boat or visit the outdoor Pirate's Cove Waterpark. A public boat launch ramp is available. Trails are available for hiking and biking.

50 Lake Fairfax Park Campground

Location: 3.5 miles east of Reston
Sites: 82 standard, 54 standard electric
Facilities: Flush toilets, showers, fire grills, fire rings, picnic tables, dump station, lake, swimming pool, lazy river, playground
Fee per night: $$$$
Management: Fairfax County Park Authority
Contact: (703) 471-5415; https://www.fairfaxcounty.gov/parks/lake-fairfax
Activities: Hiking, biking, fishing, swimming, boating
Season: Open year-round except Christmas Day
Finding the campground: Take I-66 east toward Fort Royal / Washington. Take exit 55 onto Fairfax County Parkway / SR 7100 toward Springfield / Reston / Herndon, merging toward Reston / Herndon. Merge next onto Baron Cameron Avenue / SR 606 east. Take a right onto Lake Fairfax Drive. Follow it to the park entrance.
GPS coordinates: 38.962495 / -77.321993
About the campground: This park is located in Fairfax County in northern Virginia and run by the county. Campsites are shaded or sunny. The park has great offerings that include a swimming pool featuring a lazy river, which is called the Water Mine and has a Western-style theme. Swimming here is available for a small entrance fee. There is no swimming in the 18-acre lake, but you can fish or rent a paddleboat. In addition, there is a stream stocked with trout. Senior discounts available. RV friendly up to 31 feet.

51 Burke Lake Park Campground

Location: 8 miles northwest of Woodbridge
Sites: 100 standard
Facilities: Flush toilets, showers, fire grills, fire rings, picnic tables, camp store, playground, picnic areas, boat rental, snack bar, rowboat rental, dump station
Fee per night: $$$$
Management: Fairfax County Park Authority
Contact: (703) 323-6600; https://www.fairfaxcounty.gov/parks/burke-lake
Activities: Hiking, biking, fishing, boating, volleyball
Season: Late April to end of October
Finding the campground: From I-95 south take exit 160 / Route 123 north toward Woodbridge. Follow it to the park entrance located just before the golf course.

GPS coordinates: 38.769058 / -77.301453

About the campground: This park is situated amid one of the busiest counties in Virginia but offers a nice oasis from the congestion of the DC metropolitan region beyond its borders. It features a lake that covers 218 acres and fishing for largemouth bass is quite the popular recreation here, as the lake is renowned for its healthy population of these fish. Besides largemouth bass, there are also crappie, muskie, perch, walleye, and sunfish. You will need a Virginia state fishing license. Only boats with electric motors are allowed on the lake. Or rent a rowboat to explore the lake. Burke Lake Loop Trail is almost 5 miles long and available for hiking and biking, though there are some gravel sections not suitable for road bikes. The camp store offers camping supplies, basic groceries, and ice. Campsites are first come, first served. All sites are shaded. RVs up to 25 feet, with four back-in sites. Next to Burke Lake Golf Course and a miniature golf course as well. Senior discounts available.

52 Prince William Forest Park, Oak Ridge Campground

Location: 35 miles south of Washington, DC
Sites: 100 standard
Facilities: Flush toilets, showers, fire grills, picnic tables, amphitheater, visitor center
Fee per night: $$$$
Management: National Park Service
Contact: (703) 221-7181; (877) 444-6777; www.nps.gov/prwi; online reservations available at www.recreation.gov
Activities: Hiking, biking, fishing, orienteering, cross-country skiing, snowshoeing
Season: March to November in Loop A and Loop B, April to October in Loop C
Finding the campground: From Fredericksburg take I-95 north to exit 150, Joplin Road / VA 619 West. Follow it to the park entrance, which is the second right-hand turn.
GPS coordinates: 38.599039 / -77.417459
About the campground: Located in busy northern Virginia not too far outside of Washington DC, this 14,000-acre park amazingly manages to give that "getting away from it all" feeling and with good reason: It is the largest protected natural region in the DC metropolitan area. Prince William Forest Park is a federal recreation area, and you will need to pay a park entrance fee to enter, which is good for one week. Most sites are first come, first served, with some that are reservation-only during the busy season. A few sites are accessible, as are the restrooms. There are 37 miles of trails to hike. Watch for beavers, reintroduced into the park in 1950, and eastern box turtles, in addition to the hundreds of other species of plants and animals that live in this sanctuary so close to urban sprawl. Bring your bike and choose from 12 miles of paved road biking, 9 miles of graveled road, or one of the 10 fire roads for off-road biking. Or slow the pace and fish in one of the streams that run for 18 miles through the park, which is part of the Quantico Creek Watershed, two small man-made lakes. You can fish for bluegill, largemouth bass, channel catfish, and pumpkinseed. You will need a Virginia state fishing license. Also, one regulation stipulates that you can't use live bait, and there are catch limits for bass and pickerel. If you are unclear about regulations, ask one of the friendly park rangers. The park offers family-friendly programs led by park rangers, including nature hikes and a spooky cemetery night hike, which winds through the graveyards located within the park, as well as campfire programs that kids really enjoy. Bring your compass

so you can take advantage of one unique activity: orienteering. There are thirty courses within the park suitable for a range of experience from those at the beginner's level to those with advanced skills. Quantico Orienteering Club uses the park for some of its events. If you forget your compass, you can get one from the park visitor center, along with a map, both of which you can sign out for the day. When there's snow on the ground in the off-season, the park is a great place to cross-country ski or go snowshoeing. Discounts are available for seniors and access pass holders. RV friendly up to 32 feet.

53 Lake Anna State Park

Location: In Mineral, 25 miles southwest of Fredericksburg
Sites: 23 tent only, 23 standard electric
Facilities: Flush toilets, showers, fire rings, picnic tables, boat launch, playground, picnic shelter, concession/snack bar, gift shop, information center
Fee per night: $$$$

Lake Anna State Park

Management: Virginia Department of Conservation and Recreation
Contact: (540) 854-5503; (800) 933-7275; www.dcr.virginia.gov/state_parks/lak.shtml
Activities: Swimming, hiking, biking, fishing, boating, horseback riding
Season: March to early December
Finding the campground: From Fredericksburg take I-95 south toward Richmond. Take exit 118 toward VA 606 / Thornburg, and then turn right onto Mudd Tavern Road, which will become VA 208 / Courthouse Road. Veer to the left to remain on Courthouse Road. Turn right onto Lawyers Road, then left onto State Park Lane to enter the campground.
GPS coordinates: 38.120795 / -77.822420
About the campground: Situated alongside Lake Anna, a man-made lake that is used as a coolant for the local nuclear facility. Boating and fishing are available in this extensive body of water that covers 13,000 acres; there is a convenient boat launch near the campground. There's a swimming area with lifeguards on duty, a play area for kids, and a bathhouse just off the beach. Choose from eleven trails to hike, bike, or ride a horse: There are more than 15 miles to explore, 12 of which are multiuse. Fishing is popular with largemouth bass and crappie available; fishing permit is required. The park also provides a kiddie pond and one that is accessible to people with disabilities. RVs are welcome up to 60 feet.

Central / Southern Virginia Area

This is a sprawling region that lies south of the hubbub of northern Virginia, giving it a distinct, slower-paced flavor, which is why I grouped this area together despite the amount of land area it covers. The land itself flattens out considerably from the mountains to the west, with scattered pockets of population and plenty of farmland. In many sections you will notice tobacco and soybeans growing in the fields as you pass through to your campground destination. The soil, as you travel deeper south into the state headed toward Buggs Island Lake, becomes an interesting reddish-orange color, which generally indicates a high level of clay. It is rich in iron and very distinctive. The landscape provides long, rolling roads with low levels of traffic, which you will no doubt welcome if you have traveled along one of the main interstates. I-95 is by far the most heavily traveled, especially around the capital of Richmond, but I-85 is somewhat less so, though it has only two lanes compared with the four lanes of I-95. The one thing you can count on for both as you are traveling is what seems like every so many miles an exit will pop up where you can find gas stations and restaurants.

There are battlefields and historic sites, as well as tons of recreational opportunities, in this section of Virginia.

Central Virginia Area

While the central region is more developed than the area farther south, it is still nothing compared to the northern section of the state. There are more open spaces and farmland than anything else, with areas of development. This seems to be the lake region, with six of the seven campgrounds in this area offering a lake that provides a variety of water-based recreation. As for the seventh campground—it is alongside the James River, so you can still get your water recreation fix. Whether you are packing your fishing rod, putting a boat atop your car, or pulling one behind you, there is ample opportunity to make use of them once you reach your campground destination.

In addition to water recreation, there are also miles of multiuse trails for hiking, biking, and horseback riding throughout the different parks.

Near Holliday Lake State Park is Appomattox Court House National Historical Park, where General Robert E. Lee surrendered to General Ulysses S. Grant. The McLean House, where the surrender took place, has been reconstructed. Beyond the house you can walk along the route that General Lee walked on his way to meet General Grant, and the exact spot where they met, with green fields stretching as far

	Total Sites	Max. RV Length	Hookups	Fire Ring/Grill	Toilets	Showers	Drinking Water	Dump Station	Recreation	Fee ($)	Reservable
54 Dear Creek Lake State Park	48	35	E, W	Y	F	Y	Y	Y	H, S, F B, I, C	$$$$	Y
55 Powhatan State Park	29	60	F, W	Y	F	Y	Y	N	H, F, B, C, HB	$$$$	Y
56 James River State Park	66	40	E, W	Y	F	Y	Y	Y	H, F, B, L, C, HB	$$$-$$$$	Y
57 Holliday Lake State Park	35	40	E, W	Y	F	Y	Y	Y	H, S, F, B, L, C, HB	$$$$	Y
58 Twin Lakes State Park	33	36	E, W	Y	F	Y	Y	Y	H, S, F, B, L, C, HB	$$$$	Y
59 Pocahontas State Park	116	varies	E, W	Y	F	Y	Y	Y	H, S, F, B, L, C, HB	$$$$	Y
60 Peaks of Otter Campground	144			Y	F	N	Y	Y	H, F, C	$$$	Y
61 Smith Mountain Lake State Park	50	varies	E	Y	F	Y	Y	Y	H, S, F, B, L	$$$$	Y

Max RV Length: Measured in feet
Hookups: W = Water, E = Electricity, S = Sewer
Fire Ring/Grill: Y = Yes, N = None
Toilets: F = Flush, P = Pit, V = Vault
Showers: Y = Yes, N = None
Drinking Water: Y = Yes, N = None
Dump Station: Y = Yes, N = None
Recreation: H = Hiking, S = Swimming, F = Fishing, B = Boating, L = Boat Launch, C = Cycling, HB = Horseback Riding, OHV = Off-Highway Vehicles
Fee: $ = 0-$5, $$ = $6-$10, $$$ = $11-$20, $$$$ = $21-$30+
Reservable: Y = Yes. N = No

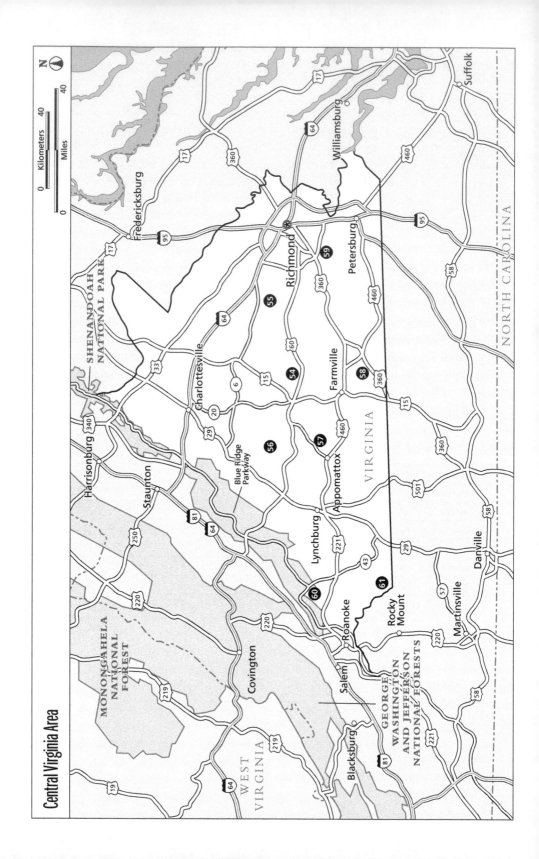

Central Virginia Area

as the eye can see in the distance. It is quite awe-inspiring to stand on a piece of history where two great men once stood when the United States was fractured.

Pocahontas State Park is close to the capital city of Richmond and makes a "world away" launch point to explore some of what Richmond has to offer, such as the Science Museum of Virginia, the Virginia Aviation Museum, and the Virginia Museum of Fine Arts, just to name a select few.

54 Bear Creek Lake State Park

Location: 54 miles west of Richmond
Sites: 11 tent only, 37 electric and water
Facilities: Flush toilets, showers, fire rings/grates, playgrounds, boat launch, boat rentals, beach area, fishing pier, picnic shelters, concession, snack bar, dump station, archery range

Bear Creek Lake State Park COURTESY VIRGINIA DEPARTMENT OF CONSERVATION AND RECREATION

Fee per night: $$$$
Management: Virginia Department of Conservation and Recreation
Contact: (804) 492-4410; (800) 933-7275; http://dcr.virginia.gov/state_parks/bea.shtml
Activities: Hiking, biking, fishing, swimming, boating
Season: March to December
Finding the campground: Take US 60 to SR 622 north, then go west on SR 629. The park entrance is located on Bear Creek Lake Road.
GPS coordinates: 37.526933 / -78.275727
About the campground: Set amid Cumberland State Forest, this campground is situated in a forested area next to Bear Creek Lake, which covers 40 acres. Rent a boat to explore the lake or spend some time at the swimming beach. Fourteen miles of multiuse trails offer a variety of options for hiking or mountain biking through the nicely wooded state forest area. Tent-only sites have a water view. RVs up to 35 feet.

55 Powhatan State Park

Location: 36 miles west of Richmond
Sites: 29 standard electric and water
Facilities: Flush toilets, showers, fire rings, fire grills, picnic tables
Fee per night: $$$$
Management: Virginia Department of Conservation and Recreation
Contact: (804) 598-7148; https://www.dcr.virginia.gov/state-parks/powhatan
Activities: Hiking, biking, horseback riding, fishing, boating
Season: March to early December
Finding the campground: From I-95 northbound take I-64 west to exit 167 for VA-617 toward Oilville/Goochland. Turn left onto SR 617 Oilville Road. Turn right onto US 250 west. Turn left on SR 632, then left onto SR 634. Continue straight onto Route 522. Turn right on Route 617 west (Old River Trail). Follow it to the campground entrance.
GPS coordinates: 37.678201 / -77.925914
About the campground: River Bend Campground is in Powhatan State Park, which runs 2.5 miles along the James River. The park offers 12 miles of multiuse trails and 9 miles of equestrian trails. You must carry a negative Coggins report copy for each horse. Cartop boat launches within the park provide easy access for canoes and kayaks (be aware of river currents and water level conditions). Boat trailer access is available just outside of the park. RVs up to 60 feet are welcome.

56 James River State Park

Location: 40 miles northeast of Lynchburg
Sites: 41 electric and water, 25 tent only/primitive
Facilities: Flush toilets, showers, fire rings, fire grill, dump station, boat launch, camp store, information center, laundry facility, nature center, picnic shelters
Fee per night: $$$–$$$$

Management: Virginia Department of Conservation and Recreation

Contact: (800) 933-7275; www.dcr.virginia.gov/state_parks/jam.shtml

Activities: Hiking, biking, horseback riding, fishing, kayaking, canoeing

Season: Tent-only sites are available year-round; electric sites from March to early December

Finding the campground: From US 29 north take US 60 toward Richmond. Turn left onto US 60, and then turn left onto Riverside Drive, which becomes River Road. Take a left onto Park Road. Follow it to the park entrance.

GPS coordinates: 37.630495 / -78.813934

About the campground: Located along 3 miles of the James River, a historic waterway, on 1,500 acres of forest and grassy meadow, this is a mostly flat, river valley park at the feet of the Blue Ridge Mountains. James River State Park Outdoor Adventures offers bicycle, canoe, kayak, and tubing rentals and shuttle service. You can make use of the cartop launch/boat launch if you bring your own boat. The James River begins its journey in the Allegheny Mountains to the west and then flows through the middle of Richmond, the state capital, on its way to where it eventually meets the Chesapeake Bay. The James River in this section is lazy and meandering, making it ideal for a relaxing river excursion. There are primitive sites available that give you a riverfront view, as well as standard sites that are equestrian and RV friendly. Depending on the camp area some sites are pull-through. Hike, bike, or ride horseback along 15 miles of trails. Fish the James River or opt for one of three ponds within the park, but be sure you have a permit. RVs up to 40 feet.

James River State Park

57 Holliday Lake State Park

Location: 34 miles east of Lynchburg
Sites: 35 standard electric and water
Facilities: Flush toilets, showers, fire rings, fire grills, picnic tables, beach/swimming area, boat launch and rental, dump station, visitor center, gift shop, snack bar, picnic shelters, playground, amphitheater
Fee per night: $$$$
Management: Virginia Department of Conservation and Recreation
Contact: (434) 248-6308; (800) 933-7275; http://dcr.virginia.gov/state_parks/hol.shtml
Activities: Hiking, swimming, biking, fishing, boating, canoeing, kayaking, horseback riding
Season: March through early December
Finding the campground: Take US 29 / US 460 east to the SR 24 south exit toward CR 60 / Appomattox. Turn right onto SR 626, then left on SR 640 (State Park Road). Follow it to the park entrance.
GPS coordinates: 37.397241 / -78.640843

Holliday Lake State Park

About the campground: The campground is located in Buckingham-Appomattox State Forest on 555 acres, a short distance (approximately 12 miles) from the famous Appomattox Court House where General Robert E. Lee surrendered to General Ulysses S. Grant, formally ending the Civil War. The site is now Appomattox Court House National Historical Park. The park's lake covers 150 acres and is stocked with a range of fish, including largemouth bass, perch, crappie, catfish, chain pickerel, and bluegill, and a stream offers trout fishing. A permit is required. The beach has a lifeguard on duty and contains a play area popular with kids and adults, diving platforms, and a volleyball net right on the beach. The park offers a bathhouse equipped with changing area, showers and toilets, and a concessionaire/snack bar. The park also rents canoes, kayaks, rowboats, or paddleboats to explore the park's one water trail. There are also six different trails from which to choose to explore the forest and its variations, which include wetlands, hardwood, and pine areas. One of the trails, the Carter Taylor Trail, is 12 miles long and great for biking, hiking, or riding a horse, while the Lakeshore Trail covers more than 6 miles of ground in its loop about the lake. At the water's edge is an old cemetery where family members of the original landowners rest. RV friendly sites, maximum length 40 feet.

58 Twin Lakes State Park

Location: 17 miles southeast of Farmville
Sites: 11 standard, 22 standard electric and water
Facilities: Flush toilets, showers, fire rings, fire grills, boat launch and rentals, dump station, picnic shelters, snack bar, gift shop
Fee per night: $$$$
Management: Virginia Department of Conservation and Recreation
Contact: (434) 392-3435; (800) 933-7275; http://dcr.virginia.gov/state_parks/twi.shtml
Activities: Swimming, hiking, fishing, biking, boating, canoeing, kayaking, horseback riding
Season: Open year-round
Finding the campground: Take US 460 east to a right turn on CR 607, then turn left to remain on 607. Take a right turn on Route 621, then a right turn onto Route 629 (Twin Lakes Road). Follow it to the park entrance.
GPS coordinates: 37.176173 / -78.273036
About the campground: Twin Lakes State Park, another historic park that was a CCC project, is located within Prince Edward Gallion State Forest and is situated on 495 acres. With two lakes from which to choose (Goodwin Lake and Prince Edward Lake), you can have two water-access vacations in one. Prince Edward Lake is the larger of the two, covering 36 acres; Goodwin sits to its west, covering 15 acres. A swimming beach is provided along with a bathhouse and concession area. You can fish for channel catfish, crappie, largemouth bass, and sunfish. Both lakes offer a boat launch, and electric-motored boats are permitted. You can also rent a canoe, kayak, paddleboat, or rowboat (available rentals vary by season). The park office sells fishing licenses. There are 6 miles of hiking trails that wind through woods and offer views of the lakes and access to Prince Edward Gallion Multiuse Trail, which runs for 8 miles and is shared with hikers, bikers, and horseback riders (a State Forest Use Permit is needed for cyclists and equestrians). RVs up to 36 feet are welcome. Located near Sailor's Creek Battlefield Historical Park, a Civil War historic site.

Twin Lakes State Park

59 Pocahontas State Park

Location: 20 miles south of Richmond
Sites: 111 standard electric and water, 5 buddy
Facilities: Flush toilets, showers, fire grills, fire rings, picnic tables, boat launch, camp store, amphitheater, concession, dump station, gift shop, laundry facility, museum, nature center, picnic area/shelters, playground, swimming pool
Fee per night: $$$$
Management: Virginia Department of Conservation and Recreation
Contact: (804) 796-4255; (800) 933-7275; www.dcr.virginia.gov/state_parks/poc.shtml
Activities: Swimming, hiking, biking, horseback riding, boating, canoeing, kayaking, fishing, volleyball
Season: Open year-round
Finding the campground: Take I-95 south to exit 61 West onto SR 10. Take CR 655 / Beach Road to the park entrance.
GPS coordinates: 37.372428 / -77.571522
About the campground: Pocahontas State Park was a CCC project, and it is the state's largest park, sitting on 7,950 acres of forested land. You have your choice of two lakes for boating and fishing: Swift Creek Lake covers 225 acres, and Beaver Lake covers 24 acres. A fishing license can be purchased at the park office. Rent a canoe, rowboat, or kayak from the park, or bring your own. Only electric-powered boats are permitted; no gas-powered boats are allowed on Swift Creek Lake. Beaver Lake is a small tributary of Swift Creek Lake and not very deep, but it does have good fishing. There is no car access for Beaver Lake and therefore no boat rentals for this section. However, you can carry in a canoe or kayak. The park offers its Pool and Aquatic Recreation Center for swimming: There is a free day of swimming for each night of camping. Throughout the park wind 90 miles of trails for hiking and biking to explore the woodlands, with one trail accessible to those with disabilities. In addition, there are three sites available that meet ADA requirements; all bathhouses are fully accessible, as well as the swimming pool, concession, and bathhouses in the aquatic area. Equestrians enjoy 10 miles of trails for horseback riding. There is a parking area for horse trailers, but there are no overnight accommodations available for horses within the park itself. Nearby resources are available. In addition, there are mountain biking trails that range from easy to expert level for single-track enthusiasts. The park offers a summer concert series on weekends. RV friendly for vehicles up to 50 feet in the buddy sites, 40 feet in the standard sites. Located just outside of Richmond and within driving range of several area Civil War battlefields.

Pocahontas State Park

60 Peaks of Otter Campground

Location: 40 miles north of Roanoke
Sites: 86 rustic, 58 RV nonelectric
Facilities: Flush toilets, fire rings/grills, picnic tables, picnic area, dump station
Fee per night: $$$
Management: National Park Service
Contact: (540) 586-7321; (877) 444-6777; https://www.nps.gov/blri/planyourvisit/camping.htm
Activities: Hiking, biking, fishing
Season: Mid-May to mid-October
Finding the campground: Located at milepost 86 on the Blue Ridge Parkway. Take I-81 to US 11 toward Buchanan. Turn right onto US 11 North/Lee Highway, then take a slight right onto SR 43 South/Parkway Drive. Turn onto the Blue Ridge Parkway. Follow it to the park entrance (milepost 86).
GPS coordinates: 37.443249/-79.604773
About the campground: This is another basic campground managed by the National Park Service, one of several located along the Blue Ridge Parkway. The Peaks of Otter is considered one of the state's natural wonders with three mountains forming a triangle with Abbott Lake in the middle. From these peaks you can view a panorama of beauty with the Blue Ridge and Allegheny Mountains and the Shenandoah Valley below. Various trails offer moderate to strenuous hiking options. Select from a range of hiking trails, from a flatter one that takes you around 24-acre Abbott Lake to one that will challenge you to reach one of these three Blue Ridge Mountain peaks in the region. The lake is stocked with bluegill and smallmouth bass that provide a great fishing opportunity. Permit is required. Campsites are shaded, and first come, first served or may be reserved in advance. A restaurant within walking distance has a store and a gift shop. Johnson Farm provides a glimpse into Appalachian home building: It is a log home that has been modified through enlargement and other changes. Polly Woods's tavern is another historic site close by; it served as a travelers' way station in the mid-nineteenth century.

61 Smith Mountain Lake State Park

Location: 40 miles southwest of Lynchburg
Sites: 26 tent only, 24 standard electric
Facilities: Flush toilets, showers, fire rings/grills, picnic tables, dump station, boat launch and rental, fishing pier, gift shop, picnic shelters, snack bar, visitor center
Fee per night: $$$$
Management: Virginia Department of Conservation and Recreation
Contact: (540) 297-6066; (800) 933-7275; http://dcr.virginia.gov/state_parks/smi.shtml
Activities: Hiking, swimming, fishing, boating, canoeing, kayaking, jet skiing
Season: Early March to early December
Finding the campground: Take US 460 to SR 122 south to the town of Moneta. Take CR 608 east to White House Road. Take CR 626 south and follow it to the park entrance.

Smith Mountain Lake State Park COURTESY VIRGINIA DEPARTMENT OF CONSERVATION AND RECREATION

GPS coordinates: 37.091904 / -79.592995

About the campground: Smith Mountain Lake is the second largest body of freshwater in the state and offers plenty of opportunities for water-related fun along its 500 miles of shoreline. Fish for bass and catfish from the pier or rent a boat. Be sure you have a fishing permit. Motorboats are permitted on this lake. The park also offers boat rentals, with a wide range of boats to select from, including kayaks, canoes, pontoon boats, and jet skis. Campsites are wooded. The park offers a range of shorter-length hikes with thirteen different trails from which to choose. RV friendly up to 50 feet depending on the site.

Southern Virginia Area

This is tobacco land in the deep southern region of Richmond. Look for the reddish-orange soil that seems to be a boon for tobacco plant growth. Virginia's largest lake is Buggs Island Lake, also known as Kerr Reservoir. It sits along the border with North Carolina just to its south.

In this area you will find that the US Army Corps of Engineers manages most of the campgrounds with seven situated along Buggs Island Lake. The John H. Kerr Dam is located there, as well as Philpott Reservoir and Lake farther west and close to Richmond. In addition, there are two campgrounds run by the National Park Service and three that are state parks.

As in the Central Virginia area, there is a wealth of water-related recreational activities to enjoy, from swimming to boating to fishing. The Smith River flows beneath the Philpott Dam and Lake area and offers excellent paddling for kayakers.

	Total Sites	Max. RV Length	Hookups	Fire Ring/Grill	Toilets	Showers	Drinking Water	Dump Station	Recreation	Fee ($)	Reservable
62 **Goose Point Campground**	63		E, W	Y	F	Y	Y	Y	H, S, F, B, L, C	$$$-$$$$	Y
63 **Horseshoe Point Campground**	49		E, W	Y	F	Y	Y	Y	H, S, F, B, L, C	$$$-$$$$	Y
64 **Salthouse Branch Campground**	90		E, W	Y	F	Y	Y	Y	H, S, F, B, L, C	$$$-$$$$	Y
65 **Fairy Stone State Park**	51	30	E, W	Y	F	Y	Y	Y	H, S, F, B, L, C, HB	$$$$	Y
66 **Roanoke Mountain Campground**	105			Y	F	N	Y	Y	H, C	$$$	N
67 **Rocky Knob Campground**	110			Y	F	N	Y	Y	H, C	$$$-$$$$	Y
68 **Staunton River State Park**	47	45	E, W	Y	F	Y	Y	N	H, S, F, B, L, C, HB	$$$$	Y
69 **Longwood Park Campground**	66		E, W	Y	F, V	Y	Y	Y	H, S, F, B, L, C	$$$-$$$$	Y
70 **Occoneechee State Park**	59	35	E, W	Y	F	Y	Y	Y	H, S, F, B, L, C, HB	$$$$	Y
71 **Rudds Creek Campground**	99		E, W	Y	F, V	Y	Y	Y	H, S, F, B, C	$$$-$$$$	Y
72 **Buffalo Park Campground**	21		E, W	Y	F, V	Y	Y	Y	H, S, F, B, L, C	$$$-$$$$	N
73 **North Bend Park Campground**	244		E	Y	F, V	Y	Y	Y	H, S, F, B, L, C	$$$-$$$$	Y

Max. RV Length: Measured in feet
Hookups: W = Water, E = Electricity, S = Sewer
Fire Ring/Grill: Y = Yes, N = None
Toilets: F = Flush, P = Pit, V = Vault
Showers: Y = Yes, N = None
Drinking Water: Y = Yes, N = None
Dump Station: Y = Yes, N = None
Recreation: H = Hiking, S = Swimming, F = Fishing, B = Boating, L = Boat Launch, C = Cycling, HB = Horseback Riding, OHV = Off-Highway Vehicles
Fee: $ = 0-$5, $$ = $6-$10, $$$ = $11-$20, $$$$ = $21-$30+
Reservable: Y = Yes, N = No

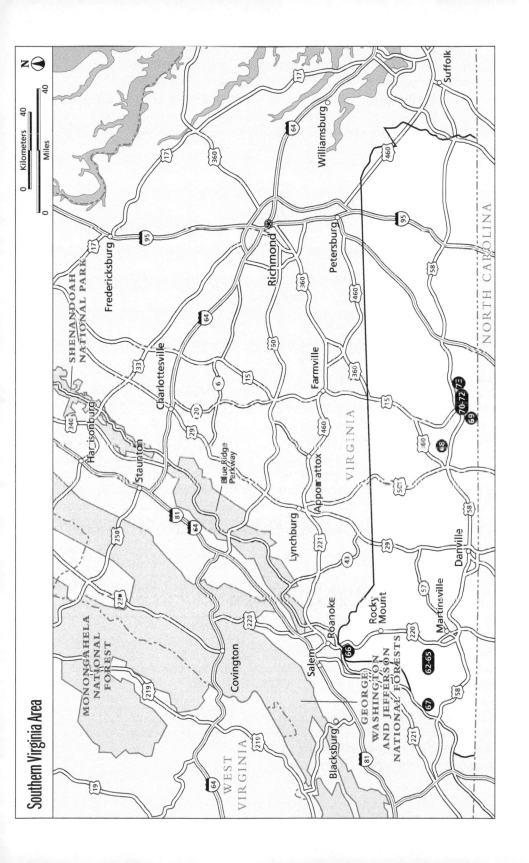

Southern Virginia Area

There are multiuse trails in some of the parks that are suitable for hiking, biking, and horseback riding. The trails are flat in the far southern section, but the closer you get to the Blue Ridge Mountains to the west, the higher your elevation and potential for a good leg workout. The Dick and Willie Passage is a rail trail that is part of the Smith River Trail system. For mountain bikers there are single-track trails located in the Jamison Mill Recreation Area next to Philpott Lake.

62 Goose Point Campground

Location: 60 miles southwest of Roanoke
Sites: 10 standard, 53 standard electric and water
Facilities: Flush toilets, showers, fire ring, picnic tables, boat ramp, playground, dump station, amphitheater, picnic shelters, fishing pier, dock, swimming beach
Fee per night: $$$–$$$$
Management: US Army Corps of Engineers
Contact: (276) 629-1847; https://www.recreation.gov/camping/campgrounds/233687
Activities: Hiking, biking, swimming, fishing, boating
Season: Open April to end of October
Finding the campground: Take US 220 to the exit for Bassett, Virginia, getting on SR 57 headed west. Follow this to Goose Point Road. Watch for a brown sign that has the park name. Take a right at the sign and follow it to the campground entrance.
GPS coordinates: 36.804465 / -80.058709
About the campground: Located along 2,900-acre Philpott Lake, this campground offers great water views as well as the Blue Ridge Mountains, as it lies at the foot of this range. There is boating and fishing along with swimming at the beach. There are hiking and biking trails that wind all around the lake, giving you plenty to do on land, too. RV friendly, but be advised that the roads leading to the campground are hilly and have narrow switchbacks, making it a challenge for larger vehicles. Use your own judgment.

63 Horseshoe Point Campground

Location: 43 miles south of Roanoke
Sites: 34 standard, 15 standard electric and water
Facilities: Flush toilets, showers, fire ring, picnic tables, beach area, boat launch, playground, dump station
Fee per night: $$$–$$$$
Management: US Army Corps of Engineers
Contact: (540) 365-7385; https://www.recreation.gov/camping/campgrounds/233515
Activities: Hiking, biking, swimming, fishing, boating
Season: Open May through end of September

Finding the campground: Take US 220 to SR 605 (Henry Road). Turn left onto Horseshoe Point Road. Follow it to the campground entrance.
GPS coordinates: 36.830078 / -80.062231
About the campground: This campground is located along Philpott Lake, covering 2,900 acres and offering a range of boating, fishing, and swimming opportunities. The convenient boat ramp allows you to launch from the campground. There is an abundance of fish, everything from bass to walleyes, but you will need a valid Virginia state fishing license. A beach provides access to swimming in the clear lake water. RV friendly.

64 Salthouse Branch Campground

Location: 46 miles south of Roanoke
Sites: 32 tent only, 14 standard, 44 standard electric and water
Facilities: Flush toilets, showers, fire ring, picnic tables, beach area, boat ramp, dock, playground, dump station, amphitheater
Fee per night: $$$–$$$$
Management: US Army Corps of Engineers
Contact: (540) 365-7005; https://www.recreation.gov/camping/campgrounds/233616
Activities: Hiking, biking, swimming, fishing, boating
Season: Open April to end of October
Finding the campground: Take US Route 220 to SR 605 (Henry Road). Turn left on Knob Church Road. Turn left onto Salthouse Branch Road. Follow it to the campground entrance.
GPS coordinates: 36.813557 / -80.038747
About the campground: This campground is located along 2,900-acre Philpott Lake, providing a range of water and land recreational activities. The lake has mostly rocky banks. Fish in the lake for walleye, bluegill, largemouth and smallmouth bass, catfish, and crappie. You will need a valid Virginia state fishing license. Also, you can boat on or swim in the lake, and there is a beach area. Choose from two 0.5-mile trails within the campground, one of which is interpretive, the other a nature trail. Near Fairy Stone State Park and Fairy Farms Wildlife Management Area. RV friendly.

65 Fairy Stone State Park

Location: 57 miles south of Roanoke
Sites: 51 standard electric and water
Facilities: Flush toilets, showers, fire ring, picnic shelters, beach area, snack bar, gift shop, boat launch/rental, playground, dump station
Fee per night: $$$$
Management: Virginia Department of Conservation and Recreation
Contact: (276) 930-2424; (800) 933-7275; http://dcr.virginia.gov/state_parks/fai.shtml
Activities: Hiking, biking, swimming, horseback riding, fishing, boating, canoeing, kayaking
Season: Open early March to early December

Finding the campground: From I-81 outside of Roanoke, take I-581 to US 220 South, then take the exit for SR 57 West to SR 346 headed north. Follow Fairystone Lake Drive to the park entrance.

GPS coordinates: 36.784806 / -80.096082

About the campground: Fairy Stone Park is one of the largest parks in the state, spread across 4,500 acres of wooded splendor. The park gets its unique name from the small stone structures found in the park. Shaped like crosses, these stones were formed ages ago when their mineral substructure crystalized. The park also features a lake that covers 168 acres next to Philpott Reservoir, though the two are not connected but are separated by a dam. The only type of powerboat allowed in the lake is electric, but gas-powered boats are allowed at the reservoir. Or rent a kayak, canoe, paddleboat, or rowboat to enjoy the lake. The lake is stocked with fish, such as pan, which are easy for anyone to catch, so it's a great place to teach a child how to fish. There are also walleye and largemouth bass in the lake, and the reservoir offers both largemouth and smallmouth bass. The park has two trail systems, the Stuarts Knob Trail system and the Little Mountain Trail system. There are 9 miles of mostly multiuse trails for hiking, bike riding, and horseback riding, and additional miles for just walking. To cool off afterward, go to the swimming beach, which offers a lifeguard (based on student availability, so contact the park's main number first), bathhouse, and concessionaire. There's a visitor center and a gift shop, which also carries camping supplies should you discover you missed packing something important. RV friendly up to 30 feet.

Fairy Stone State Park Courtesy Virginia Department of Conservation and Recreation

66 Roanoke Mountain Campground

Location: 9 miles south of Roanoke
Sites: 74 standard, 31 RV
Facilities: Flush toilets, fire ring/grill, dump station
Fee per night: $$$
Management: National Park Service
Contact: (540) 745-9681; www.nps.gov/blri/index.htm
Activities: Hiking, biking
Season: Mid-May to mid-October
Finding the campground: Milepost 120.4 on the Blue Ridge Parkway. Take US 220 south to the Blue Ridge Parkway exit. Take a right onto the exit and follow it to the park entrance at milepost 120.4, located off Mill Mountain Spur.
GPS coordinates: 37.229460 / -79.951801
About the campground: This is the next campground after Peaks of Otter headed south along the Blue Ridge Parkway and located in Roanoke. There are no shower facilities, but there is drinking water available. Also, three of the sites are accessible. No reservations: sites are first come, first served. Mill Mountain Zoo is nearby in Roanoke, the largest city off the Parkway. There are multiple hiking trails around the campground from which to choose and biking trails nearby.
Note: This campground may be temporarily closed. Check with the office listed above for current information.

67 Rocky Knob Campground

Location: 8 miles south of Floyd
Sites: 76 tent only, 34 RV nonelectric
Facilities: Flush toilets, fire rings, fire grills, picnic tables, dump station, picnic area, picnic shelter
Fee per night: $$$–$$$$
Management: National Park Service
Contact: (877) 444-6777; https://www.recreation.gov/camping/campgrounds/233324
Activities: Hiking, biking
Season: Mid-May to mid-October
Finding the campground: Milepost 167 on the Blue Ridge Parkway. Take US 221 to SR 8, then take the exit on the left onto the Blue Ridge Parkway, taking a right onto the Parkway. Follow it to the park entrance at milepost 167.
GPS coordinates: 36.831591 / -80.344728
About the campground: This is the last campground located within the state heading south along the Blue Ridge Parkway and within the Rocky Knob Recreation area, with 4,000 acres of forest surrounding it. This campground's claim to fame is that it is one of the first established sites along the Parkway. There are no shower facilities, but there is drinking water available. Located near Mabry Mill, a picturesque old gristmill worth seeing. The campground is also located near Rock Castle Gorge, named for its crystalline quartz rock formations, and which covers more than 3,500 acres with trails running throughout; one trail is accessible from the campground. RV friendly.

68 Staunton River State Park

Location: 18 miles east of South Boston
Sites: 13 tent only, 14 standard electric and water, 20 electric and water pop-up and tent campers
Facilities: Flush toilets, showers, fire rings, picnic tables, laundry facility, bathhouse, snack bar, pool/waterslides, boat launch, picnic shelters, amphitheater, visitor center
Fee per night: $$$$
Management: Virginia Department of Conservation and Recreation
Contact: (434) 572-4623; (800) 933-7275; http://dcr.virginia.gov/state_parks/sta.shtml
Activities: Swimming, hiking, biking, horseback riding, fishing, boating, waterskiing
Season: March to early December
Finding the campground: Take US 360 to SR 344. Follow it to the park entrance.

Staunton River State Park Courtesy Virginia Department of Conservation and Recreation

GPS coordinates: 36.698122 / -78.676806

About the campground: Staunton River State Park is one of the original six state parks created in Virginia and is recognized as both a National Historic Landmark and a Virginia Historic Landmark. It is located on the eastern shore of Buggs Island Lake (the largest lake in the state) to the east of Occoneechee State Park and between the Staunton River and Dan River that spill into the lake. The park stretches across more than 2,400 acres and still has structures built through the CCC project in the 1930s. There is an Olympic-size pool with a 70-foot waterslide and a log slide, making it a hit with bigger kids, as well as a wading pool/water playground just for smaller kids. Choose from six different trails to explore along the rivers and the lake, sheltered by trees, with one multiuse trail for bikers, hikers, and horseback riders. Fish in the lake or the rivers for perch, bluegill, bass, and crappie; you can purchase a Virginia fishing license from the park's office. There is a boat launch, but no boat rentals are handled by the actual park: Either bring your own or rent from a private rental company outside of the park. Motorboats permitted. RV friendly for vehicles up to 45 feet. Located just south of Staunton River Battlefield State Park, a Civil War historic site.

69 Longwood Park Campground

Location: 4 miles south of Clarksville
Sites: 32 standard, 34 standard electric and water
Facilities: Flush toilets, vault toilets, showers, fire rings, picnic tables, boat ramp, beach, playground, dump station, picnic shelters
Fee per night: $$$–$$$$
Management: US Army Corps of Engineers
Contact: (434) 374-2711; (877) 444-6777; https://www.recreation.gov/camping/campgrounds/233545
Activities: Hiking, biking, fishing, boating, swimming
Season: Open early April to end of October
Finding the campground: From Clarksville take SR 15 headed south. Follow it to the campground entrance.
GPS coordinates: 36.576727 / -78.548817
About the campground: This campground, like Occoneechee State Park, is situated on the 50,000-acre Buggs Island Lake, also known as John H. Kerr Reservoir. It sits south of Occoneechee State Park on the opposite side of the lake, so it also offers stunning water views and is close to the North Carolina state line. There are hiking and biking trails within driving distance. If you like to boat and fish, there's plenty of opportunity for both. The lake offers largemouth bass, crappie, and catfish; a permit is needed. There's a boat ramp and a marina available for use. Along the lake, there is a beach where you can swim, making it a popular site for kids. Campsites have gravel bases, so consider bringing a tarp to place beneath your tent. RV friendly.

70 Occoneechee State Park

Location: 1 mile east of Clarksville
Sites: 9 standard, 39 standard electric and water, 11 equestrian
Facilities: Flush toilets, showers, fire grills, picnic tables, boat launch/rental, marina, bike rental, gift shop, picnic areas/shelters, playground, dump station, amphitheater, visitor center, museum
Fee per night: $$$$
Management: Virginia Department of Conservation and Recreation
Contact: (434) 374-2210; (800) 933-7275; http://dcr.virginia.gov/state_parks/occ.shtml
Activities: Hiking, biking, swimming, fishing, boating, horseback riding, horseshoes, volleyball, waterskiing
Season: March to early December
Finding the campground: Take I-85 to US 58 west at South Hill. Follow it to the park entrance.
GPS coordinates: 36.624131 / -78.525834
About the campground: This campground is situated on the largest lake in Virginia, Buggs Island Lake, also known as John H. Kerr Reservoir, which was created by the dam that was built here

Occoneechee State Park

and shares the state line with North Carolina. Occoneechee State Park is named for the Native Americans who once lived in this region, the Occoneechi, whom you can learn more about at the visitor center. Also, you can learn about the plantation that once existed here during the nineteenth century, which, along with its graceful terrace gardens, was burned to the ground by a fire presumably caused by candles on a Christmas tree. The campground welcomes tents or RVs, with some sites right on the lakefront and others allowing for RVs up to 35 feet in length. An equestrian campground offers 11 sites and 11 covered stalls for horse lovers. There are 3.1 miles of walking trails for exploring the forest and the lakefront, with a 15-mile multipurpose trail (out and back) for use by bikers, horseback riders, or hikers. There are a total of three boat ramps, and motorboats are allowed. If you don't have your own, you can rent either a pontoon boat or a fishing boat. The lake covers 48,000 acres, giving you plenty to explore. Fishermen can rejoice in the selection and renowned size of the fish, including striped bass, perch, and bluegill. Permit is required. This area is in the Piedmont region, characterized by rolling flatlands that are situated at the foot of the Blue Ridge Mountains. One thing that's very noticeable is the reddish-orange soil, indicating a high clay concentration that is ideal for pine trees and tobacco farming. You can see tobacco farms along your drive to the campground, as well as fields covered in low-lying soybean crops. Some spots along the lake have a white, sandy shoreline, which along with the pine trees, give this region the feel of a rugged coastline along the ocean. John H. Kerr Dam is nearby and has a visitor center. Six of the standard sites are situated right on the waterfront, along with six of the standard water and electric sites.

71 Rudds Creek Campground

Location: Located in Boydton, 7 miles northeast of Clarksville
Sites: 24 standard, 75 standard electric and water
Facilities: Flush toilets, vault toilets, showers, fire rings, picnic tables, swimming beach, boat ramp, playground, dump station, picnic shelters, amphitheater
Fee per night: $$$-$$$$
Management: US Army Corps of Engineers
Contact: (434) 738-6827; (877) 444-6777; https://www.recreation.gov/camping/campgrounds/233610
Activities: Hiking, biking, fishing, boating, swimming
Season: Open April to October
Finding the campground: From Boydton take SR 58 headed west. Turn at the sign for the recreation area and campground.
GPS coordinates: 36.657490 / -78.442252
About the campground: Another US Army Corps of Engineers campground that offers amenities similar to the other US Army Corps of Engineers campgrounds located along Buggs Island Lake, the John H. Kerr Reservoir. The Joseph S. J. Tanner II Environmental Education Center is nearby, which provides programs and exhibits during the summer season. This whole area offers an abundance of hiking and biking trails and plenty of opportunities for wildlife and bird watchers. All campsites have gravel bases, so bring some type of tarp for ground cover if you are pitching a tent.

72 Buffalo Park Campground

Location: Located in Boydton, 10 miles northeast of Clarksville
Sites: 10 standard, 11 standard electric and water
Facilities: Flush toilets, vault toilets, showers, fire rings, picnic tables, boat ramp, swimming beach, playground, dump station, picnic shelters
Fee per night: $$$–$$$$
Management: US Army Corps of Engineers
Contact: (434) 374-2063; (877) 444-6777; https://www.recreation.gov/camping/campgrounds/233442
Activities: Hiking, biking, fishing, boating, swimming
Season: Open May to September
Finding the campground: From Clarksville take US 58. Turn right (north) on Buffalo Springs Road. Turn right onto Carter's Point Road. Follow it to the campground entrance.
GPS coordinates: 36.661125 / -78.628404
About the campground: Located along John H. Kerr Reservoir, this lakeside campground is also run by the US Army Corps of Engineers and is yet another site from which to go out and enjoy all this recreational and wildlife management area has to offer. All campsites are first come, first served and have gravel padding, so a tarp as ground cover is recommended. RV friendly.

73 North Bend Park Campground

Location: Located in Boydton, 23 miles east of Clarksville
Sites: 106 standard, 138 standard electric
Facilities: Flush toilets, vault toilets, showers, fire rings, picnic tables, fishing pier, playgrounds, swimming beach, boat launches, dump station, picnic area, amphitheater
Fee per night: $$$–$$$$
Management: US Army Corps of Engineers
Contact: (434) 738-0059; (877) 444-6777; https://www.recreation.gov/camping/campgrounds/233563
Activities: Hiking, biking, fishing, boating, swimming
Season: April to end of October
Finding the campground: Take I-58 west to SR 4 / Buggs Island Road. Go to the right of the dam and follow the road to the campground entrance.
GPS coordinates: 36.586067 / -78.308100
About the campground: Another campground alongside John H. Kerr Reservoir, aka Buggs Island Lake. The 50,000-acre body of water has a fishing pier where, as long as you have a fishing permit, you can try your luck in catching largemouth bass, crappie, and catfish. It is accessible to people with disabilities. There are also three different sites from which to launch your boat and a couple of beach areas for swimming. There is a biking and jogging trail, and you can visit nearby local Wildlife Management areas for bird watching, wildlife viewing, and additional hiking. More hiking and biking trails are within driving distance. Campsites are gravel, so bring a tarp for a tent base. Some campsites are available as first come, first served. RV friendly.

Tidewater / Hampton Roads / Chesapeake Bay / Eastern Shore Area

Welcome to Virginia's coastal area, which sits astride the Chesapeake Bay and next to the Atlantic Ocean, and where the two great bodies of water meet. This area is a huge draw for maritime history buffs, colonial history buffs, and nature lovers.

This region features the bustling ports of Hampton Roads and Portsmouth, which include major shipping and shipbuilding operations and the home of the United States Coast Guard Atlantic Fleet, and Norfolk, which supports the United States Navy's Atlantic Fleet and the largest naval station in the world. Colonial Williamsburg is located in this area and is as close to a walk back in time as you can get. If you stay at a campground in this region, make time for a day trip to tour this beautifully preserved slice of time. You can also cut your costs for a family vacation that includes trips to the Busch Gardens Williamsburg theme park and to the naval area of Norfolk by staying at one of the campgrounds in this area. All of the campgrounds are well developed and offer great amenities.

The area is characterized by its flat, coastal plain, featuring pine forests in the Tidewater area; wild, sandy beaches along the Eastern Shore; and developed beaches in Virginia Beach in the southeastern corner of the state. With access to water trails in the area, you can explore the waters and various tributaries of the Chesapeake region.

Tidewater / Hampton Roads Area

In this area there are two campgrounds run by their local recreation and parks departments, one run by a county, and two state parks.

This area is rich with recreation opportunities, especially for anyone interested in Colonial- and Revolutionary-era history. Make time to go see Colonial Williamsburg. The colonial architecture and pristine, landscaped yards are stunning, and you can also do tours of many of the buildings, including the famous Raleigh Tavern and the Governor's Palace. Obtain a Patriot's Pass for admission to all of the historic buildings, the Abby Aldrich Rockefeller Folk Arts Center and DeWitt Wallace Decorative Arts Gallery, and other shops and homes.

Farther south of Williamsburg is Historic Jamestowne, the first permanent English settlement—predating the landing in Plymouth, Massachusetts—and now a Colonial National Historical Park. The one remaining piece of the settlement is the Old Church Tower, and archaeological digs continue to find where foundations and streets once stood. Jamestown Settlement is a living history museum next to it that has reproductions of the original ships that brought the settlers, the *Susan Constant*, the *Godspeed*, and the *Discovery*, as well as Powhatan Indian Village, also a historical recreation. There is an entrance fee for the historical park and to the Jamestown Settlement. Yorktown is south of this area and features the Yorktown Victory Center and

	Total Sites	Max. RV Length	Hookups	Fire Ring/Grill	Toilets	Showers	Drinking Water	Dump Station	Recreation	Fee ($)	Reservable
74 **Chickahominy Riverfront Park**	161		E, W, S	Y	F	Y	Y	N	H, S, F, B, L, C	$$$$	Y
75 **Chippokes Plantation State Park**	50	30, 50	E	Y	F	Y	Y	Y	H, S, F, C	$$$$	Y
76 **Newport News Park Campsites**	188		E, W	Y	F	Y	Y	Y	H, F, B, L, C	$$$$	Y
77 **First Landing State Park**	183	50	E, W	Y	F	Y	Y	Y	H, S, F, B, L, C	$$$$	Y
78 **Northwest River Park Campground**	66	50	E	Y	F	Y	Y	Y	H, S, F, B, C	$$$$	Y

Max. RV Length: Measured in feet
Hookups: W = Water, E = Electricity, S = Sewer
Fire Ring/Grill: Y = Yes, N = None
Toilets: F = Flush, P = Pit, V = Vault
Showers: Y = Yes, N = None
Drinking Water: Y = Yes, N = None
Dump Station: Y = Yes, N = None
Recreation: H = Hiking, S = Swimming, F = Fishing, B = Boating, L = Boat Launch, C = Cycling, HB = Horseback Riding, OHV = Off-Highway Vehicles
Fee: $ = 0–$5, $$ = $6–$10, $$$ = $11–$20, $$$$ = $21–$30+
Reservable: Y = Yes, N = No

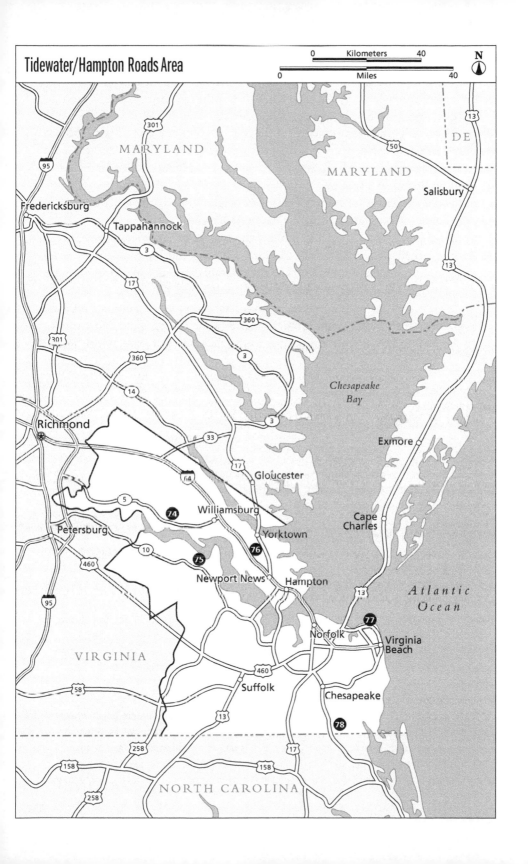

Kilometers

Miles

N

MARYLAND

MARYLAND

DE

Salisbury

Fredericksburg

Tappahannock

Chesapeake Bay

Exmore

Richmond

Gloucester

Cape Charles

Williamsburg

Yorktown

Petersburg

Newport News

Hampton

Atlantic Ocean

VIRGINIA

Norfolk

Virginia Beach

Suffolk

Chesapeake

NORTH CAROLINA

Yorktown Battlefield. Yorktown gained fame as the location where Cornwallis, commander of the British forces during the Revolutionary War, was defeated through the joint efforts of the Americans and the French. It was the last major battle of the war.

Norfolk, Portsmouth, and Newport News are the cities in the Port of Hampton Roads region, and Hampton is located in this area, too. All of these cities are packed with museums and sightseeing opportunities, including the Virginia Air and Space Center, Mariners' Museum, Virginia War Museum, the National Maritime Center, and Norfolk Botanical Gardens.

You could also travel for a part of your camping stay to visit Virginia Beach and walk the 3 miles of boardwalk along the Atlantic Ocean.

There is a unique ecological area in the southeast corner of the state, where Dismal Swamp Canal connects Virginia and North Carolina and is the oldest operating waterway in the country, running through Great Dismal Swamp. Lake Drummond is the second largest natural lake and a favorite of kayakers and fishermen.

Once again, you may need a vacation from your vacation, because not only are there dozens of recreational opportunities outside of the campground, but you may also find it hard to leave your campsite due to the abundance of recreational opportunities within.

74 Chickahominy Riverfront Park

Location: 10 miles west of Williamsburg
Sites: 161 standard (electric, water, and sewer sites available)
Facilities: Flush toilets, showers, fire rings, picnic tables, swimming pools, boat ramp, fishing pier, playgrounds, picnic shelters, camp store
Fee per night: $$$$
Management: James City County Parks and Recreation
Contact: (757) 258-5020; https://www.jamescitycountyva.gov/Facilities/Facility/Details/Chickahominy-Riverfront-Park-2
Activities: Hiking, biking, swimming, fishing, boating, canoeing, kayaking
Season: April to October
Finding the campground: Take I-64 east to exit 205, SR 33 headed west, then exit toward New Kent Airport. Merge onto New Kent Highway. Take a left onto US 60 east / Pocahontas Trail. Turn right onto SR 155 / North Courthouse Road, then left on Boulevard Road / SR 155. Turn left onto Sturgeon Point Road. Take a left onto John Tyler Memorial Highway / SR 5. Follow it to the park entrance.
GPS coordinates: 37.265166 / -76.872257
About the campground: If you like to swim, this 140-acre park offers two outdoor pools. You can also explore the Chickahominy River and Gordon Creek by boat: Rent a canoe, kayak, or paddleboard, or bring your own. The Chickahominy Water Trail is one of several water trails in this area, routes that have been developed to highlight natural and historic sites along the river. There is a fishing pier and boat ramp available. Some campsites have a waterfront view, as this campground

is situated on a bluff overlooking the Chickahominy River. Call the park office to reserve. Your camping fee includes use of the pool and the boat ramp.

75 Chippokes Plantation State Park

Location: 34 miles west of Newport News, 38 miles southeast of Hopewell
Sites: 50 standard electric
Facilities: Flush toilets, showers, fire rings, picnic tables, swimming pool, dump station, camp store, gift shop, picnic shelters, snack bar, visitor center, laundry facility
Fee per night: $$$$
Management: Virginia Department of Conservation and Recreation
Contact: (757) 294-3728; (800) 933-7275; http://dcr.virginia.gov/state_parks/chi.shtml
Activities: Hiking, biking, swimming, fishing
Season: March to early December

Chippokes Plantation State Park COURTESY VIRGINIA DEPARTMENT OF CONSERVATION AND RECREATION

Finding the campground: Take I-95 to SR 10 east toward Hopewell. At the intersection for SR 10 and SR 31, turn left to stay on SR 10. At the stop light, take a right turn, then turn left onto Alliance Road. Follow it to the park entrance.

GPS coordinates: 37.135938 / -76.725626

About the campground: This park is located on the James River, where it creates Cobham Bay, and is recognized as one of the oldest working farms in the country, having been in existence since 1617. It continues as a working farm run by the state and is used as a living historic exhibit demonstrating farming methods from the eighteenth and nineteenth centuries. Within the park is the Chippokes Farm and Forestry Museum, which has an exhibit of antique farm and forestry equipment. You can also tour the Chippokes Mansion, carriage house, and surrounding formal gardens on weekends when they are open. You can fish in the river, but you must have a Virginia fishing license. The park offers canoe trips, including instruction, during which you can tour Lower Chippokes Creek. You can register through the Reservation Center (800-933-7275). The Olympic-size swimming pool has free admittance for campers. There are two campgrounds within the park, with campground A having sites that offer more shade. RV friendly up to 30 feet in campground A; larger vehicles up to 50 feet can be accommodated in campground B. The park is a nice launch point from which to explore historic Williamsburg, Jamestown, and Yorktown, all just across the James River. You can take the Jamestown-Scotland Ferry across: It is free. Otherwise, you need to drive south to cross the James River over into Newport News and head north.

76 Newport News Park Campsites

Location: Newport News

Sites: 24 standard, 43 standard electric, 121 standard electric and water

Facilities: Flush toilets, showers, fire grills, picnic tables, playgrounds, dump station, camp store, laundry facility, picnic shelters, boat rentals, boat launch, bike rentals, disc golf course, airplane model flying field, archery range, discovery center

Fee per night: $$$$

Management: Newport News Parks and Recreation

Contact: (757) 888-3333; (800) 203-8322; https://www.nnva.gov/2340/Camping

Activities: Hiking, biking, fishing, boating, canoeing, kayaking, disc golf, archery

Season: Open year-round

Finding the campground: Take I-64 west to exit 250B / Jefferson Avenue. Follow this road to the park entrance.

GPS coordinates: 37.188425 / -76.558304

About the campground: This park is located in the port city of Newport News and covers 8,000 acres featuring woodlands and lakes. Fish for northern pike, sunfish, and chain pickerel in two of the freshwater lakes. You will need a Virginia state fishing license; you can obtain one conveniently at the park's camp store. You can rent a canoe, rowboat, or paddleboat from the camp office and explore the reservoir. Watch for beaver and other wildlife. A boat launch is available, but gas-powered boats are not allowed. There are more than 30 miles of trails suitable for hiking and biking. You can rent a bike or bring your own. There is also an all-terrain trail just for mountain bikers. If you like to create airplane models and fly them, the park offers a 30-acre flying field. In addition, there is an archery range and an eighteen-hole disc golf course. You can rent or purchase discs in the park if you don't have your own. Also, there are two public golf courses available. The Discovery Center has displays depicting nature scenes and historic events and an arboretum that is beautiful, especially when in bloom in the spring. Newport News has a lot of Civil War historic sites and is just one of the many stops listed on the Virginia Civil War Trails. Campsites are wooded. RV friendly. Senior discounts available.

77 First Landing State Park

Location: 6.5 miles north of Virginia Beach
Sites: 75 standard, 108 standard electric and water
Facilities: Flush toilets, showers, fire grills, picnic tables, picnic area, picnic shelters, laundry facility, camp store, concessionaire, dump station, boat launch
Fee per night: $$$$
Management: Virginia Department of Conservation and Recreation
Contact: (757) 412-2300; (800) 933-7275; http://dcr.virginia.gov/state_parks/fir.shtml
Activities: Hiking, biking, swimming, boating, fishing, crabbing, kayaking
Season: March to early December

First Landing State Park COURTESY VIRGINIA DEPARTMENT OF CONSERVATION AND RECREATION

Bald cypress stumps, First Landing State Park COURTESY VIRGINIA DEPARTMENT OF CONSERVATION AND RECREATION

Finding the campground: Take I-64 to Northampton Boulevard / US 13 North, exit 282. Turn right onto Shore Drive / US 60, which is the last possible exit before the Chesapeake Bay Bridge Tunnel. Follow it to the park entrance.

GPS coordinates: 36.920057 / -76.049868

About the campground: First Landing State Park is the most visited state park in Virginia with about a million visitors each year. Its history and proximity to major tourist attractions account for this, as well as its beautiful location. The park's name is the giveaway: It was the location of the first landing of the Virginia Company, which then traveled just a short distance north and settled Jamestown. Located on a peninsula that juts out into the Chesapeake Bay, close to where the Bay meets the Atlantic Ocean, it is situated just north of Virginia Beach, a popular beachside tourist destination. The park sits on 2,888 acres and has more than 1 mile of beach frontage with swimming available right there in the Bay. Because there are no lifeguards, it is considered "swim at your own risk," so use caution. The currents may be especially strong due to the confluence of these two great bodies of water. There are large cypress trees, sand dunes, and lagoons located within the park, making the landscape unique as far as campgrounds go. Watch for egrets and osprey, birds that are denizens of this type of environment. You can fish or go crabbing from an area called the Narrows, located between two smaller bay areas, but you will need a Virginia saltwater license. There is a boat ramp located here, as well, for launching motor boats or smaller boats such as a kayak. Bring your own or rent from local outfitters. Also, consider Back Bay National Wildlife Refuge, a glorious refuge that covers 9,000 acres and offers a unique mix of beach areas, woodlands, and an abundance of wildlife including bald eagles. Within the park, choose from nine different trails offering 20 miles of hiking. Bald Cypress Trail is accessible to people with disabilities. Bikes are permitted only on Cape Henry Trail. The camp store offers camping supplies, bike rentals, fishing/crabbing supply rentals, and concession-style food items. The park is close to a military training base, so don't be alarmed if you hear various training exercises. RV friendly up to 50 feet.

78 Northwest River Park Campground

Location: Located in Chesapeake, 14 miles west of Virginia Beach
Sites: 26 standard, 40 standard electric
Facilities: Flush toilets, showers, fire rings, fire grills, picnic tables, laundry facility, dump station, miniature golf course, horseshoe court, volleyball courts, geocaching, playground
Fee per night: $$$$
Management: Chesapeake Parks and Recreation
Contact: (757) 421-7151; www.cityofchesapeake.net
Activities: Hiking, biking, swimming, fishing, boating, canoeing, kayaking, geocaching
Season: April to end of November
Finding the campground: From Norfolk take I-464 south. As the interstate comes to an end, stay to your left so you can take SR 168 south. Take exit 8B, Hillcrest Parkway East, just before the toll booth. Turn right onto Battlefield Boulevard, then turn left onto Indian Creek Road. Follow it to the park entrance located on the right.
GPS coordinates: 36.586129 / -76.152640

About the campground: This park covers more than 760 acres along the Northwest River and is listed as part of the Virginia Bird and Wildlife Trail, offering a year's worth of bird-watching opportunities for bird lovers, including birds like great egrets and blue herons and the pileated woodpecker. It is a year-round park that offers water- and land-based recreational opportunities. To reserve in advance, you must either mail in an application or reserve in person. Lake Lesa covers 300 acres and is stocked with bass, catfish, bluegill, and crappie. You must have a Virginia state fishing license. The lake is also stocked with trout some months of the year, which requires a special trout-fishing license. Another area from which to fish is a pier located on the Northwest River, where you can catch perch and stripers. Rental boats are available for the lake only, and you can select from a kayak, canoe, or paddleboat. There are 7 miles of hiking trails that range from 0.25 mile to more than 2 miles. The 2-mile Molly Mitchell Trail is accessible to people with disabilities in one section. One of the trails has a wooden bridge that features unique carved posts. If you are into geocaching, there are twenty sites scattered throughout the park. And if you like stargazing and time your visit right, the Back Bay Amateur Astronomy Club sets up telescopes once a month, weather permitting, for a free viewing opportunity of the night sky. RV friendly up to 50 feet.

Chesapeake Bay / Eastern Shore Area

Camping by the water—this area may have less than a handful of campground options, but what wonderful options they are, with one of the campgrounds here on the Atlantic Ocean and the other two situated along major rivers that feed into the Chesapeake Bay.

The Chesapeake Bay region is one of those areas where you have campgrounds within easy reach of major urban centers. You can travel in any direction from your campsite to make a day trip of any of the area's attractions, but one of the biggest draws for this area is the access to water, water, and still more water. Whether you are a boater, a fisherman, or just like to swim, there are plenty of options from which to choose. River cruise operators and canoe and kayak outfitters, as well as nature parks, preserves, and wildlife refuges dot the region.

You may be surprised by how seemingly desolate the area on the Eastern Shore is compared to the Western Shore. The Eastern Shore is characterized by its amazingly relaxed atmosphere and the wild nature of undeveloped coastline. Chincoteague National Wildlife Refuge is located here. Though it does not have a campground, it is within easy reach from Kiptopeke State Park. It features sand dunes and beach area, marshes and forests, and plays host to more than 300 bird species. Also, it is the site of the annual Chincoteague Pony Swim and Auction every year in July. Visit Assateague Lighthouse, which stands more than 140 feet tall and is located in the farthest northeastern corner of Virginia.

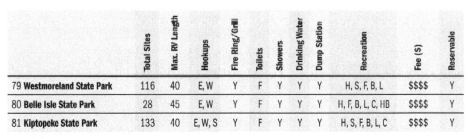

	Total Sites	Max. RV Length	Hookups	Fire Ring/Grill	Toilets	Showers	Drinking Water	Dump Station	Recreation	Fee ($)	Reservable
79 **Westmoreland State Park**	116	40	E, W	Y	F	Y	Y	Y	H, S, F, B, L	$$$$	Y
80 **Belle Isle State Park**	28	45	E, W	Y	F	Y	Y	Y	H, F, B, L, C, HB	$$$$	Y
81 **Kiptopeke State Park**	133	40	E, W, S	Y	F	Y	Y	Y	H, S, F, B, L, C	$$$$	Y

Max RV Length: Measured In feet
Hookups: W = Water, E = Electricity, S = Sewer
Fire Ring/Grill: Y = Yes, N = None
Toilets: F = Flush, P = Pit, V = Vault
Showers: Y = Yes, N = None
Drinking Water: Y = Yes, N = None
Dump Station: Y = Yes, N = None
Recreation: H = Hiking, S = Swimming, F = Fishing, B = Boating, L = Boat Launch, C = Cycling, HB = Horseback Riding, OHV = Off-Highway Vehicles
Fee: $ = 0–$5, $$ = $6–$10, $$$ = $11–$20, $$$$ = $21–$30+
Reservable: Y = Yes, N = No

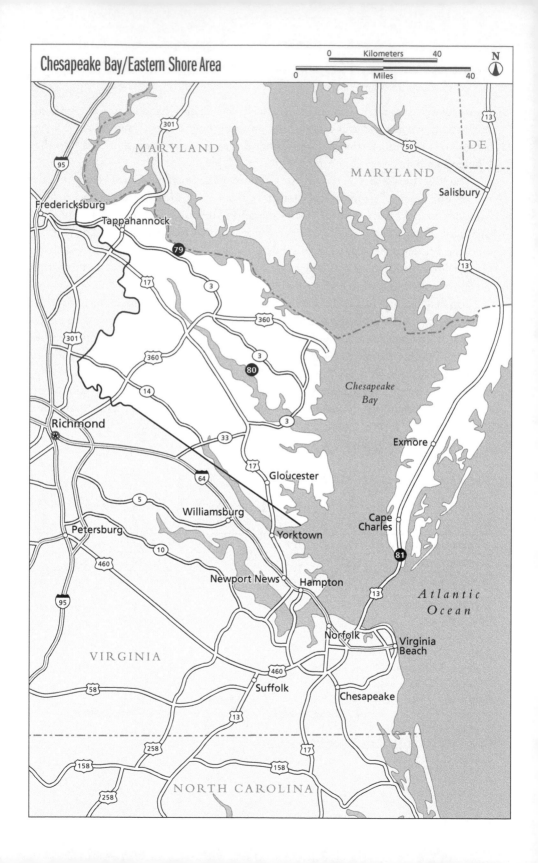

Kilometers

0   40

0   40

Miles

N

MARYLAND

MARYLAND

DE

Salisbury

Fredericksburg

Tappahannock

Chesapeake
Bay

Exmore

Richmond

Gloucester

Cape
Charles

Williamsburg

Yorktown

Petersburg

Newport News   Hampton

VIRGINIA

Norfolk   Virginia
Beach

Atlantic
Ocean

Suffolk

Chesapeake

NORTH CAROLINA

79 Westmoreland State Park

Location: 42 miles southeast of Fredericksburg
Sites: 74 standard, 42 standard electric and water
Facilities: Flush toilets, showers, fire rings, box grills, camp store, laundry facility, bathhouse, swimming pool, dump station, gift shop, boat launch, boat rental, snack bar, picnic shelters, playground, visitor center
Fee per night: $$$$
Management: Virginia Department of Conservation and Recreation
Contact: (804) 493-8821; (800) 933-7275; http://dcr.virginia.gov/state parks/wes.shtml
Activities: Hiking, swimming, boating, kayaking, fishing
Season: March to early December
Finding the campground: From I-95 south take SR 3 east. Follow it to the park's entrance, taking a left turn onto SR 347.
GPS coordinates: 38.158926 / -76.866328
About the campground: This park is situated on 1,311 acres along the Potomac River. The Horsehead Cliffs rise majestically above the water. When you make a reservation, you are guaranteed the site type you reserve, but you can't reserve a specific site or select which campground

Westmoreland State Park COURTESY VIRGINIA DEPARTMENT OF CONSERVATION AND RECREATION you'd like (out of A, B, or C). When you arrive, a park attendant will assign your site and ensure you get what fits best with your needs for space and equipment. As a camper at the park, you are not charged to swim in the pool or for launching your boat. There are seven trails from which to choose for hiking; just one of the trails is available for biking. The beach trail gives a breathtaking view of the Potomac River. Electric wheelchairs are permitted on the trails. You can fish in the river for striped bass and bluefish, but you do need a Virginia fishing license. There's also a pond, Rock Spring, which holds bass, crappie, catfish, and bream. Motorboats are permitted, which you can launch from the park boat ramp. Kayaks and paddleboats are available for rent during the summer months and most weekends during the off-season. Also, you can reserve a spot to participate in an interpretive kayak tour of the shoreline, launched from Osprey Boat House. About an hour away is Fredericksburg, which has Civil War battlefields, and Kings Dominion, a large amusement park. Located close to the birthplaces of both Robert E. Lee, the famous general of the Confederate Army, and George Washington. RV friendly up to 40 feet.

80 Belle Isle State Park

Location: 20 miles southeast of Warsaw
Sites: 28 standard electric and water
Facilities: Flush toilets, showers, fire rings, fire grills, picnic tables, playground, picnic shelters, laundry facility, dump station, camp store, boat launch, fishing pier, and canoe, kayak, and bike rentals
Fee per night: $$$$
Management: Virginia Department of Conservation and Recreation
Contact: (804) 462-5030; (800) 933-7275; http://dcr.virginia.gov/state_parks/bel.shtml
Activities: Hiking, biking, horseback riding, fishing, boating, canoeing, kayaking
Season: March to early December
Finding the campground: Take SR 3 east to SR 354. Turn right and follow it for a few miles, and then turn right again onto SR 683. Follow it to the park entrance.
GPS coordinates: 37.776894 / -76.597956
About the campground: This park is located in what's called a "coastal estuary," where salt water and freshwater meet, creating the estuarine environment oysters and crabs thrive in. (The Chesapeake Bay is the largest estuary in the United States.) Covering 739 acres with more than 7 miles of frontage along the lower portion of the Rappahannock River, an area otherwise very developed, the park makes a nice oasis. It offers wetlands, coves, and marshes for exploration by boat. Naturalists will enjoy the fact that there are no fewer than eight different types of wetlands within the park. You can explore the area by renting a canoe, kayak, or motorboat from the park, or rent a bike. You can also bring your own boat and launch from the ramp. Look for a diverse range of wildlife that includes hawks, blue herons, and turkeys, as well as deer, groundhogs, and various amphibians and reptiles. Equestrian trails and hiking trails also run through the park. The fishing pier is accessible and park trails are wheelchair accessible. The property, which was once a plantation, is listed on the National Register of Historic Places. The Belle Isle Mansion and the Belle Isle Guest House are not part of the park; they are privately owned and can be rented. RV friendly up to 45 feet.

Belle Isle State Park COURTESY VIRGINIA DEPARTMENT OF CONSERVATION AND RECREATION

81 Kiptopeke State Park

Location: 35 miles north of Norfolk
Sites: 47 tent only, 86 standard electric, water, and sewer
Facilities: Flush toilets, showers, fire rings, fire grills, picnic tables, camp store, gift shop, picnic shelters, fishing pier, boat launch, beach area, playground, dump station
Fee per night: $$$$
Management: Virginia Department of Conservation and Recreation
Contact: (757) 331-2267; (800) 933-7275; http://dcr.virginia.gov/state_parks/kip.shtml
Activities: Hiking, biking, boating, kayaking, swimming, fishing, crabbing
Season: March to early December
Finding the campground: From the Chesapeake Bay Bridge Tunnel, travel north on US 13. Turn left on Route 704 west to the park entrance. The tunnel does have a pricey toll, so be prepared to pay twelve dollars or more, depending on how many axles your vehicle has. If you are coming in from the north, down through Maryland on US 13, you will avoid the tunnel.

Kiptopeke State Park COURTESY VIRGINIA DEPARTMENT OF CONSERVATION AND RECREATION

GPS coordinates: 37.170322 / -75.980997

About the campground: This unique park, which features sand dunes and extensive water views, sits on 536 acres on the farthest eastern stretch of Virginia: its Eastern Shore, which is a peninsula that runs between the Chesapeake Bay and the Atlantic Ocean. Virginia is the southern section of the peninsula with Maryland to the north. The park itself faces onto the Chesapeake Bay, which is a bird lover's paradise, recognized as a major flyway for birds as they migrate to distant points. Extensive studies of bird populations have taken place here for the past five decades through the Coastal Virginia Wildlife Observatory. Volunteers capture, collect data, tag, and release these migratory birds to track their journeys. During the fall, you can go to the Bird Banding Station and observe their work. It is also home to a research area where birds of prey such as hawks and osprey are studied; the hawk observatory is among the top observatories of its kind in the country. Motorboats and cartop boats such as kayaks can be launched for no fee if you're camping. Parking is limited in the boat launch area, so there is a small fee if you want to park your boat trailer there. If you fish from the pier, you don't need a state fishing license. However, fishing from your boat or from the shore requires a Virginia saltwater fishing license. The southern section of the beach is best for that, along with crabbing, while the northern end of the beach has a swimming area during the summer season. There is no lifeguard, so use caution. There are sunken ships that create a somewhat protected swim area. This northern section also stretches for about 0.5 mile along the Bay, providing a nice panoramic view north and south. There are also 4 miles of hiking and biking trails, with four of the bike trails named after birds. Various programs are available, including fishing clinics, guided hikes, canoeing programs (for a fee), beach bonfires, and during the fall, weekly birding programs. If you come late enough in the fall, you will be treated to a hayride around the park. Just a few miles south is the Eastern Shore of Virginia National Wildlife Refuge Visitor Center, considered one of the country's top five visitor centers. For a truly unusual experience, you can also get in your car and catch a ferry over to Tangier Island, located in the middle of the Chesapeake Bay and accessible only by boat or by small plane. It was first visited by Captain John Smith in 1608 and was settled in 1620 and is now a crabbing community. And if you would like to visit the other side of Virginia's mainland, take the Chesapeake Bay Bridge / Tunnel to get there. It is 20 miles long and the section of the bridge that is above water will remind you of the Florida Keys, as it seemingly skims just above the surface. RV friendly up to 40 feet.

Introduction to
West Virginia

Introduction to West Virginia

Welcome to West Virginia, one of the original thirteen colonies with a rich history. It is nicknamed the "Mountain State" and is the birthplace of such famous people as Devil Anse Hatfield (of Hatfield and McCoy fame), Chuck Yeager, Pearl S. Buck, Don Knotts, Mary Lou Retton, Henry Louis Gates Jr., Jennifer Garner, and Brad Paisley. Its capital is Charleston, located in the southwestern area of the state.

West Virginia's tourism slogan is "Wild and Wonderful," and the state lives up to it tenfold. This may not be the Wild Wild West, but West Virginia, one of the ten smallest

Dome of the Capitol building in Charleston, West Virginia

Wildflowers in Metro Valley / Hatfield-McCoy Mountains Area, West Virginia

states, sure is rugged for a state located in the eastern portion of the country. It does a lot with a little, packing quite the punch in terms of geography. My son summed it up perfectly for me, as we enjoyed our travel time in the state, when he said, "I feel sorry for anyone who tries to invade us from the East Coast." The mountain passes can give your vehicle quite the workout, and all I could think in many spots was "Thank goodness I don't have to walk or ride my bike up this," and that was just on the major highways.

If you are an outdoors enthusiast, here are two words for you that best describe the state: outdoors mecca. There are many enterprising outfitters who have made it their business to help get people outside, whether it is white-water rafting one of the many rivers, mountain biking some of the hundreds of miles of forested trails, climbing rock formations, or boating on one of the lakes. Or you can design your own outdoor adventure with campgrounds all over the state providing the perfect launch point for exploring. You can hike, bike, or ride your horse starting from one of the many trailheads that begin right in the campground area or within easy driving distance.

Rhododendrons are the state flower. In addition, you will see wildflowers all over the state, including one with rose-hued flowers that stands tall and proud along roadsides but has the unflattering name of Joe Pye Weed, as well as diverse wildlife and ecosystems.

Climate

West Virginia's mountains can provide a welcome respite from summer's heat, a natural cooling effect, while areas in lower elevations are subject to a bit more heat and humidity. One thing you will notice, though, is the fog that shrouds the trees in the early morning hours, which is attributed to the forested mountains and valleys that roll throughout; it is considered one of the foggiest states. The western section of the state sees less rain than the higher elevations in the eastern portion around the Allegheny Mountains, again due to ridges and valleys. If you like snow, you will not be disappointed by what you can find in the eastern section of the state, with many campgrounds open for snowshoeing and cross-country-skiing enthusiasts.

Geography

Winding roads will give your arms a workout while driving. In sections trees form an overhanging canopy, providing shade and a feeling of being embraced and welcomed by this beautiful landscape. Roads twist left and right, sometimes quite sharply, presenting curves in the middle of which you're not quite sure what to expect on the other side. If you're traveling on a main highway such as in the central mountain region, when you see ridge upon ridge stacked one after the other, know this is what creates the switchbacks on the back roads and makes them seem to stretch on forever.

In short, when you travel in West Virginia, you will soon learn why it is referred to as the "Mountain State."

Something else that you will discover is how different that mountain terrain can be from one mountainous region to the next. Some mountains are large and sprawling, while others seem to be tightly packed together, rising up into the sky to what feels like neck-stretching heights. Spruce Knob is the highest peak in the state at 4,863 feet.

There are two panhandles to the state: One is in the far northwestern section of the state, stretching up between Pennsylvania to the east and Ohio to the west, and one is in the northeastern section between Maryland and Virginia. From Harpers Ferry in the northeastern panhandle, you can see all three states from one particular vantage point. This is also where the Shenandoah River and the Potomac River meet.

Several major rivers run through West Virginia: the Cheat, the Monongahela (the "Mon"), the New River, the Ohio, the Greenbrier, and the Kanawha. These provide water recreation opportunities in addition to the many lakes, streams, and creeks throughout the state, drawing fishermen, boaters, white-water kayakers, rafters, and swimmers. The New River is recognized as one of the oldest rivers on Earth, though there is fierce debate on where it ranks in the "old" category. There are plenty of guides and outfitters in the area.

The eastern section of the state is dominated by the Monongahela National Forest that stretches more than 920,000 gorgeous acres. You will find mountain ash, red spruce, and balsam fir trees, which are just a few of the approximately seventy tree species just in this area. Spruce Knob is located here. The Monongahela National Forest is divided into five ranger districts, and the campgrounds located in each one are operated by these individual districts of the Forest Service. Farther east the bulk of the forest area is in a section of the George Washington and Jefferson National Forests, which overlaps the state line with Virginia.

Some interesting features in Monongahela National Forest include the Cranberry Glades Botanical Area and Cranberry Wilderness Area, the Dolly Sods Wilderness Area, and the Sinnett-Thorn Mountain Cave System. The Cranberry Wilderness Area features red spruce trees. The Cranberry Glades are bogs, a neat wetland with a wheelchair-accessible boardwalk that can be used to tour the area and see the unusual plants that grow there. It is located in the southwestern section of Monongahela National Forest. Dolly Sods Wilderness Area is also located there, in the northern section. It sits at a high altitude and resembles a landscape you would find in Canada, making it a very unusual find. Just think: You do not need a passport to get a glimpse. There are heath barrens, meadows, and wind-stunted trees, as well as bogs of sphagnum moss (also called peat moss, which you may be familiar with from bags you have seen at garden centers). I always wondered who Dolly Sods was, and now I know that Dolly Sods is not a "who" but a "what": The designation is partially derived from the name of a family who lived in the area in the eighteenth century and partially derived from the term that locals used for a mountaintop meadow. The Sinnett-Thorn

Mountain Cave System is an area that is not easily accessed; it has very strict policies for entrance and rules that must be followed. Recently, this caving system, in addition to many others in eastern states, has been closed due to the spread of white nose syndrome, which is killing off the bat population. It is suspected that the syndrome is being tracked from cave system to cave system on caving enthusiasts' clothing. Large limestone caverns are found in the eastern section of the state, from the southern region and north up to the Seneca Rocks area in Monongahela National Forest.

North and south of Monongahela National Forest are a couple of areas that have mineral springs, long believed to be curative of all that ails you. Berkeley Springs sits in the northeastern panhandle, and White Sulphur Springs is situated in the lower southeastern quadrant of the state.

History

Native Americans were of course this region's earliest denizens; there are ancient man-made, cone-shaped mounds used for ceremonial burials still in existence, as well as hundreds upon hundreds of archaeological sites across the state.

The first settler to make a permanent home in the region was Morgan Morgan. His son, Zackquill Morgan, founded the city of Morgantown, from whom it derives its name. There were skirmishes and bloodshed between the Native Americans who lived here and the settlers who continued to move in, and this was considered frontier country, complete with forts. Eventually a treaty was signed. Today, Prickett's Fort State Park has a fort that was recreated from the original that stood there in 1774. While the park does not have a campground, it is worth a day trip if you are camping in the area, because it gives you a glimpse into life on the frontier in this region. Daniel Boone lived in the region that is now Charleston before he headed farther west.

Once upon a time, West Virginia used to be simply the western section of Virginia. In 1863 it became its own state, apparently because it did not want to secede from the Union during the Civil War. There are multiple Civil War Historic Trails across the state, showcasing battlefields, homes, and other historic sites. It was in the town of Phillipi that the first land battle of the Civil War took place. John Brown famously led an insurrection in Harpers Ferry, seizing the town's armory. He was surrounded and outnumbered, and just as soon captured, and later hanged for treason. Droop Mountain was the site of the last major Civil War battle in the state and is now preserved as a state park. It is also considered the state's oldest park.

The state was rich in coal, natural gas, and oil; mining became a dominant industry in the late nineteenth century. Railroads were built to carry coal and timber from the forest areas, and many of these railroads are still in use supporting the state's current hottest industry: tourism. West Virginia is rich in outdoor resources and scenic beauty. Many of those railroad paths have been turned into multiuse trails enjoyed by cyclists, horseback riders, and hikers.

Major Tourist Attractions

By far the number one major tourist attraction in West Virginia is the outdoor recreational opportunities that it offers across the state. That might be my bias, but if you are at all passionate about being outdoors, this state will slake your thirst. However, there are other tourist attractions worth mentioning, and we will take a look at outdoor recreational opportunities in the next section.

In the northeastern panhandle, Berkeley Springs State Park offers spa treatments, including baths and a public swimming pool fed by the warm springs, and there is a spigot in one area where you can fill up jugs of the mineral-rich water. It was a favorite of George Washington, who it is said returned many times to take the waters. Also in this area is Harpers Ferry National Historical Park, where the abolitionist John Brown's raid took place. The area is a walk back in time and is representative of what the town looked like in the nineteenth century.

Southeast of the panhandle is what is known as the Potomac Highlands, prominently featuring Monongahela National Forest. The outdoors itself is a major tourist attraction, with rock climbers traveling to 1,000-foot-high Seneca Rocks to work their technical skills, and cyclists hauling their mountain bikes and backpacks to explore the miles of trails throughout the forest or to visit the unusual geographic anomalies that are Dolly Sods Wilderness Area and Cranberry Glades Wilderness Area. It makes for scenic driving along winding roads, and there are train rides that can be taken for a different means of seeing the area. Cass Scenic Railroad State Park offers rides on its steam-driven locomotives, as do others in the area. The National Radio Astronomy Observatory is located in Green Bank and its Science Center offers educational programs and exhibits, and tours of the world's largest fully steerable telescope. There are also famous ski resorts in this area: Canaan Valley, Snowshoe Mountain, and Timberline. Civil War sites bring history alive at Fort Mill Ride and Droop Mountain Battlefield State Park.

The north-central section of the state is referred to as Mountaineer Country and is home to West Virginia State University in Morgantown. Many of the small towns within this region have historic sites and downtown areas. Prickett's Fort State Park is located in Fairmont, providing living history programs for visitors to learn about frontier life. Phillipi, the site of the first major Civil War land battle, is located here and features an old covered bridge, one of many covered bridges in the area.

The northern panhandle juts up between Ohio and Pennsylvania. In this area you will find the Gothic-style West Virginia Penitentiary, which offers ghost-hunting tours and looks like it could play the lead role in a horror movie. Part of West Virginia's ancient history features mounds created by the Adena people who once lived here and built the mounds for ceremonial burials. Grave Creek Mound Archaeological Complex offers a glimpse back into this ancient time. This region also offers such casinos as Wheeling Island Casino and Mountaineer Casino.

A dry streambed in West Virginia's Mountain Lakes region

South of this area is the Mid-Ohio Valley region, where the millionaires of the oil and gas era once lived. One draw is the Blennerhassett Island Historical State Park. To get there, you need to take a riverboat called a sternwheeler. The oldest continuously operating movie theater is in Spencer. There are also historic parks that preserve a snapshot of Civil War history in the region.

The southwestern corner of the state is the Metro Valley region, home of the Hatfields and McCoys, the most famous feuding families in history. It is also coal-mining country, and there are various sites that pay tribute to this legacy, including the Coal Miner's Memorial and Coal Heritage Museum, and even an annual coal festival located in Madison. The capital, Charleston, is located in this region and features a can't-miss golden dome on its capitol building, as well as cultural draws, including such museums and venues as State Museum, Huntington Museum of Art, and Clay Center for the Arts and Sciences. For history lovers Tu-Endie-Wei and Point Pleasant Battle Monument State Park preserve an area where a nasty frontier battle took place.

The central region of the state is known as the Mountain Lakes area, featuring five major lakes. Wildlife management areas preserve the region's green spaces. There are Civil War Discovery Trails in this area, including Carnifex Ferry Battlefield State Park, which occasionally features reenactments that draw history buffs.

In the south-central section of the state, Beckley Exhibition Coal Mine is devoted to all things coal, offering coal car tours through underground areas and a museum. Tamarack is unique, offering the best of West Virginia's arts, crafts, and foods. To the east of this area is the New River and Greenbrier Valley area, where the famous Greenbrier resort is located in White Sulphur Springs. For scenic drives consider traveling the Midland Trail, Paint Creek Trail, or Coal Heritage Trail. In Lewisburg visit Lost World Caverns for a look-see underground on a self-guided tour.

In addition, there are many festivals that occur all over throughout the year, drawing tourists from everywhere.

Recreational Opportunities

West Virginia has in its possession quite the incredible, awe-inspiring gold mine: acres and acres, mile upon mile, of outdoor opportunities.

Horseback riding: For equestrians there are some really great trails in the state, thanks in large part to the rail trails that are multiuse, such as Blackwater Canyon Rail Trail, Allegheny Highlands Trail, Panhandle Rail Trail, Gauley Mountain Trail, Greenbrier River Trail, and North Bend Rail Trail, to name just a few. Also, the accommodating nature of many of the state parks, such as Pipestem Resort, Cacapon Resort, Lost River and Babcock State Parks, which provide stables, or Camp Creek State Park, which provides camping for both equestrians and their horses, makes getting out by horseback possible. And that's just the state parks; you will also find other campgrounds that are somewhat primitive in nature but well placed next to equestrian-friendly trailheads. There are also many outfitters that provide lessons and trail rides, including some within the state parks and forests.

Fishing: There are so many places to fish, the avid angler may need to book many a camping trip to hit them all. Just in Monongahela National Forest alone, there are 576 miles of trout streams. Trout fishing is popular in this region, with many streams and lakes stocked with native brook trout and rainbow trout. All across the state you will also find fishing available for smallmouth and largemouth bass, another popular fish, as well as muskellunge, channel catfish, and walleye. Favorite fishing spots abound throughout the state. For example, Stonecoal Lake offers excellent muskie fishing, while nearby Stonewall Jackson Lake in the state park offers great trout fishing. For the biggest naturalized population of trout, many point to the Upper Elk River area, though they have a catch-and-release program there. Kids under the age of 15 can fish for free. Fishermen over that age can purchase a license at a local sporting goods store, by calling (304) 558-2758, or by visiting www.wvfish .com. There are year-round fishing, open season for trout, catch-and-release, and fly-fishing-only streams. In addition, many of the campgrounds provide fishing piers, often accessible to people with disabilities, as well as boat launches and convenient shoreline areas.

Hiking: You could walk your whole lifetime and still miss quite a few feet of trail in West Virginia. That may be only mild exaggeration, but the West Virginia State Park system wants to encourage hiking and offers a unique challenge to hikers: a special hiking program. Register for a small fee and start logging miles in one of the many parks, forest, or wildlife management areas. You'll start chalking up rewards for reaching various plateaus, including a hiking staff at 25 miles and cane shields after the next designated levels. As if the natural scenic beauty of these trails weren't incentive enough for hikers to want to walk and walk some more! In addition to the numerous trails found in all of the parks and forest areas, there is also the Appalachian Trail in the southeastern section of the state, picking up again in the northeastern panhandle, and the Allegheny Trail that starts in the southern region and travels 300 miles north to the Mason–Dixon Line. The multiuse rail trails offer additional mileage suitable for hikers, including the Mon River Rail Trail, Greenbrier River Rail Trail, and North Bend Rail Trail.

Biking: Whether you are a recreational or serious, adrenaline-pumping cyclist, West Virginia offers some amazing trails suitable for a range of bikes. The mountain biking here is some of the best on the East Coast, and West Virginia is considered a world-class destination by many, with more than 1,000 miles of mountain bike trails to choose from. This would be a challenge in many states, but West Virginia has gone out of its way to accommodate mountain bikers. You may want to check out the Gauley Mountain Trail, a challenging favorite of riders. For example, roots and rocks more than a foot tall can make this somewhat short-distance trail (about 11 miles round-trip) more like Mother Nature's version of an obstacle course. Sometimes it is not the distance; it is the technical aspects that make a trail tops. In addition, Monongahela National Forest can claim about 700 trails for mountain bikers to get muddy on, so you can have fun trying to discover your own "favorite." Or if grassy meadows are more your speed, the Cranberry Back Country area on the southern end of Monongahela National Forest provides a different experience. The variety of rail trails throughout the state also provides miles of options for individuals and families to see the countryside by two wheels. North Bend Rail Trail offers 72 miles, the New River Rail Trail is 75 miles in length, and Greenbrier River Trail is 78 miles long. That's just a few of the many options, including many trails that you can start on right from your campsite. For road cyclists all of the mountainous roads provide abundant lung-taxing opportunities. Just exercise caution, especially around any of those blind corners you will find on switchback roads. State helmet laws dictate that kids under the age of 15 must wear a helmet when riding a bike or as a passenger on a bike (think tandem bikes and kiddie carriers), and some jurisdictions have helmet laws for other age ranges, so know before you go.

Water sports: You wouldn't know West Virginia was a land-locked state judging by its incredible number of water-based opportunities, ranging from rafting to boating to swimming. Lakes, rivers, and streams are the water-based playgrounds, and many of the parks also offer swimming pools in addition to the natural amenities. There are many white-water rafting outfitters near the major rivers that offer guided white-water trips as well as the benefit of local experience. White-water rafting is popular on the Shenandoah River from the Harpers Ferry area. This would be a day trip from one of the campgrounds closest to West Virginia's eastern panhandle, as there are no nearby offerings of public campgrounds. The Cheat River offers white-water rafting and kayaking with Class III and IV rapids and is located in the Morgantown area in the north-central area of the state. Gauley River in the south-central area of the state provides renowned white-water kayaking and rafting when the water is released at Summersville Dam in the fall. It offers more than 100 rapids in a gorgeous river canyon, giving it the status of having more Class IV and Class V rapids than any other river in the East. Raft or kayak on the Elk River, also located in the central region, or the New River Gorge in the south near Beckley. Kayak or canoe the Coal River Walhonde Water Trail, located in the southwestern region, which offers 88 miles of flat water and the occasional ripple of minor rapids. The southeastern region offers the New River Gorge area, considered some of the best and biggest white water in the East, very popular for rafting. Many campgrounds are situated on lakes and rivers and offer beach and swimming areas, boat rentals, and boat launches, greatly expanding the number of opportunities to enjoy water-based fun.

Snow sports: There are a few downhill skiing resorts, including Canaan Valley Resort and Conference Center, which is a state park, as well as Timberline Resort in Davis, and Winterplace Ski Resort located in Ghent in the southeastern region, which also holds the state's largest tubing park. Blackwater Falls State Park and Canaan Valley State Park offer flat trails that work well for cross-country skiing and snowshoeing, and the rail trails become excellent cross-country skiing trails when the snow falls. Many of the roads in the campgrounds can be used in the winter when snowed over for snowshoeing and cross-country skiing.

Rock climbing: West Virginia has a solid reputation in the climbing world for providing some of the best climbing opportunities in the East. Seneca Rocks in Monongahela National Forest is a climbing mecca, with more than 400 mapped routes. US Army paratroopers trained here back in World War II. These rock formations are about 1,000 feet tall, making them an eye-catching, awe-inspiring visual in this area as they rise up over the North Fork River. The New River Gorge National Recreation Area tops out with more than 2,000 developed routes, amazing views, and diverse climbing opportunities. Coopers Rock State Park near Morgantown also offers climbing opportunities. There are outfitters located in all of these areas that provide climbing lessons and trips.

Caving: There are commercial caverns you can pay a fee to visit and tour that are suitable for tourists, including Organ Cave, the second largest cave in the East. (Virginia lays claim to the largest with Luray Caverns.) In addition, there are Lost World Caverns, Seneca Caverns, and Smoke Hole Caverns for anyone craving a subterranean view of the state. There are hundreds more caves that are for the serious spelunker, and I recommend you get in contact with a local spelunking organization to learn more before venturing into one, as there are strict rules and regulations designed to protect you as well as the fragile cave environments.

ATV: There are more than 500 miles of professionally designed public trails available to ATV and ORT enthusiasts located in the southwestern section of the state and known as the Hatfield-McCoy Trails. Every user must have his or her own User Permit, even if they are just riding as a passenger. Trails range from beginner to pro level. Outfitters in the area offer tours, equipment, and passes to the trails.

Geocaching: Go treasure hunting for geocaches with your GPS. West Virginia State Parks is an avid participant in this fun game, which is taking place on an international level. Individuals, groups, and families can all enjoy the hunt while enjoying their camping stay.

Golf: There are golf courses all over the state, but many of the state parks offer amazing golfing opportunities, including Cacapon Resort State Park, Canaan Valley Resort State Park, North Bend State Park, Twin Falls Resort State Park, and Tygart Lake State Park.

Overview of Camping in the State

I recommend, if possible, camping during the weekdays if you want to escape crowds. In many of the parks, there are much smaller numbers of people during the week and you will feel like you have the area almost to yourself. This depends on the park, of course. The more off the beaten path, the better for finding fewer people. The closer the parks are to main highways and cities, the busier they seem to be.

Reservations are accepted by mail, phone, and walk-in. State parks accept only mail-in reservations in the late winter, between February 15 and March 14, and these are first come, first served. Their policies seem to be pretty firm; many of the reservation forms state that mail-in applications must be postmarked on or after February 15 or else they will be returned to sender. Once they are received, they are sorted by the postmark and then randomly opened, and you can submit a maximum of three reservations in one envelope, so at least no one gets an unfair advantage. You can download a reservation form from the state park's web address, provided in each listing below. On the form will be the details for that particular location. Phone reservations are taken beginning on March 15 at the individual park, and walk-ins are taken as they come starting April 1. For most state parks reservation season covers from the Friday prior to Memorial Day through Labor Day. Reservations can be made at least two days in advance at campgrounds that offer reservable sites. A minimum reservation of two nights along with a deposit and a handling charge is required. The parks cannot guarantee that a specific campsite number can be reserved for you, but they do their best to assign it if possible.

The public campgrounds in West Virginia are administered by West Virginia State Parks, West Virginia State Forests, the USDA Forest Service, and the US Army Corps of Engineers. The state parks and forests and the campgrounds run by the US Army Corps of Engineers tend to be very well developed, and the wildlife management areas tend to be more primitive.

Most campsites can accommodate six people per site, and larger group camping areas are available, too. Only one tent or RV is permitted in a site at state parks, and if your group is larger than six people, there is a charge for each additional guest. Developed campsites have water, picnic tables, and grills, and they provide marked paths to bathhouses and toilets.

Swimming is prohibited in nondesignated areas within state parks, forests, and wildlife management areas. When in doubt, ask someone in authority who can give you the correct answer.

Weather can be a factor in opening and closing a campground, so check with the campground just in case if you are traveling in the off-season. Also, at least one campground was closed due to flooding during the writing of this guidebook, so it isn't a bad idea to make sure everything is a go, before you go, especially if you are counting on a first-come, first-served campground.

Special note on firewood: The overwhelming majority of campgrounds have a firewood quarantine in effect, which means you cannot bring firewood from outside the campground into the campground where you are staying. You must purchase your firewood from the place you camp, because it is sourced locally. The reason is the potential for transporting into the state some very destructive insects, plants, and diseases that could be in the wood and that will kill native trees. This is one way to be a nice guest and not bring the equivalent of bed bugs with you to your temporary camping home.

Travel Tips

Navigation

I recommend that, even though you may be partial to your GPS, an online mapping service, or maps, you bring all of them with you. Some back roads are simply not marked, though locals take those roads for granted and are more than happy to help out a lost traveler. The great majority of parks within the state, however, are right off main roads, have great signage, and are easy to find. There were really only one or two parks where I wished I had brought my compass, because after so many switchbacks, I could not tell north from south. That may have been because I was traveling between locations and didn't always begin each leg of my journey from a main road, so maybe the advice here is to always begin from a major highway, which is easy to do since the state is conveniently bisected by interstates.

Driving considerations

In particular, be aware of "CR" routes, which are county routes. If you like leisurely drives, these do provide the perfect pace. However, some can narrow down to one lane, leaving you to wonder what to do should a car come in the opposite direction, since your only option is a ditch or drop-off on the side. Some spots on these roads can become quite hilly, and the road may even turn to gravel quite suddenly. That happened to us on one particularly memorable trip that we still talk about. I was reassured by the full gas tank I had, and if nothing else, this type of travel will force you to slow down.

There are "Backways" such as CR 17 that will take you through beautiful scenery, while also reminding you why West Virginia's tagline is "Wild and Wonderful." You will find plenty of both on your camping adventure.

Throughout West Virginia you will see "Falling Rock" signs for areas where the road has been hewn out of a mountain. Keep an eye out, just in case.

Brief Description of the Regions

Northern Panhandle / Mid-Ohio Valley / Metro Valley / Hatfield-McCoy Mountains Area: This region hugs the western section of the state from north to south, along the state line with Ohio to the north and Kentucky to the south.

Mountaineer Country / Mountain Lakes / Eastern Panhandle / Potomac Highlands Area: This region covers the north-central, northeastern, and eastern sections of the state, sharing a state line with Pennsylvania to the north, Maryland in the upper eastern panhandle area, and Virginia to the east and southeast.

New River / Greenbrier Valley Area: This region covers the south and southeastern portion of the state, sharing a state line with Virginia.

These different areas match the state's tourism department designations, and they make perfect sense in terms of what is close to what when it comes to driving and geography. Within each section you will be provided with more in-depth information about that particular area.

Northern Panhandle / Mid-Ohio Valley / Metro Valley / Hatfield-McCoy Mountains Area

The Northern Panhandle area stretches up between Ohio and Pennsylvania like a finger raised for attention, forming the northwestern border of the state. The Mid-Ohio Valley, Metro Valley, and Hatfield-McCoy Mountains areas form the western section of the state, sharing the border with Ohio on the north and Kentucky on the south.

In the southwest and central region, the mountains become steeply mounded, rising up like piles of salt that have been closely poured together to squeeze as many as possible into a tight space. It is in this lower quadrant that the capital of Charleston can be found.

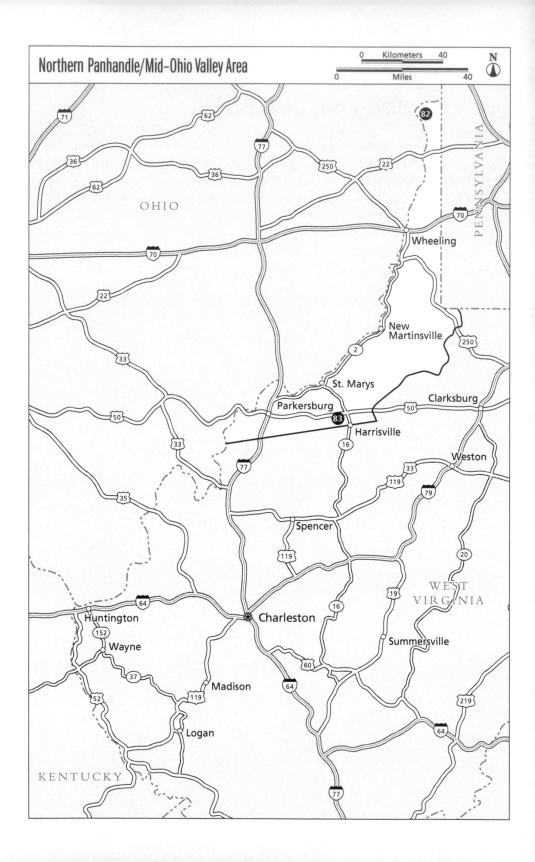

Northern Panhandle / Mid-Ohio Valley Area

Tomlinson Run State Park is the northernmost campground in the state, situated next to the Ohio River. There are multiple wildlife management areas in this region, providing plenty of green spaces and keeping overdevelopment at bay. Grave Creek Mound State Park is outside of Moundsville, just south of Wheeling. While it does not have a campground, it is worth a side trip to see the archaeological site and learn about some ancient West Virginian history, well before there was a "West Virginia." Also, the Suspension Bridge, noted for being the first bridge to cross the Ohio River, is in Wheeling. There are just two parks in this area.

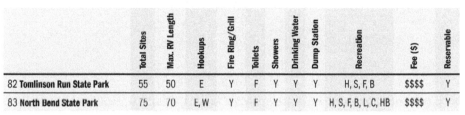

	Total Sites	Max. RV Length	Hookups	Fire Ring/Grill	Toilets	Showers	Drinking Water	Dump Station	Recreation	Fee ($)	Reservable
82 **Tomlinson Run State Park**	55	50	E	Y	F	Y	Y	Y	H, S, F, B	$$$$	Y
83 **North Bend State Park**	75	70	E, W	Y	F	Y	Y	Y	H, S, F, B, L, C, HB	$$$$	Y

Max RV Length: Measured in feet
Hookups: W = Water, E = Electricity, S = Sewer
Fire Ring/Grill: Y = Yes, N = None
Toilets: F = Flush, P = Pit, V = Vault
Showers: Y = Yes, N = None
Drinking Water: Y = Yes, N = None
Dump Station: Y = Yes, N = None
Recreation: H = Hiking, S = Swimming, F = Fishing, B = Boating, L = Boat Launch, C = Cycling, HB = Horseback Riding, OHV = Off-Highway Vehicles
Fee: $ = 0–$5, $$ = $6–$10, $$$ = $11–$20, $$$$ = $21–$30+
Reservable: Y = Yes, N = No

82 Tomlinson Run State Park

Location: 19 miles north of Weirton
Sites: 16 tent only, 39 electric
Facilities: Flush toilets, showers, fire grills, picnic tables, store, dump station, laundry facility, picnic shelters, playground, swimming pool with waterslide, boat rental
Fee per night: $$$$
Management: West Virginia State Parks & Forests
Contact: (304) 564-3651; (800) 225-5982; www.tomlinsonrunsp.com
Activities: Hiking, swimming, basketball, volleyball, horseshoes, miniature golf, disc golf, fishing, boating
Season: April to October

Tomlinson Run State Park Courtesy West Virginia Department of Commerce (www.wv commerce.org)

Finding the campground: Take SR 8 north to where it intersects with SR 2. Follow the signs to the park entrance.
GPS coordinates: 40.541550 / -80.575568
About the campground: The park sits at the upper northernmost panhandle section of West Virginia, the finger that juts up between Pennsylvania to the east and Ohio to the west. There is a swimming pool located here, which is naturally quite popular with kids and offers a waterslide. With access to ponds and lakes, you can rent a paddleboat or rowboat, or fish for bass, catfish, and trout. A fishing permit is required. Tomlinson Run is a stream that flows through a deep gorge on its way to the Ohio River. Hiking trails wind throughout the park, including Laurel Trail, which is a loop around the gorge area. The campground is located near what was Jamboree USA, relocated to the southern end of the state in the New River Gorge area. RVs up to 50 feet.

83 North Bend State Park

Location: 4 miles northeast of Cairo
Sites: 23 standard, 26 standard electric (River Run Campground); 26 standard electric and water (Cokeley Campground)
Facilities: Flush toilets, showers, fire grills, swimming pool, dump station, tennis courts, picnic areas, picnic shelters, fishing pier, boat launch, canoe launch, boat rentals, bike rentals, nature programs, playgrounds, gift shop, amphitheater, miniature golf course
Fee per night: $$$$
Management: West Virginia State Parks & Forests

North Bend State Park COURTESY WEST VIRGINIA DEPARTMENT OF COMMERCE (WWW.WV
COMMERCE.ORG)

Contact: (304) 643-2931; (800) 225-5982; www.northbendsp.com
Activities: Hiking, biking, horseback riding, swimming, boating, fishing, canoeing, kayaking, tennis,
miniature golf
Season: Open mid-April to October
Finding the campground: If you are driving east, take US 50 to SR 31 toward Cairo. Follow it to
the campground entrance. If you are driving west, take SR 16 toward Harrisville. Follow It to the
campground entrance. Be forewarned: Online map directions may be inaccurate, so be careful if
using them.
GPS coordinates: 39.218748 / -81.077507
About the campground: This park is situated in the valley area that is the North Fork of the
Hughes River. The bend in the river is where the park got its name. There are two campgrounds
located in this park, which is situated next to a 305-acre lake that is actually 8 miles of river. One
of the two campgrounds is River Run Campground, which opens in early April and has a smaller
fee. The second one is Cokeley Campground, which opens in early May and has a slightly higher
fee. River Run Campground has a pond and nature trails, and the Hughes River runs alongside
it, providing some waterfront sites. Cokeley Campground features a play area. Some campsites
are accessible as are two fishing platforms. Fish for bass, muskie, catfish, and crappie. You must
have a valid West Virginia state fishing license. You can bring a boat or launch a cartop boat from
the canoe launch site. If you bring a motorboat, ***please note:*** there is a horsepower limit of 9.9.
Fourteen hiking trails range from 0.5 mile to 4.5 miles in length, providing access to overlooks
and geological formations, pond views, and even one self-guiding, Interpretive trail featuring braille
signs. There's also a fitness trail and a multiuse trail for hikers, bikers, and equestrians to share.
RV friendly up to 70 feet.

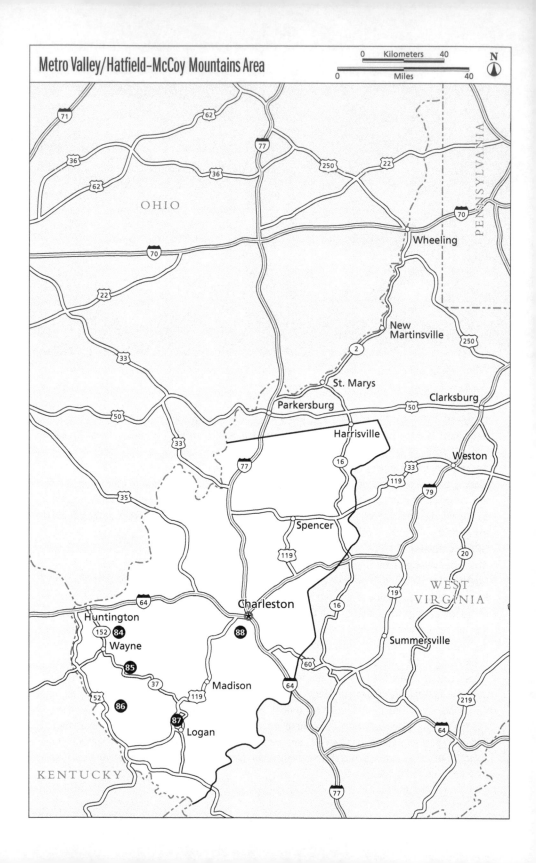

Kilometers

Miles

N

OHIO

PENNSYLVANIA

Wheeling

New Martinsville

St. Marys

Parkersburg

Clarksburg

Harrisville

Weston

Spencer

Charleston

Huntington

Wayne

WEST VIRGINIA

Summersville

Madison

Logan

KENTUCKY

Metro Valley / Hatfield-McCoy Mountains Area

This area offers an array of recreational opportunities for the camping enthusiast. If you elect to stay around the Metro Valley region, you have access to city-life options for day trips. This section is home to Charleston, the state capital, and Huntington with shopping, restaurants, museums, and a bustling arts scene. Kanawha State Forest, located in this area, is a birders' paradise.

Farther west in the Hatfield-McCoy area, you're going to be treated to some rugged terrain. This area offers the greatest number of miles for ATV and ORV enthusiasts to enjoy. For cartop boaters, you can paddle down the Coal River Walhonde Water Trail. Campgrounds such as Cabwaylingo State Forest will give you a wonderful sense of isolation in the midst of mountain splendor.

	Total Sites	Max. RV Length	Hookups	Fire Ring/Grill	Toilets	Showers	Drinking Water	Dump Station	Recreation	Fee ($)	Reservable
84 **Beech Fork State Park**	275	70	E, W, S	Y	F	Y	Y	N	H, S, F, B, L, C	$$$$	Y
85 **East Fork Campground**	167		E, W	Y	F, P	Y	Y	Y	H, S, F, B, L, C	$$$-$$$$	Y
86 **Cabwaylingo State Forest**	25	30	E, W	Y	F	Y	Y	Y	H, S, F	$$$-$$$$	Y
87 **Chief Logan State Park**	26	30	E, W, S	Y	F	Y	Y	Y	H, S, F, C	$$$$	Y
88 **Kanawha State Forest**	40	20	E, W	Y	F	Y	Y	Y	H, S, F, C	$$$$	Y

Max RV Length: Measured in feet
Hookups: W = Water, E = Electricity, S = Sewer
Fire Ring/Grill: Y = Yes, N = None
Toilets: F = Flush, P = Pit, V = Vault
Showers: Y = Yes, N = None
Drinking Water: Y = Yes, N = None
Dump Station: Y = Yes, N = None
Recreation: H = Hiking, S = Swimming, F = Fishing, B = Boating, L = Boat Launch, C = Cycling, HB = Horseback Riding, OHV = Off-Highway Vehicles
Fee: $ = 0-$5, $$ = $6-$10, $$$ = $11-$20, $$$$ = $21-$30+
Reservable: Y = Yes, N = No

84 Beech Fork State Park

Location: 12 miles south of Huntington
Sites: 226 standard electric, 49 standard electric, water, and sewer
Facilities: Flush toilets, showers, fire grills, picnic tables, laundry facility, playgrounds, camp store, tennis court, basketball court, horseshoe pit, volleyball court, nature program, swimming pool, snack bar, boat launch, boat rentals, picnic areas, picnic shelters, softball field

Beech Fork State Park COURTESY WEST VIRGINIA DEPARTMENT OF COMMERCE (WWW.WV
COMMERCE.ORG)

Fee per night: $$$$
Management: West Virginia State Parks & Forests
Contact: (304) 528-5794; (800) 225-5982; www.beechforksp.com
Activities: Hiking, biking, swimming, fishing, boating, canoeing, kayaking, tennis, horseshoes, volleyball, softball, basketball
Season: Open year-round
Finding the campground: Take I-64 to exit 18 in Barbourville. Take US 60 west, and then take a left onto SR 10 headed south for several miles to SR 10 north. Turn left on Hughes Branch Road and follow it to the end, and then take a left. Follow it to the campground entrance.
GPS coordinates: 38.307258 / -82.348827
About the campground: This park is the westernmost state park, located not too far from the borders with Ohio and Kentucky, and it spreads across 3,100 acres. The campground is huge and offers many amenities. The camp store on-site is available from April to October and offers a range of groceries, camping supplies, and fishing supplies, as well as hand-dipped ice cream. The swimming pool is available for a small admittance fee and is open six days a week, closed on Mondays, and it has a snack bar. For the game courts you can rent equipment from the camp store. Fish in the 760-acre Beech Fork Lake for largemouth bass, hybrid striped bass, walleye, saugeye, catfish, and bluegill. You will need a valid West Virginia state fishing license that you can obtain from the park's office. You can rent a canoe, kayak, rowboat, or pedal boat to explore the lake or bring your own. There is a boat launch available from April to November; *please note:* there is a 10-horsepower limit on motors. The park naturalist provides different programs for campers, including nature hikes, scavenger hunts, and other family-friendly activities. There is a fitness trail

and four hiking and biking trails ranging in length from less than 1 mile for a nature trail to a more strenuous trail that is 5 miles, Lost Trail. Campsites are reservable through Labor Day, then revert to a first-come, first-served basis until the season starts back up in mid-May. There are four different campground areas offering 275 sites, with 99 of these sites available situated next to the lake. RV friendly up to 70 feet. Senior discounts available.

85 East Fork Campground

Location: 12 miles southeast of Wayne
Sites: 1 tent only, 166 standard electric and water
Facilities: Flush toilets, pit toilets, showers, fire grills, picnic tables, playground, dump station, boat ramp, fishing dock, swimming beach, basketball courts, volleyball courts, amphitheater
Fee per night: $$$–$$$$
Management: US Army Corps of Engineers
Contact: (304) 849-5000; (800) 225-5982; https://www.recreation.gov/camping/campgrounds/233493
Activities: Hiking, biking, swimming, fishing, boating, waterskiing, basketball, volleyball
Season: Early May to mid-October
Finding the campground: Take I-64 to exit 8, SR 152 headed south. When you reach the town of Wayne, take SR 37 headed east. Follow it to the campground entrance.
GPS coordinates: 38.078352 / -82.315595
About the campground: This campground offers a large number of campsites and is beautifully situated on the eastern shore of East Lynn Lake, which spreads for 12 miles along the East Fork of Twelvepole Creek. It is surrounded by trees thanks to its proximity to East Lynn Lake Wildlife Management Area on the southeastern portion of the lake. This site is managed by the US Army Corps of Engineers. There are several hiking trails in the area from which to choose, and the trailhead for East Fork Trail is in the campground; the trail is 1.5 miles long. Make use of the swimming beach when you finish your hike or bike ride through the woods. The lake offers about twenty-nine different species of fish, including black crappie, red-breast sunfish, and several varieties of bass and muskellunge, making this a prime fishing spot. Fishing requires a valid West Virginia state fishing license. There is a fishing dock available, which is accessible to people with disabilities, and a boat ramp. Flush toilets are also accessible. RV friendly.

86 Cabwaylingo State Forest

Location: 58 miles south of Huntington, near the Kentucky state line
Sites: 19 standard, 6 standard electric and water
Facilities: Flush toilets, showers, fire pits, picnic tables, dump station, swimming pool, basketball court, volleyball courts, picnic areas, picnic shelters, playgrounds
Fee per night: $$$–$$$$
Management: West Virginia State Parks & Forests
Contact: (304) 385-4255; (800) 225-5982; www.cabwaylingo.com

Cabwaylingo State Forest COURTESY WEST VIRGINIA DEPARTMENT OF COMMERCE (WWW.WV COMMERCE.ORG)

Activities: Hiking, swimming, basketball, volleyball, fishing
Season: April through end of October
Finding the campground: From Huntington take SR 152 headed south. Turn left onto Missouri Branch Road, headed east, and follow it to the campground entrance.
GPS coordinates: 37.981052 / -82.357279
About the campground: This campground is more isolated than most, with very few people because of its remote, out-of-the-way location, but it is a beautiful area and perfect if you crave peace, quiet, and the sounds of nature. The forest covers more than 8,100 acres. Its unique name comes from a few letters of each of the four counties it stretches into. It features a swimming pool and a kiddie wading pool, available to campers for a small entrance fee. **Please note:** The pool is closed on Mondays and Tuesdays. With seven hiking trails to choose from, you should be able to get in one hike a day for a week or group them together for longer jaunts. These trails vary in length, ranging from 1 to 3 miles, and level, taking you through forested areas to rock overhangs, a fire tower, a waterfall, and other points within the park. One is the Sleepy Hollow Trail, where you will see the waterfall and rock ledges; it is a somewhat moderate hike. You can fish for trout in Twelvepole Creek, which meanders through the forest. You must have a valid West Virginia fishing license, which you can pick up at the park office. There are two campgrounds at this location: Tick Ridge Campground has 20 rustic sites, while Spruce Creek Campground is a newer addition with some electric and water hookups. You can reserve up to a year in advance, which is recommended by forest staff. Close to East Lynn Lake Wildlife Management Area just to the north. RV friendly up to 30 feet and some pull-through sites.

87 Chief Logan State Park

Location: 53 miles southwest of Charleston, 4 miles north of Logan
Sites: 12 standard electric and water, 14 standard electric, water, and sewer
Facilities: Flush toilets, showers, fire grills, picnic tables, swimming pool, waterslide, tennis courts, basketball court, miniature golf course, picnic areas, picnic shelters, playground, dump station, wildlife center, amphitheater, museum
Fee per night: $$$$
Management: West Virginia State Parks & Forests
Contact: (304) 792-7125; (800) 225-5982; www.chiefloganstatepark.com
Activities: Hiking, swimming, biking, fishing, tennis, miniature golf, basketball
Season: March through November
Finding the campground: Take US 119 south. Once you pass through the town of Chapmanville, turn left on SR 119/90 (Logan Road), headed east. Follow it to the park and campground entrance.
GPS coordinates: 37.897346/-82.001342
About the campground: This state park covers more than 3,000 acres and offers a range of amenities, including a swimming pool with a waterslide and a lake. There are twelve trails covering 18 miles for hiking and mountain biking, ranging in difficulty from easy to challenging and ranging in length from 0.5 mile to 6 miles. One of the trails is a 1-mile fitness trail, which has fitness stations spaced out along its length. This area is coal country, and some of the trails run alongside old mine openings and abandoned coal mines. Use caution on the trails: Stay on the designated trail, as wandering off can be dangerous. There are lots of cliffs you may suddenly come upon that could be quite hazardous. You can also visit the park's museum, which is centered on the history of coal mining in the region. Tennis, miniature golf, and basketball courts are available for a small fee, and you can rent equipment. There is a fee to swim in the pool as well. One unique thing that makes this a very family-oriented park is the wildlife exhibit, featuring a range of West Virginia animals, including black bears, owls, bobcats, wild boar, and reptiles—a nice, safe way to get close to nature while camping. Performances are often scheduled at the amphitheater, so check with the park office. ATV trails are close to the park. RVs up to 30 feet.

88 Kanawha State Forest

Location: 7 miles south of downtown Charleston
Sites: 21 standard, 25 standard electric and water
Facilities: Flush toilets, showers, fire grills, picnic tables, dump station, playgrounds, swimming pool
Fee per night: $$$$
Management: West Virginia State Parks & Forests
Contact: (304) 558-3500; (800) 225-5982; www.kanawhastateforest.com
Activities: Hiking, biking, fishing, swimming, basketball, volleyball, archery range, shooting range
Season: Mid-April to early December

Kanawha State Forest

Finding the campground: From I-64 take exit 58A south onto US 119. Take a left onto Oakwood Road (the second stop light). Take a left to remain on Oakwood Road (it is before George Washington High School just ahead). Turn right onto Bridge Road. Take a right onto Connell Road. When you reach the bottom of Connell Road, take a sharp left on Kanawha Forest Drive. Follow it to the park entrance.

GPS coordinates: 38.259080 / -81.668330

About the campground: This 9,300-acre park has ample hiking and biking trails and plenty of space to spread out. For recreation there is also a swimming pool with a small fee for use. This is also a very mountain-bike-friendly park, with nine different trails to choose from that have been set aside specifically for mountain bikes—something you do not usually find available year-round. Distances range from 0.75 mile to 2.5 miles, varying from level and moderate to technically challenging. Hikers of all levels will appreciate the 25 miles of hiking trails available spread over fourteen different trails, ranging from 0.25 mile to 2 miles and varying from easy to difficult. In addition, there is a paved trail with braille interpretive sign areas. Ellison Pond offers fishing on its two acres stocked with trout, bass, and bluegill. A fishing license is required. The shooting range is another unusual find: It is free but you can only use paper targets. The park is located in the state capital, Charleston, close to the downtown area. There is a waterfront walkway that runs alongside Kanawha River, and Daniel Boone State Park is here as well. The forest itself is a big draw for those interested in bird-watching, boasting habitat for nineteen different species of warblers. If you come by way of Charleston, you will drive past stately homes on your way to the park, before the road tightens up as you approach the park entrance. Closer to the campground is a unique area called the Shoppes at Trace Fork that offers several little independent eateries should you get tired of camp cooking or would like a treat. To get a campsite, you can claim one that's not already taken or reserved; a campground attendant will be around to register you. Or reserve in advance through mail-in registration before February 15, or call the main park's number when call-in reservations are accepted starting March 15. The park itself is RV friendly up to 26 feet. Vehicles more than 26 feet are not recommended due to the roads leading to the park. It will be a tight squeeze for vehicles any larger. Senior discount of 10 percent is available.

Mountaineer Country / Mountain Lakes / Eastern Panhandle / Potomac Highlands Area

The area around Morgantown and Fairmont in the north-central, eastern section of the state is like a roller-coaster ride: You go up and down highways to get to your destination. Depending on the type of vehicle you drive, you will feel the engine digging in to make it up one steep section to crest the mountain, and then you will need to scramble for your brakes as your vehicle careens wildly down the other side. Big engines do well climbing these steep roads, so if you drive something smaller, stick to the right lane.

I-79 has a technology corridor outside of Fairmont, and there is a lot of activity in the area as is befitting a major university region: This is where West Virginia University is located, home of the Mountaineers. Hence, you have officially entered Mountaineer Country.

Farther south in the central region, known as the Mountain Lakes area, you leave the more densely populated region to the north behind. Richly green, forested mountains are nestled against each other with nooks and crannies folding in as much mountain space as can possibly be squeezed in by the foot. It is less populated, and there is a lot less traffic on the roads; there are towns dotted sporadically on the map, leaving plenty of green space for sightseeing. Peaks and valley abound. Mist hovers among the trees during the early morning hours, giving the air a crisp autumn feeling even in the peak of summer.

Mountaineer Country Area

This bustling area is home to major towns such as Morgantown, Fairmont, and Clarksburg, each with charming, historic downtown areas. There are also some great water recreation opportunities in this area, including Cheat Lake, Cheat River, Monongahela River, Tygart Lake, Tygart River, and West Fork River. You can try white-water rafting on the Cheat River and Little Sandy Creek or kayak one of the other waterways. Boating is popular on 1,800-acre Cheat Lake and Tygart Lake, as well.

There are multiple trails in this area. The Mon River Rail Trail is in this region, beginning at Prickett's Fort State Park and headed north, in sections, to the Pennsylvania border. It is a multiuse trail for cyclists and hikers.

Prickett's Fort State Park is unique, a living history park that shows what frontier life was like in this area where the fort, which has been reproduced, once stood. There is no campground in this park, but it is within easy driving distance. Another interesting park that does not have camping facilities but is within easy driving distance is Cathedral State Park. It has a very old hemlock forest with trees that are more than 90 feet tall. Another day trip to consider would be to Cranesville Swamp for some wildlife viewing in its arboreal bog, one of a couple of unusual ecological niches in the state.

	Total Sites	Max. RV Length	Hookups	Fire Ring/Grill	Toilets	Showers	Drinking Water	Dump Station	Recreation	Fee ($)	Reservable
89 **Chestnut Ridge Regional Park**	62		E, W	Y	F, P	Y	Y	Y	H, S, F, B, C	$$$-$$$$	Y
90 **Coopers Rock State Forest**	50		E	Y	F	Y	Y	N	H, F, C	$$$$	Y
91 **Tygart Lake State Park**	36	70	E, W	Y	F	Y	Y	Y	H, S, F, B, L	$$$$	Y

Max RV Length: Measured in feet
Hookups: W = Water, E = Electricity, S = Sewer
Fire Ring/Grill: Y = Yes, N = None
Toilets: F = Flush, P = Pit, V = Vault
Showers: Y = Yes, N = None
Drinking Water: Y = Yes, N = None
Dump Station: Y = Yes, N = None
Recreation: H = Hiking, S = Swimming, F = Fishing, B = Boating, L = Boat Launch, C = Cycling, HB = Horseback Riding, OHV = Off-Highway Vehicles
Fee: $ = 0-$5, $$ = $6-$10, $$$ = $11-$20, $$$$ = $21-$30+
Reservable: Y = Yes, N = No

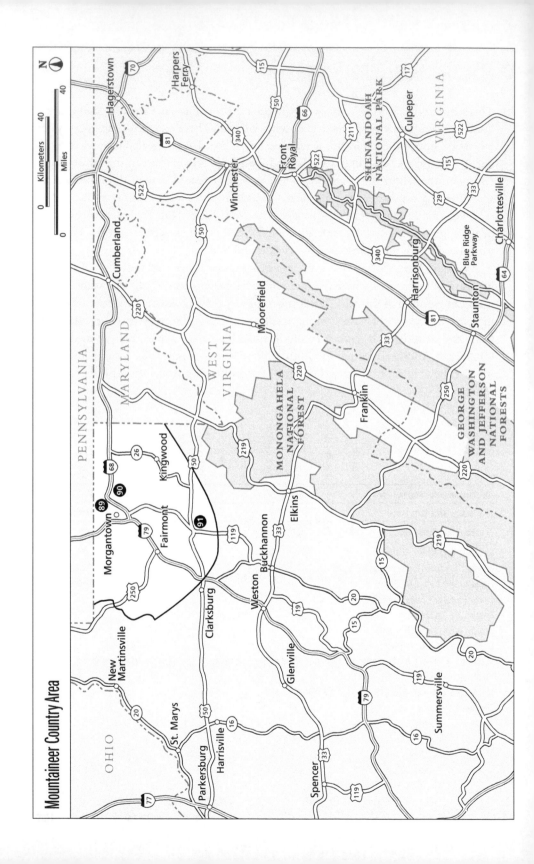

Mountaineer Country Area

89 Chestnut Ridge Regional Park

Location: 10 miles northeast of Morgantown
Sites: 50 standard, 12 standard electric and water
Facilities: Flush toilets, pit toilets, showers, fire rings, picnic tables, picnic shelters, playground, dump station, snack bar
Fee per night: $$$–$$$$
Management: Monongalia County Recreation
Contact: (304) 594-1773; (888) 594-3111; www.chestnutridgepark.com
Activities: Hiking, biking, swimming, fishing, cross-country skiing, sledding, rock climbing (wall), paddleboating, volleyball
Season: Open year-round
Finding the campground: Take I-68 to exit 15 toward Coopers Rock, veering to the right. Go up to the stop sign and take a right again, following signs for the park. Take a left on Sand Springs Road, then a left on Chestnut Ridge Camp Road. Follow it to the park entrance.
GPS coordinates: 39.680296/-79.780629
About the campground: This campground is fortunate to sit within Coopers Rock State Forest as well as the West Virginia University

Chestnut Ridge Regional Park

Forest, so it is surrounded by about 16,000 acres of trees. There are two lakes in the park and fishing and paddleboating available at Feather Lake. A fishing license is not required within the park, and you can buy bait at the main office located next to Feather Lake. The park offers a summer concert series. An old, one-room schoolhouse sits on the property, as well as an old stone baking oven that used to supply the camp with bread. RV friendly.

90 Coopers Rock State Forest

Location: 13 miles east of Morgantown
Sites: 25 primitive, 25 electric
Facilities: Flush toilets, fire pit, showers, picnic tables, picnic shelters, camp store, laundry facility
Fee per night: $$$$
Management: West Virginia State Parks & Forests
Contact: (304) 594-1561; (800) 225-5982; www.coopersrockstateforest.com
Activities: Hiking, biking, fishing, cross-country skiing, rock climbing

Coopers Rock State Park

Season: April to November

Finding the campground: From I-68 west take exit 15 for Coopers Rock. Turn left toward Coopers Rock. Follow this road to the park entrance.

GPS coordinates: 39.655567 / -79.787777

About the campground: The park is located just south of Chestnut Ridge State Park. A nice wooded drive helps you release any traveling stress you may have accrued. There are two camp-grounds: McCollum, which offers the electric sites, and Rhododendron, which offers primitive, tent-only sites. Get set up at your site or continue on and you will reach a couple of parking areas to access trails for hiking or biking; continue even farther on to reach the end of the park. There you will find a concession stand and trails that lead to a breathtaking scenic outlook, complete with viewing platforms that, with a quarter, will buy you the ability to scope out the scene up close. Below the overlook is the Cheat River Gorge. Trees stand like soldiers all around, and to the west you can see the town of Morgantown. You may see people carrying what looks like smallish plastic mattresses on their backs: Those are mats used for rock climbing in case of falls. There are large rock structures in this park, from boulders to cliffs, and rock climbing is one of the park's recreational offerings—but you must register with the camp office first. In addition, there are more than 50 miles of forested trails to explore, and rhododendrons are in abundance. One special site is the Henry Clay Iron Furnace Trail, which boasts a large stone outdoor furnace that was used in the 1800s to make iron. Another trail brings you out at Cheat Lake, which is located a few miles up the road just west of the park off I-68, where you can also go swimming or boating. There are also designated skiing trails suitable for cross-country skiing. Creeks run in spots throughout the park, and one has been dammed to create a pond. Six people are permitted per site, and there is an additional charge for each person extra. Senior citizens can get a 10 percent discount.

91 Tygart Lake State Park

Location: Grafton, 16 miles southeast of Fairmont

Sites: 26 standard, 10 standard electric and water

Facilities: Flush toilets, showers, fire rings, picnic tables, dump station, boat ramp, playground, gift shop

Fee per night: $$$$

Management: West Virginia State Parks & Forests

Contact: (304) 265-6144; (800) 225-5982; www.tygartlake.com

Activities: Hiking, swimming, boating, canoeing, kayaking, fishing, golfing

Season: Mid-April through October

Finding the campground: Take US 119 toward Grafton. Take US 50 to South Grafton. Follow the signs to the park entrance.

GPS coordinates: 39.280194 / -80.010803

About the campground: Swimming is available at the newly renovated beach with an updated bathhouse, sandy beach, picnic, and game area. Select from five hiking trails. The 10-mile-long lake, covering 1,750 acres, is a boater's dream: Rent a fishing or pontoon boat from the marina or rent a slip for your own boat. Or bring your canoe or kayak and explore the lake's quiet coves. Fish for bass, walleye, perch, crappie, carp, northern pike, and more in Tygart Lake's deep waters. The fish are not stocked but breed freely in the clean water. You must have a valid West Virginia

Tygart Lake State Park

state fishing license. In addition, the park has partnerships with two local golf courses so that park visitors who are avid golfers won't miss any time out on the links. Prickett's Fort State Park is just to the northwest of the park in Fairmont. There you can learn more about frontier history, and if you want to take your bike, Prickett's park offers access to the Rails to Trails Mon River Trail section, which goes up to the Pennsylvania state line. Tygart Lake State Park is also located just north of historic Anna Jarvis House Museum; she was the founder of Mother's Day. The house was used by General McClellan for his headquarters during the Civil War. RV friendly up to 70 feet.

Mountain Lakes Area

This area is aptly named, because there is water, water everywhere. One surprise you will find in this section is one park's lake where it is clear enough that you can go scuba diving, if that happens to be one of your hobbies. This is a water recreationist's heaven with plenty of boating and fishing opportunities from which to choose. There are also plenty of trails for hikers and bikers.

History buffs will enjoy the Civil War Discovery Trail locations scattered throughout the region, with Carnifex Battlefield State Park, Droop Mountain Battlefield State Park, and Bulltown Historic Area in the area.

	Total Sites	Max. RV Length	Hookups	Fire Ring/Grill	Toilets	Showers	Drinking Water	Dump Station	Recreation	Fee ($)	Reservable
92 **Cedar Creek State Park**	60		E, W	Y	F	Y	Y	Y	H, S, F, B, C	$$$$	Y
93 **Stonewall Resort State Park / Briar Point Campground**	46		E, W, S	Y	F	Y	Y	N	H, S, F, B, L, C	$$$$	Y
94 **Bulltown Campground**	196		E	Y	F	Y	Y	Y	H, S, F, B, L, C, HB	$$$$	Y
95 **Audra State Park**	65			Y	F	Y	Y	Y	H, S, F	$$$	Y
96 **Gerald Freeman Campground at Sutton Lake**	150		E, W, S	Y	F	Y	Y	Y	H, S, F, B, L, C	$$$$	Y
97 **Bakers Run-Mill Creek Campground at Sutton Lake**	79		E, W, S	Y	F	Y	Y	Y	H, S, F, B, L, C	$$$$	Y
98 **Bee Run Campground at Sutton Lake**	10			Y	V	N	Y	N	H, S, F, B, L, C, HB	$$	Y
99 **Holly River State Park**	88		E	Y	F	Y	Y	Y	H, S, C, HB	$$$$	Y
100 **Kumbrabow State Forest / Mill Creek Campground**	13	20	E	Y	P	Y	Y	N	H, F	$$$	Y
101 **Battle Run Campground**	117		E	Y	F	Y	Y	Y	H, S, F, B, L, C	$$$-$$$$	Y

Max RV Length: Measured in feet
Hookups: W = Water, E = Electricity, S = Sewer
Fire Ring/Grill: Y = Yes, N = None
Toilets: F = Flush, P = Pit, V = Vault
Showers: Y = Yes, N = None
Drinking Water: Y = Yes, N = None
Dump Station: Y = Yes, N = None
Recreation: H = Hiking, S = Swimming, F = Fishing, B = Boating, L = Boat Launch, C = Cycling, HB = Horseback Riding, OHV = Off-Highway Vehicles
Fee: $ = 0–$5, $$ = $6–$10, $$$ = $11–$20, $$$$ = $21–$30+
Reservable: Y = Yes, N = No

Top: Pull-through camp site, suitable for RVs
Bottom: RV-friendly campgrounds abound.

Mountain Lakes Area

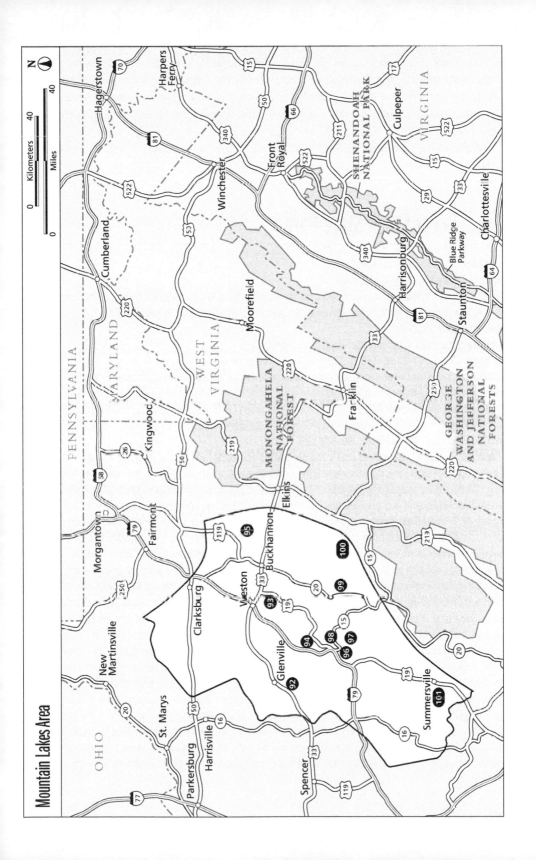

The Trans–Allegheny Lunatic Asylum is located in Weston and operates now for tours, both historic and haunted. It is considered the largest hand–cut stone building in the country, and it does resemble something out of a horror movie. This area is also known for its glass works, with many galleries offering blown glass and other creations.

Many of the campgrounds offer waterfront campsites suitable for tent camping or RVs.

92 Cedar Creek State Park

Location: 7 miles south of Glenville
Sites: 66 standard electric and water
Facilities: Flush toilets, showers, fire grills, picnic tables, camp store, dump station, laundry facility, boat rental, swimming pool, volleyball court, tennis court, miniature golf, horseshoe pit
Fee per night: $$$$
Management: West Virginia State Parks & Forests
Contact: (304) 462-7158; (800) 225-5982; www.cedarcreeksp.com
Activities: Hiking, swimming, biking, fishing, paddleboating, volleyball, tennis, miniature golf
Season: Early April to mid-October
Finding the campground: Take I-79 to SR 5 West (toward Glenville). Take US 33 / US 119 south. Turn left onto CR 17 / Cedar Creek Road. Follow it to the park entrance.
GPS coordinates: 38.882548 / -80.854128
About the campground: Tucked into a remote part of the state well off the beaten path, this is a beautiful, peaceful park if you want solitude. One clue will be the signs that promote the route as a "Backway" as opposed to the usual "Scenic Way" signs elsewhere in the state! It is highly recommended, even if you get directions to the contrary, that you take US 33, especially if driving an RV. Taking other county route options will put you on very narrow roads that allow room for at most one car and turn to gravel in sections. But once you reach this secluded parcel, there is plenty to enjoy in its tranquil setting on more than 2,500 acres along Cedar Creek. There is a swimming pool with paid admission available. In addition, you can take advantage of the volleyball net, the tennis court, and miniature golf for a minimal fee. Numerous hiking trails offer 14 miles of exploring options. Also, there are several spots to enjoy a picnic lunch, whether at a picnic area or on the well-kept grounds near the historic one-room schoolhouse. The creek runs through the campground, so you can hear the soft trickle of water as you sleep at night if you get one of the creek-side campsites. The park offers advance reservations through mail (very specific dates between February and March) or call-in; payment must be received seven days in advance for a minimum of two nights on ten of its campsites. Or opt for walk-in. The park offers fishing in three different lakes, each stocked with a variety of fish, depending on the season. With a valid West Virginia State fishing license, you can fish for trout that have been stocked early in the year, or catfish that are stocked in June, in addition to other species. Or rent a paddleboat to enjoy the water. Park activities are also available, posted on bulletin boards by the camp's naturalist headquarters. The camp store offers camping supplies, food items, and souvenirs. RV friendly up to 70 feet.

Cedar Creek State Park

93 Stonewall Resort State Park / Briar Point Campground

Location: Roanoke, 24 miles southwest of Buckhannon
Sites: 5 tent, 41 standard with electric, water, and sewer
Facilities: Flush toilets, showers, fire grills, picnic tables, picnic shelters, playground, marina, boat launch, restaurants, snack bar
Fee per night: $$$$
Management: West Virginia State Parks & Forests
Contact: (304) 269-8889; (800) 225-5982; www.stonewallresort.com/accommodations/briar_point_camp_ground/
Activities: Hiking, biking, swimming, boating, kayaking, fishing, geocaching, golf
Season: Open year-round
Finding the campground: Take I-79 to US 19 exit 91 toward Roanoke. Turn left onto US 19 headed south. Follow it to the park entrance.
GPS coordinates: 38.946373 / -80.491025
About the campground: A very RV-friendly campground situated on a peninsula that juts out into Stonewall Jackson Lake, providing lakeside campsites for both tents and RVs. Located within Stonewall Resort, the campground has a lush Arnold Palmer Signature golf course at its entrance, and campsites look out over woods and across the water on one side, the resort and water on the other. Boat and kayak rentals are available. You can get a resort activity pass for a fee. The lake is 26 miles long and available for fishing and boating. Mooring posts are available for your boat on a first-come, first-served basis. Make reservations in person or by phone up to one year in advance, though specific sites cannot be guaranteed. Senior discounts of 10 percent are available.

94 Bulltown Campground

Location: 44 miles southwest of Clarksburg
Sites: 196 standard electric
Facilities: Flush toilets, showers, fire grills, picnic tables, dump station, playground, swimming beach, picnic areas, boat ramp, horseshoe pit, basketball court
Fee per night: $$$$
Management: US Army Corps of Engineers
Contact: (304) 452-8006; https://www.recreation.gov/camping/campgrounds/233443
Activities: Hiking, biking, swimming, fishing, boating, waterskiing, horseshoes, horseback riding
Season: End of May to September
Finding the campground: Take I-79 to exit 67 for US 19 toward Flatwoods headed north. Follow it to the campground entrance.
GPS coordinates: 38.793542 / -80.561372
About the campground: This rather large campground is situated next to Burnsville Lake in central West Virginia, in the Bulltown Historic Area famous for a Civil War battle that took place here. Located at the foot of the Allegheny Mountains, the campground has beautiful mountain views.

Stonewall Resort State Park

Little Kanawha River runs near the campground, so between the lake and the river, there are abundant fishing opportunities. A fishing permit is required. Launch a boat using the boat ramp and explore the lake. There are trails available for hiking, biking, and horseback riding. Visit the beach area and swim in the cool waters of the lake. The campground is right next to Burnsville Lake Wildlife Management Area and south of Stonewall Jackson Lake. Many campsites are located next to the lake for a nice, partially shaded water view. RV friendly, but be forewarned that the roads leading to the campground are narrow and winding.

95 Audra State Park

Location: Buckhannon, 36 miles southeast of Clarksburg
Sites: 26 standard, 39 standard electric
Facilities: Flush toilets, showers, fire grills, picnic tables, picnic shelters, playground, dump station, laundry facility, camp store, concessions
Fee per night: $$$

Audra State Park

Management: West Virginia State Parks & Forests
Contact: (304) 457-1162; (800) 225-5982; www.audrastatepark.com
Activities: Hiking, swimming, fishing, kayaking
Season: Mid-April to mid-October
Finding the campground: Take I-79 south to exit 115 toward Stonewood / Nutter Fork. Turn left onto Route 20 heading south (after several miles, take a right to remain on this route). Take a left on Route 119 north. Follow it to the park entrance.
GPS coordinates: 39.039622 / -80.066044
About the campground: Situated on Middle Fork River, Audra State Park is tucked among verdant woodlands in the Buckhannon Watershed area. Swim or fish in Middle Fork River, which runs more like a stream over rocks in this section, depending on water levels and rain amounts. Walk along the boardwalk that has been built along Alum Cave's ledge, which overhangs the walkway. When water is high enough, white-water kayaking may be possible (check daily water flows for the Monongahela River basin / Middle Fork River at Audra). All campsites are first come, first served, and reservations are not taken. Some campsites are alongside the river, while others are nestled in among trees and thickets of rhododendrons. There are also some sites accessible to people with disabilities. The park is close to a couple of historic covered bridges and the West Virginia State Wildlife Center. It is south of Phillipi, a town that holds the distinction of being the site of the first land battle of the Civil War, which was very mild in comparison to the bloodier battles to come. Roads in the region around the park are narrow along US 119. RV friendly. Senior discount of 10 percent available Memorial Day to Labor Day.

96 Gerald Freeman Campground at Sutton Lake

Location: 70 miles north of Charleston
Sites: 113 standard electric, 37 electric, water, and sewer
Facilities: Flush toilets, showers, fire grills, picnic tables, playground, picnic areas, picnic shelters, dump station, laundry facility, horseshoe pits, basketball court, boat ramp, marina, boat rental, snack bar
Fee per night: $$$$
Management: US Army Corps of Engineers
Contact: (304) 765-7756; (877) 444-6777; https://www.recreation.gov/camping/campgrounds/233678
Activities: Hiking, biking, swimming, fishing, boating
Season: Open end of April to end of November
Finding the campground: Take I-79 south to exit 67 headed east toward Flatwoods. Take a right on SR 4. Turn left on SR 15. Follow it to the campground entrance.
GPS coordinates: 38.679983 / -80.546925
About the campground: This campground is located along the northwestern section of 1,440-acre Sutton Lake and near the Elk River Wildlife Management Area. Enjoy fishing for catfish, bass, crappie, and sunfish. A fishing permit is required. The Elk River, which is below the dam and called the Downstream Area, provides stocked trout as well as walleye and muskie. There is an accessible pier located in this section. This location has a marina called the Snak Shak, where you can rent a boat; it has a boat launch as well. Swimming beaches are available over at Bee Run Day Use

Area and at the South Abutment Day Use Area, but there are no lifeguards so use caution. There is ample opportunity for hiking and biking: You can make use of the fire roads and also trails used by hunters (I recommend that you not use these when it is hunting season) that weave around the lake and in the Wildlife Management Area. For equestrians horseback riding is allowed in nonrecreation areas. Some campsites are reservable during the season and the rest are first come, first served.

97 Bakers Run–Mill Creek Campground at Sutton Lake

Location: 70 miles north of Charleston
Sites: 45 standard, 21 standard electric, 5 standard electric and water, 8 standard electric, water, and sewer
Facilities: Flush toilets, showers, fire grills, picnic tables, playground, dump station, horseshoe pits, volleyball courts, boat ramp, picnic areas
Fee per night: $$$$
Management: US Army Corps of Engineers
Contact: (304) 765-5631; https://wvtourism.com/company/bakers-run-campground/
Activities: Hiking, biking, swimming, fishing, boating
Season: Open late May to mid-October
Finding the campground: Take I-79 south to exit 62, the Sutton / Gassaway exit. Follow it to the campground entrance.
GPS coordinates: 38.635367 / -80.591314
About the campground: This is another campground option located along the southern side of 1,440-acre Sutton Lake and near the Elk River Wildlife Management Area, managed by the US Army Corp of Engineers. If you like to fish, there are catfish, bass, crappie, and sunfish in the lake, and the Elk River, which is dammed here, is stocked with trout, in addition to having walleye and muskie. Shoreline fishing is available. There is an accessible pier located in this section known as the Downstream Area. A fishing permit is required for all spots. Swimming beaches are available over at Bee Run Day Use Area and at the South Abutment Day Use Area, but there are no lifeguards so use caution. For hiking and biking use the fire roads and the trails used by hunters, which go around the lake and extend well into the Wildlife Management Area. For equestrians horseback riding is allowed in nonrecreation areas. There is a mix of waterfront and wooded campsites. Some campsites are reservable during the season, and the rest are first come, first served.

98 Bee Run Campground at Sutton Lake

Location: 70 miles north of Charleston
Sites: 10 primitive sites
Facilities: Vault toilets, fire grills, picnic tables, winter boat launch ramp, boat marina, beach, playgrounds, picnic shelters
Fee per night: $$
Management: US Army Corps of Engineers

Contact: (304) 765-2816; https://wvtourism.com/company/bee-run-campground/
Activities: Hiking, biking, swimming, fishing, boating, horseback riding
Season: April to early December
Finding the campground: Take I-79 south to exit 67 headed east toward Flatwoods. Follow it to the campground entrance.
GPS coordinates: 38.666380 / -80.678032
About the campground: This is a more primitive campground located along the northeastern side of 1,440-acre Sutton Lake and near the Elk River Wildlife Management Area. It is next to the Bee Run Day Use Area, where you will find water amenities such as a boat ramp, a marina, and a beach, as well as a playground and picnic shelters. These are not in the campground proper. There is no drinking water available, so you will need to bring your own for cooking, cleaning, and drinking. A shower house is located nearby. Enjoy fishing for catfish, bass, crappie, and sunfish. The Elk River, which is dammed here, offers stocked trout as well as walleye and muskie. There is an accessible pier located in this section known as the Downstream Area below the Elk River dam. You must have a valid West Virginia state fishing license. For equestrians horseback riding is allowed in the nonrecreation areas. Sutton Lake Marina is located in the day-use area here. For swimming make use of the swimming beach, but there is no lifeguard so use caution. There are different selections for hiking and biking: You can make use of the fire roads and also trails used by hunters (I recommend that you not use these when it is hunting season) that wind around the lake and through the Wildlife Management Area. Some campsites are reservable during the season, and the rest are first come, first served. RV friendly.

99 Holly River State Park

Location: 34 miles south of Buckhannon
Sites: 88 standard electric
Facilities: Flush toilets, showers, fire grills, picnic tables, dump station, laundry facility, swimming pool, tennis courts, volleyball court, basketball court, horseshoe pit, croquet and shuffleboard areas, nature programs
Fee per night: $$$$
Management: West Virginia State Parks & Forests
Contact: (304) 493-6353; (800) 225-5982; www.hollyriver.com
Activities: Hiking, swimming, biking, tennis, basketball, horseshoes, croquet, shuffleboard, volleyball, cross-country skiing, horseback riding
Season: April through end of November
Finding the campground: From Buckhannon to the north or Webster Springs to the south, take I-79 to SR 20. Follow it to the campground entrance.
GPS coordinates: 38.665337 / -80.354525
About the campground: Covering almost 8,300 acres, this park is the second largest state park in the state. It is tucked into a valley and surrounded by tall mountains that are thick with trees, which gives it a sense of being miles from anything. This park is located not too far from what is considered the state's rainiest spot in Pickens, so keep that in mind when packing for your camping trip. There is a swimming pool available for a small fee, but **please note:** It is closed on Mondays and Wednesdays. Game courts are also available for a small fee. During the summer

months, park rangers offer nature programs that include hikes, movies, and even hayrides. Choose from one of ten trails around and through the park, leading to an overlook, 10-foot-high waterfalls, and campground facilities, and ranging in length from 0.5 mile to 10 miles. The waterfalls feature small caves in which you can watch the waterfalls from the inside. Use caution as rocks are slippery when wet. One trail, Ridge Road, is multiuse for hikers, cyclists, cross-country skiing, and horseback riding, offering 6 miles of potential recreation. Also, the park features an old, one-room schoolhouse, the Windy Gap School. Most campsites are first come, first served, while a portion of them are reservable in advance. RV friendly.

100 Kumbrabow State Forest / Mill Creek Campground

Location: 24 miles south of Elkins
Sites: 13 primitive, 1 pull-through RV site
Facilities: Pit toilets, showers, fire pits, picnic tables, laundry facility, picnic shelters, picnic areas, playgrounds
Fee per night: $$$
Management: West Virginia State Parks & Forests
Contact: (304) 335-2219; (800) 225-5982; www.kumbrabow.com
Activities: Hiking, fishing
Season: Mid-April to October
Finding the campground: Take US-219 to SR 219-16 (Kumbrabow Forest Road). Follow it to the state forest entrance.
GPS coordinates: 38.642954 / -80.090552
About the campground: Spend some time in this remote area that covers almost 9,500 acres of the state's highest-elevation forest. Streams run throughout the forest, weaving alongside rhododendrons, mountain laurel, gorgeous and varied stands of trees, and small waterfalls. The park's name is derived from three families who once lived here. There are eight trails located within the forest area, spread across Rich Mountain and Mill Ridge and ranging from just 0.5 mile to 3.5 miles in length. You can combine trails to create a longer hike at one of many cross points. Pack a picnic and take it to the top of Mill Ridge, using the Mill Ridge Fire Trail. From there you get mountain and valley views from a picnic table that is provided. Fish for native brook trout, but you will need a valid West Virginia state fishing license. Sites are rented first come, first served or by advance reservation. It is a self-registration location, so bring the exact fee amount. Showers are coin operated. RV friendly, though RVs more than 20 feet in length may be challenged in finding a site that fits. There is one pull-through site, which can accommodate an RV up to 60 feet.

101 Battle Run Campground

Location: 3 miles west of US 19, 9 miles south of Summersville
Sites: 110 standard electric, 7 walk-to primitive sites
Facilities: Flush toilets, showers, fire grills, picnic tables, picnic shelters, playground, laundry facility, dump station, picnic areas, boat ramp, fishing dock, swimming beach

Fee per night: $$$-$$$$
Management: US Army Corps of Engineers
Contact: (304) 872-3459; (877) 444-6777; https://www.recreation.gov/camping/campgrounds/233422
Activities: Hiking, biking, swimming, fishing, boating, waterskiing, scuba diving, rock climbing, kayaking
Season: Last week in May to first week in October
Finding the campground: Take US 19. Turn onto SR 129 headed west. Follow it to the campground entrance.
GPS coordinates: 38.222069 / -80.905620
About the campground: Located next to Summersville Lake, the largest lake in West Virginia at 2,700 acres, this campground is run by the US Army Corps of Engineers. With 60 miles of shoreline and surrounded by forests, the lake is renowned for its water quality. Sheer cliff faces rise from the clear lake water, providing a gorgeous backdrop to your water recreation–based activities. They also extend down about 100 feet into the water, providing scenery for scuba divers. The campground sits on the southern shore of the lake, which means an abundance of waterfront campsites. You can dock your boat right at your campsite if you want. The Summersville Lake Marina and a dive shop are located 11 miles from the campground, and you can rent a pontoon boat or kayak there, or make arrangements to scuba dive at one of the few outdoor locations that offers the kind of water suitable for scuba diving, a rare treat for an inland state. Lake visibility is reported to be anywhere from 20 feet to 45 feet, depending on how much rainfall has occurred. There is a boat ramp, which is accessible to people with disabilities, as well as a fishing dock, also accessible. Fish for largemouth and smallmouth bass, catfish, walleye, and panfish, and on occasion the state will stock the area below the dam with trout. You will need a valid West Virginia state fishing license to fish in the lake. There are nature, hiking, and biking trails available in the area. The swimming beach is nice and long, but there are no lifeguards so use caution. There is a day-use fee in the swimming area. Campsites are reservable; a few of the campsites are primitive, walk-to sites, just in case the campground fills up quickly and you are desperate for a spot. The Summersville Lake Wildlife Management Area is nearby. Also, Carnifex Ferry Battlefield State Park is just up the way from the campground to the west. This campground makes a nice base camp for white-water rafters as well, as the Gauley River is located close by. In addition, there is excellent technical rock climbing in the region.

Eastern Panhandle / Potomac Highlands Area

The Eastern Panhandle is the gateway into West Virginia from the east and the first introduction to the mountainous terrain of the state. Shepherdstown is West Virginia's oldest town at 250 years old. Harpers Ferry and Berkeley Springs are also here. This area does not have any public campgrounds. The first one you will reach is just south of the Maryland border in the northwestern section of the panhandle, located just beyond Keyser—Robert W. Craig Campground on Jennings Randolph Lake.

Sections of the George Washington and Jefferson National Forests are in the southeastern section of the panhandle and farther south, both along the Virginia state line. These areas feature a smattering of campgrounds managed by the USDA Forest Service.

To the southwest of the Eastern Panhandle, you will enter the Potomac Highlands area, characterized most significantly by the sprawling expanse of Monongahela National Forest. This area holds the heaviest concentration of campgrounds in the entire state; most of them are run by one of the districts of the USDA Forest Service. Just four state parks are located here. A notable highlight of the area is the Highland Scenic Highway, which is a National Forest Scenic Byway that runs from Richwood in the southwestern section of Monongahela National Forest, where you travel along SR 39/55 over to Cranberry Visitor Center and then turn north onto SR 150 as it heads into higher elevations. This is considered the Parkway section and offers several scenic overlooks where you can pull off for the view over the Allegheny Highlands before ending after 43 miles at US 219. SR 150 has no snow removal in the off-season, but people use it for snowmobiling and cross-country skiing. Dolly Sods Wilderness area is also located here, covering more than 32,000 acres and featuring bogs, meadows, and barrens covered in heath—quite unusual features and worth the drive to see.

In this lower southwestern section, you will find Cranberry Glades Botanical Area near Hillsboro, where you will find bogs, a southern version of the arctic tundra region normally found in Canada. There are programs offered by the Nature Center here to learn more about the area. This Canaan Valley area offers a lot of wetland areas to explore either by hiking or biking.

This area offers some of the best cycling, with trails that range from easy and suitable for families to more advanced trails that provide a challenge for the most serious enthusiasts. The Greenbrier River Trail runs alongside Monongahela National Forest, Watoga State Park (an excellent launch site), and Seneca State Forest to the north, providing 78 miles of multiuse rail trail. Because it runs mostly next to the river, the trail is flat and is used by cyclists, hikers, equestrians, and when there is snow, cross-country skiers.

In this lower southwestern section, you will find hundreds of miles for hiking, including the Allegheny Trail, which offers 330 miles of trekking. It runs from

	Total Sites	Max. RV Length	Hookups	Fire Ring/Grill	Toilets	Showers	Drinking Water	Dump Station	Recreation	Fee ($)	Reservable
102 Robert W. Craig Campground	81		E	Y	F	Y	Y	Y	H, S, F	$$$$	Y
103 Hawk Recreation Area	15			Y	V	N	Y	N	H, C	$	N
104 Horseshoe Recreation Area and Campground	25	53	E	Y	F, V	N	Y	N	H, F	$$$	Y
105 Blackwater Falls State Park	65	70	E	Y	F	Y	Y	Y	H, S, F, B, L, C, HB	$$$$	Y
106 Canaan Valley Resort State Park	37	45	E, W, S	Y	F	Y	Y	Y	H, S, C	$$$$	Y
107 Red Creek Campground	12			Y	V	N	Y	N	H, C	$$$	N
108 Trout Pond Recreation Area	50		E	Y	F	Y	Y	Y	H, S, F, B, L, C	$$$-$$$$	N
109 Big Bend Campground	41			Y	F	N	Y	Y	H, S, F, B	$$$$	Y
110 Seneca Shadows Campground	78		E	Y	F, V	Y	Y	Y	H, S, F	$$$-$$$$	Y
11 Bear Heaven Recreation Area Campground	8			Y	V	Y	N	N	H, F	$$	N
112 Stuart Recreation Area and Campground	25	53	E	Y	F	Y	Y	Y	H, S, F	$$$$	Y
113 Laurel Fork Campground	14	53		Y	V	N	Y	N	H, F	$$	N
114 Spruce Knob Lake Campground	42			Y	V	N	Y	N	H, F, B, L	$$$-$$$$	Y
115 Brandywine Recreation Area	35			Y	F	Y	Y	Y	H, S, F, B, C	$$$	N
116 Seneca State Forest	10			Y	V	Y	Y	N	H, S, F, B, C	$$$	Y
117 Tea Creek Campground	28			Y	V	N	Y	N	H, F, C	$$	N
118 Cranberry Campground	30	40		Y	V	N	Y	N	H, F, C	$$	N
119 Bishop Knob Campground	54	40		Y	V	N	Y	N	H, F, C	$$	N
120 Big Rock Campground	5			Y	V	N	Y	N	F	$$	N
121 Summit Lake Campground	33	53		Y	V	N	Y	N	H, S, F, B	$$	N
122 Day Run Campground	12			Y	V	N	Y	N	H, F, C	$$	N
123 Watoga State Park	88		E	Y	F	Y	Y	Y	H, S, F, B, C	$$$$	Y
124 Pocahontas Campground	8			Y	V	N	Y	N	H, F, C	$$	N

Max RV Length: Measured in feet

Hookups: W = Water, E = Electricity, S = Sewer

Fire Ring/Grill: Y = Yes, N = None

Toilets: F = Flush, P = Pit, V = Vault

Showers: Y = Yes, N = None

Drinking Water: Y = Yes, N = None

Dump Station: Y = Yes, N = None

Recreation: H = Hiking, S = Swimming, F = Fishing, B = Boating, L = Boat Launch, C = Cycling, HB = Horseback Riding, OHV = Off-Highway Vehicles

Fee: $ = 0-$5, $$ = $6-$10, $$$ = $11-$20, $$$$ = $21-$30+

Reservable: Y = Yes, N = No

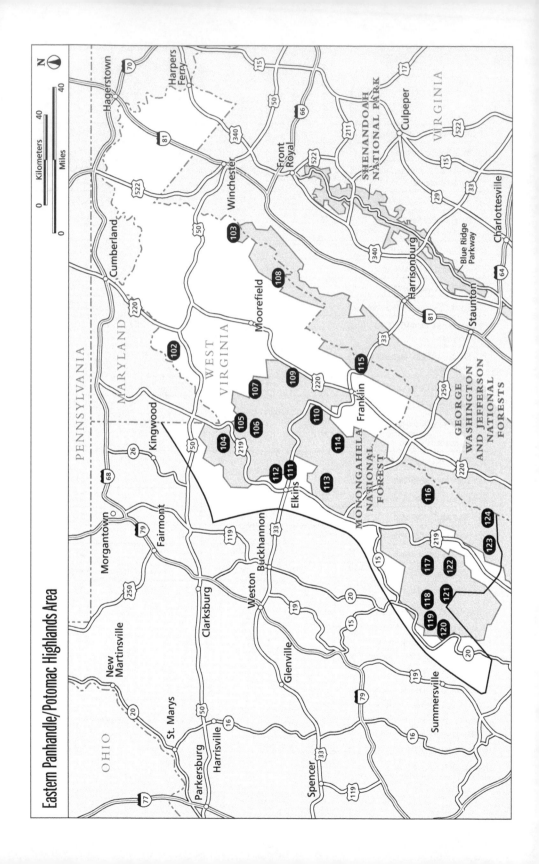

Eastern Panhandle/Potomac Highlands Area

Blackwater Falls

Seneca Rocks in the Potomac Highlands Area

the West Virginia and Pennsylvania border to the north and south, down through Monongahela National Forest, before ending at the Appalachian Trail at the state line with Virginia. There are about 20 miles that are not completed yet in the southern-most section. All the campgrounds and recreation areas have their own miles of trails, so all you need to do is step off from your campsite.

If you like to fish, you will certainly have a selection of places to go, with miles of streams and several lakes that provide fishing and other water recreation opportunities. Good luck trying to do it all, and enjoy feeling like a kid again as you have to pull yourself away each evening from "playing outside."

102 Robert W. Craig Campground

Location: 16 miles west of Keyser
Sites: 9 standard, 72 standard electric
Facilities: Flush toilets, showers, fire grills, picnic tables, picnic shelter, dump station, playground, camp store, horseshoe pits, basketball court, amphitheater, swimming beach
Fee per night: $$$$
Management: US Army Corps of Engineers
Contact: (304) 355-2346; (800) 444-6777; https://www.recreation.gov/camping/campgrounds/233604?q=Robert%20W%20Craig

Activities: Hiking, swimming, fishing, waterskiing

Season: May to end of September

Finding the campground: Take US 50 headed east. Turn left on SR 42 headed north. Take a right on SR 46 headed east. Follow it to the campground entrance.

GPS coordinates: 39.420079 / -79.112975

About the campground: Located near the Maryland state line in the northeastern panhandle of the state, this campground is situated so that 952-acre Jennings Randolph Lake can be observed just below. Swim or fish in the lake; there is a nice swimming beach available along the lakeshore. Bring a boat for motoring around, fishing, or waterskiing. To use the boat launches, either Howell Run or Maryland, you will need to drive outside the campground. There are some unique interpretive trails to explore that will be of interest to anyone who likes to learn a bit about nature. To begin with, there are 8 miles of nature trails from which to choose. One such trail is the Songbird Trail, which is great for birding enthusiasts. The High Timber Trail features twenty-eight different varieties of labeled trees. In addition, there are hiking trails that you can take from the campground to explore beyond its boundaries. The North Branch of the Potomac River is located nearby, which is popular for white-water rafting and trout fishing. RV friendly. Accepts Interagency Senior and Interagency Access Passes.

1O3 Hawk Recreation Area

Location: 4 miles south of Capon Springs, 34 miles northwest of Strasburg

Sites: 15 standard

Facilities: Vault toilets, fire grills, picnic tables

Fee per night: $

Management: USDA Forest Service / George Washington and Jefferson National Forests / Lee Ranger District

Contact: (540) 984-4101; www.fs.usda.gov

Activities: Hiking, biking

Season: Open middle of April to middle of December

Finding the campground: From I-81 take exit 296 west for Virginia SR 55. Once you have crossed over the state line into West Virginia, this route becomes West Virginia SR 55. Take a right turn onto FR 502 (this is a sharp right turn that goes onto a gravel road, so use caution). Take a left onto FR 347 and follow it to the campground entrance on the right.

GPS coordinates: 30.116516 / -78.498893

About the campground: This Forest Service campground is the northernmost campground located within GWJ National Forests in the Allegheny Mountains. It is pretty primitive, but at no fee the price is right. Drinking water is available, which is a plus for a no-fee campground. You can access Tuscarora Trail from this campground, an extensive hiking trail that is a sort of side jaunt from the Appalachian Trail, starting from the section in Shenandoah National Park and meandering up into West Virginia and Maryland before rejoining the Appalachian Trail again in Pennsylvania. There are also great mountain-biking opportunities in the area. Campsites are wooded. RVs are not recommended, only because of the challenge of getting to the park entrance.

104 Horseshoe Recreation Area and Campground

Location: 7 miles northeast of St. George
Sites: 12 standard, 13 standard electric
Facilities: Flush toilets, vault toilets, fire rings, picnic tables, picnic areas
Fee per night: $$$
Management: USDA Forest Service / Monongahela National Forest / Cheat Ranger District / Ohio / WV YMCA
Contact: (304) 478-2481; (877) 444-6777; www.fsda.us.gov
Activities: Hiking, fishing
Season: Open end of May to early September
Finding the campground: Take SR 72 headed northeast. Take SR 5 toward St. George. Turn south on SR 1. Take a left onto SR 7. Follow SR 7 to the recreation and campground entrance. (Drive past YMCA Camp Horseshoe and continue to the recreation area entrance.)
GPS coordinates: 39.181426 / -79.599626
About the campground: Situated along Horseshoe Run, this campground is located in the far north section of Monongahela National Forest and comes under the jurisdiction of the Forest Service. Fish for trout in Horseshoe Run, but you will need the following: a valid West Virginia state fishing license, a National Forest stamp, a Conservation stamp, and a trout stamp. You can also wade or swim in the river but use caution. There are a few hiking trails in the area ranging in length from 0.33 mile to almost 2 miles. The nearby Allegheny Trail offers a much longer option. Vault toilets are accessible. A few campsites are reservable, but the majority are first come, first served. Hand pumps are available for drinking water. RV friendly up to 53 feet.

105 Blackwater Falls State Park

Location: 43 miles northeast of Elkins
Sites: 35 standard, 30 standard electric
Facilities: Flush toilets, showers, fire rings, picnic tables, playground, laundry facility, dump station, nature center, sledding hill, indoor pool, boat dock, stables, volleyball court, basketball court
Fee per night: $$$$
Management: West Virginia State Parks & Forests
Contact: (304) 259-5216; (800) 225-5982; www.blackwaterfalls.com
Activities: Hiking, biking, swimming, fishing, cross-country skiing, sledding, boating, tennis, volleyball, basketball, horseback riding
Season: Open end of April through October
Finding the campground: Take I-79 to SR 33 east in Weston. When you reach the town of Harman, take SR 32 north toward Davis. Follow it to the campground entrance.
GPS coordinates: 39.107657 / -79.495100
About the campground: This park covers more than 2,300 acres within the boundaries of the Monongahela National Forest and features a feast for the eyes from the stunning Elakala Falls to Lindy Point looking into Blackwater Canyon. The name "Blackwater" is from the dark color of the water, the result of drainage of bog-type areas in the Canaan Valley. The bogs in this area are similar

Top: Blackwater Falls State Park COURTESY WEST VIRGINIA DEPARTMENT OF COMMERCE
(WWW.WVCOMMERCE.ORG)
Campground at Blackwater Falls State Park

to the ones found at Cranberry Glades to the south. Pendleton Lake is also located within park boundaries. No less than eighteen trails are offered with 20 miles just for hiking. Some trails offer more than 10 miles exclusively for cross-country skiing. There is a horseback riding trail near the stables and a couple of trails that allow cycling. Blackwater Canyon Rim Trail leads to Olson Tower, a fire tower that looks out over Otter Creek Wilderness and Blackwater Canyon. Nature programs are offered by the park naturalist, so look for notices at the park office. Blackwater Lodge has a small indoor pool that campground guests can use for a small fee, but there is no swimming permitted in Pendleton Lake. Blackwater River offers catch-and-release fishing within the park area, and Pendleton Lake is another option. All fishing requires a valid West Virginia state fishing license. One unique offering is a sledding hill, useable should you have an early or late snow. Another unique feature is the Farm Discovery Center, helping people stay in touch with their agricultural roots so they understand how their food is grown. There are hands-on activities that are family friendly. Most campsites are first come, first served, but about twenty are reservable. RV friendly up to 70 feet.

106 Canaan Valley Resort State Park

Location: 35 miles northeast of Elkins
Sites: 3 primitive, 34 standard electric, water, and sewer
Facilities: Flush toilets, showers, fire pits, picnic tables, dump station, swimming pool, waterslide, tennis court, miniature golf course, picnic shelters, playground, nature center, restaurant, paintball, climbing wall, Eurobungy, geocaching course
Fee per night: $$$$
Management: West Virginia State Parks & Forests
Contact: (304) 866-4121; (800) 225-5982; https://www.canaanresort.com/accommodations/camping/
Activities: Hiking, biking, swimming, cross-country skiing, downhill skiing, geocaching, tennis, golf, climbing wall, paintball
Season: Open year-round
Finding the campground: Take US 33 east toward Elkins. Take a slight right onto SR 92 south. Continue straight onto Randolph Avenue. Turn left onto CR 33 / Seneca Pike, and then take a left onto US 33 / SR 55 headed east. Take a sharp left onto SR 32, then a left onto Main Lodge Road. Follow it to the campground.
GPS coordinates: 39.024302 / -79.465024
About the campground: This campground is situated next to a resort and conference center in the Monongahela National Forest, and the amenities reflect this close relationship. When it is not ski season, it is hiking and biking season, with trails that lead you through bogs and forest land. You can rent a bike at the resort or bring your own. There are 18 miles spread across eleven trails to explore, and many of them are linked to even longer trails within the Monongahela National Forest. They range in distance from 0.125 mile to 2.5 miles and from easy to difficult terrain. The trails are good for touring bikes, and many also permit mountain bikes; there are 11 miles just for mountain bikers. One trail takes you to Bald Knob and provides a gorgeous view of the Canaan Valley. The ski lift is available for mountain bikers to access the mountain areas, which can be done with the purchase of a lift ticket. It is also available during the fall for an outstanding view of fall foliage in Canaan Valley itself and the surrounding mountains—a wonderful way to see the

Top: Canaan Valley Region COURTESY WEST VIRGINIA DEPARTMENT OF COMMERCE (WWW.WV
COMMERCE.ORG)
Bottom: Playground at Canaan Valley Resort State Park

foliage. There is a swimming pool featuring a waterslide. In addition, there is a rock wall for climbing and a "Eurobungy" to jump on, both for a fee. If you are into geocaching, you can rent a GPS system or bring your own to participate in locating one of five hidden caches. You can fish in the lake or one of the many streams, but you must have a valid West Virginia state fishing license. Cross-country skiing and snowshoeing are winter options for those hiking trails. There is downhill skiing as well, for which the resort is quite popular and well known. There is a golf course located here, offering eighteen holes, as well as a miniature golf course. Reservations for campsites are for a minimum of two nights in a row, on a first-come, first-served basis, during the season. RV friendly up to 45 feet (with one pull-through site up to 50 feet).

107 Red Creek Campground

Location: 20 miles north of Petersburg
Sites: 12 standard
Facilities: Vault toilets, fire grills, picnic tables
Fee per night: $$$
Management: USDA Forest Service / Monongahela National Forest / Potomac Ranger District
Contact: (304) 257-4488; www.fs.usda.gov
Activities: Hiking, biking
Season: Mid-April to December
Finding the campground: Take SR 22 / 55 to SR 4, Jordan Run Road. Turn left on FR 19. Take a right turn on FR 75. Follow it to the campground entrance.
GPS coordinates: 39.032274 / -79.315935
About the campground: This primitive campground is conveniently located next to the Dolly Sods Wilderness, which does not have its own developed campground. The wilderness area is considered a unique treasure, as its plants and climate have been compared to those of the tundra usually found in northern Canada, an unusual environment this far south. There are about 45 miles of hiking trails through Dolly Sods, which is a popular location for backpackers. Blackbird Knob Trail is more than 9 miles long and leads to trails farther into Dolly Sods. A spigot provides water directly from a natural spring, but it must be boiled to ensure safety. All campsites are first come, first served, and reservations are not taken. Vault toilets are accessible to people with disabilities. RV friendly, but note that the road to the campground is narrow.

108 Trout Pond Recreation Area

Location: 13 miles south of Wardensville, 48 miles west of Strasburg, VA
Sites: 36 standard, 14 standard electric
Facilities: Flush toilets, showers, fire rings, picnic tables, swimming beach, boat ramp, picnic areas, dump station, playground
Fee per night: $$$-$$$$
Management: USDA Forest Service / George Washington and Jefferson National Forests / Lee Ranger District

Top: The Dolly Sods Wilderness
Bottom: A trailhead in the Dolly Sods Wilderness Area

Contact: (304) 897-6450; www.fs.usda.gov
Activities: Hiking, biking, fishing, swimming, boating
Season: Open early May to end of November
Finding the campground: From I-81 take SR 48 west. When you cross the Virginia state line into West Virginia, it will become SR 55. Continue on, and then take a left on SR 23/10. Take a right on SR 259/5. Turn left onto Forest Service Road 500. Follow it to the entrance for the recreation area.
GPS coordinates: 38.959530/-78.741625
About the campground: This campground is located in GWJ National Forests and offers two lakes: Rock Cliff Lake and Trout Pond. The swimming beach is located at Rock Cliff Lake, which is man-made and covers seven acres. Trout Pond, covering two acres, is the only natural lake within the state. It was created by a sinkhole that occurred and then filled with spring water fresh off the mountain. It offers native brook trout for fishermen. You can fish from the banks along Rock Cliff Lake or the fishing dock. There are a couple of hiking trails from which to choose: one going around Trout Pond or a more strenuous trail that goes up Long Mountain and Devil's Hole Mountain. No gas-powered boats allowed, but electric motor, sailboats, and cartop boats are welcome. Showers are wheelchair accessible. RV friendly.

109 Big Bend Campground

Location: 10 miles southwest of Petersburg
Sites: 41 standard
Facilities: Flush toilets, fire rings, picnic tables, picnic area, dump station
Fee per night: $$$$
Management: USDA Forest Service/Monongahela National Forest/Potomac Ranger District/American Land and Leisure
Contact: (304) 257-4488; (800) 444-6777; www.fs.usda.gov
Activities: Hiking, fishing, swimming, boating, tubing, canoeing, kayaking, cave exploration
Season: April through late October
Finding the campground: From Petersburg take US 33 to SR 55 headed west. Take a left on SR 28/11, Smoke Hole Road, headed south. At CR 2, take a left (also Smoke Hole Road). Follow it to the campground entrance.
GPS coordinates: 38.889710/-79.238785
About the campground: Situated next to the South Branch of the Potomac River in the Smoke Hole Canyon, this nice, quiet Forest Service campground is tucked in the far northeastern end of the Monongahela National Forest. Because of its location along a bend in the river, it makes a nice spot for wading, swimming, and tubing or bring a canoe or kayak and paddle along for a different way to see this beautiful area. Boating works best when the water level is high, which means in the spring after snow melt; the level may drop considerably during the summer. You can also fish here, but you will need the following per state fishing regulations: a valid West Virginia state fishing license, a National Forest stamp, a Conservation stamp, and a trout stamp. For hikers there is a trail in the campground that is 1 mile long or you can venture into areas nearby that have miles of maintained trails. There are caves in the area for exploring. Some campsites are reservable; the rest are first come, first served. There is drinking water available. RV friendly.

110 Seneca Shadows Campground

Location: 1 mile east of Seneca Rocks
Sites: 25 standard, 13 standard electric, 40 walk-to-only tent sites
Facilities: Flush toilets, vault toilets, showers, fire pits, fire grills, picnic tables, dump station
Fee per night: $$$–$$$$
Management: USDA Forest Service/Monongahela National Forest/Potomac Ranger District/ American Land and Leisure
Contact: (304) 567-3082; (304) 257-4488; (877) 444-6777; www.fs.usda.gov
Activities: Hiking, rock climbing, fishing, swimming, kayaking, cave exploration
Season: Mid-April to third week in October
Finding the campground: From Elkins take US 33 headed east. Follow it to the campground entrance, which is on the right.
GPS coordinates: 38.823723/-79.386534
About the campground: Situated in the Spruce Knob-Seneca Rocks National Recreation Area, this beautifully laid out campground affords a view of Seneca Rocks, meadows, and mountains, and there is plenty to explore here. Seneca Rocks is quite popular with rock climbers, who travel from all over to scale its challenging 900-foot-tall rock face. If you are not a climber, you can observe the climbers from the campground (bring your binoculars), as the rock face can be seen from most campsites. There are also hiking trails available, including the Seneca Rocks Trail, about a 1-mile-long trek that leads to Seneca Rocks, and Sunrise Loop, which is about 0.5 mile long. You will need to drive to longer hiking and biking trails. While you are out, visit the local swimming hole that is located about 1 mile from the campground. If you want to fish, the North Fork of the

A campsite at the Seneca Shadows Campground

South Branch of the Potomac River is located nearby. Also, you can fish in Seneca Rocks behind the visitor center, but it is catch and release. You will need the following per state fishing regulations: a valid West Virginia state fishing license, a National Forest stamp, a Conservation stamp, and a trout stamp. There are two caves in the area that can be explored. Toilets and showers are wheelchair accessible. Campsites are mostly wooded, and there are three loops. I have also listed the walk-to campsites, which means you will have a short trek with your camping gear to your site location. The bonus is that these sites have some of the best views of the rocks. Some campsites are first come, first served, located in Loop A and Loop C, while others in Loop B and Loop C and some of the walk-to sites can be reserved in advance. RV friendly.

111   Bear Heaven Recreation Area Campground

Location: 14 miles southeast of Elkins
Sites: 8 standard
Facilities: Vault toilets, showers, fire rings, picnic tables, picnic area
Fee per night: $$
Management: USDA Forest Service / Monongahela National Forest / Cheat Ranger District
Contact: (304) 478-2000; www.fs.usda.gov
Activities: Hiking, fishing, rock climbing
Season: Mid-April to December
Finding the campground: Take US 33 headed east from Elkins. At FR 91, turn left headed northbound. (This will be at the top of Shavers Mountain.) Follow this to the campground entrance on the left.
GPS coordinates: 38.932273 / -79.680515
About the campground: Located in Monongahela National Forest, this primitive campground is a part of the Forest Service. It is situated along a ridgetop next to Otter Creek Wilderness Area. For recreation you can fish in Otter Creek, but you must have the following to meet regulations: a valid West Virginia state fishing license, a National Forest stamp, a Conservation stamp, and a trout stamp. Hikers can take advantage of the proximity to Otter Creek Wilderness trails, but these require some level of skill because of a lack of signage and because you will need to cross streams by foot. If you want to stay closer to camp, Middle Point Trail is almost 4 miles in length and can be found off FR 91, the entrance road. Rock outcrops in the area may be suitable for experienced climbers. All campsites are first come, first served, so there are no reservations available at this site. These sites are best suited for tent camping, as sites have irregular spacing that may be challenging for larger RVs. There is no drinking water available, so you will need to bring your own for cooking, cleaning, and drinking.

112   Stuart Recreation Area and Campground

Location: 6 miles northeast of Elkins
Sites: 25 standard electric

Facilities: Flush toilets, showers, fire rings, picnic tables, picnic areas, swimming beach, dump station, horseshoe pit, picnic shelters
Fee per night: $$$$
Management: USDA Forest Service / Monongahela National Forest / Cheat Ranger District / American Land and Leisure
Contact: (304) 636-5070; (304) 567-3082; (877) 444-6777; www.fs.usda.gov
Activities: Hiking, swimming, fishing, horseshoes
Season: Open mid-April to early October
Finding the campground: From Elkins take SR 219 to SR 33 headed east. Turn left on Old Route 33 headed north. Take a left onto Highway 6, where there is a sign for the Stuart Recreation Area. Follow it to campground entrance.
GPS coordinates: 38.918691 / -79.772922
About the campground: This campground is located next to a bend in the Shavers Fork River, offering prime fishing for regularly stocked trout. To fish here, you will need the following: a valid West Virginia state fishing license, a National Forest stamp, a Conservation stamp, and a trout stamp. You can also swim in the river, and a beach located in the day-use area provides convenient access to the water. It is a beautiful swimming spot with stone outcroppings. Use caution, as there is no lifeguard on duty. There is one hiking trail, the River Loop, which offers 2 miles alongside the river. Drinking water is located throughout the campground. Toilets are accessible. Several of the campsites are reservable, but the majority are first come, first served. RV friendly up to 53 feet.

113 Laurel Fork Campground

Location: 29 miles southeast of Elkins
Sites: 14 standard
Facilities: Vault toilets, fire rings, picnic tables
Fee per night: $$
Management: USDA Forest Service / Monongahela National Forest / Greenbrier Ranger District
Contact: (304) 456-3335; www.fs.usda.gov
Activities: Hiking, fishing
Season: Mid-April to December
Finding the campground: Take US 33/55 to FR 14, and turn right heading south. Take a left on FR 423 heading east. Use caution: This is a gravel road. Follow it to the campground entrance.
GPS coordinates: 38.740622 / -79.692124
About the campground: This more primitive campground is situated next to the Laurel Fork River, which runs right down the middle of the campground within the Laurel Fork Wilderness Area. Because it's alongside the river, it can be prone to flooding. Fish for trout and native brookies in the river, which will require that you have a valid West Virginia state fishing license. It is also located in what is called the Middle Mountain area of the Monongahela National Forest and provides access to trails that lead into the Wilderness Area. Vault toilets are wheelchair accessible. Drinking water is available from a hand pump station. Sites are first come, first served and mostly unshaded. RV friendly up to 53 feet in length.

114 Spruce Knob Lake Campground

Location: 23 miles southwest of Harman
Sites: 30 standard, 12 walk-to sites
Facilities: Vault toilets, fire rings, fire grills, picnic tables, pier, boat ramp
Fee per night: $$$–$$$$
Management: USDA Forest Service / Monongahela National Forest / Potomac Ranger District / American Land and Leisure
Contact: (304) 567-3082; (304) 257-4488; (877) 444-6777; www.fs.usda.gov
Activities: Hiking, boating, canoeing, kayaking, fishing
Season: Open mid-April to early October
Finding the campground: From Elkins take US 33 headed eastbound. Take a right on SR 29 headed south. Turn left on FR 1. Follow it to the campground entrance.
GPS coordinates: 38.707622 / -79.587797
About the campground: This campground is located in the Spruce Knob-Seneca Rocks National Recreation Area and close to Spruce Knob, the highest point in the state at 4,863 feet. The campground itself is supposed to be at the highest elevation in the state as well. Spruce Knob Lake is located within 1 mile, offering various water recreation activities. You can fish in the lake that was built expressly for fishing and is regularly stocked with trout or in one of several creeks in the area. You must have the following to fish in this area: a valid West Virginia state fishing license, a National Forest stamp, a Conservation stamp, and a trout stamp. Bring your boat and launch it from the ramp. The only type of motored boat allowed on the lake is electric. You can also launch a cartop boat here, such as a canoe or kayak, to explore the 25 acres of water. For hikers there are 60 miles of hiking trails available in the area, including the 1-mile Big Bend River Loop. The campground is situated atop a ridge that looks down over the lake, and this higher elevation makes for either a cool breeze or a strong wind, depending on the weather. Some campsites are available first come, first served and others are reservable. For walk-to sites you will have to walk about 75 feet from your vehicle to your site. Toilets and sites are accessible to people with disabilities. RV friendly. The road leading to the campground is a bit rugged and gravelly in spots with switchbacks, which may make it challenging for larger vehicles.

115 Brandywine Recreation Area

Location: 2 miles east of Brandywine
Sites: 35 standard
Facilities: Flush toilets, showers, fire grills, picnic tables, picnic area, swimming beach, dump station
Fee per night: $$$
Management: USDA Forest Service / George Washington and Jefferson National Forests / North River Ranger District
Contact: (540) 432-0187; www.fs.usda.gov
Activities: Hiking, fishing, biking, swimming, boating
Season: Open mid-May to mid-December

Finding the campground: From Harrisonburg, Virginia, head west on SR 33. Cross the state line into West Virginia and continue on. Follow the road to the park entrance just a few miles from the state line.

GPS coordinates: 38.599682 / -79.199623

About the campground: Located in the GWJ National Forests near the state line next to Virginia. This campground features Brandywine Lake, which covers 10 acres and has a sandy swimming beach. Nonmotorized boats are welcome. You can also fish in the creeks that run through the campground or the lake, which is stocked with trout. You will need a valid West Virginia state fishing license to do so. For hiking you can choose the more strenuous High Knob Trail that is a straight climb of 2 miles along the Shenandoah Mountain ridgeline up to the fire tower. It is one of just three fire towers still in existence in GWJ National Forests and gives you a view out over several other "knobs," including Spruce Knob in West Virginia. Saw Mill Loop is an easier option that is almost 4 miles in length with creek views. RV friendly for smaller RVs.

116 Seneca State Forest

Location: 4 miles south of Dunmore

Sites: 10 standard

Facilities: Vault toilets, coin-operated showers, fireplaces, picnic tables, drinking water, laundry facility, picnic areas, picnic shelters, boat rentals, playground, fishing pier

Fee per night: $$$

Management: West Virginia State Parks & Forests

Contact: (304) 799-6213; (800) 225-5982; www.senecastateforest.com

Activities: Hiking, biking, fishing, boating, swimming

Season: April to first week of December

Finding the campground: Take SR 39 eastbound, then take SR 28 headed north. Follow it to the campground entrance.

GPS coordinates: 38.296340 / -79.929489

About the campground: This campground is situated in the state's oldest "state forest," a nicely secluded location with the Greenbrier River running along its boundary. The forest itself covers more than 11,600 acres and is considered one of the largest in the state. Swimming is allowed in the river, but use caution. There is also Seneca Lake, which covers four acres and provides fishing for bass, bluegill, and trout. Fish from the pier or take out a boat: Rent a canoe, rowboat, or paddleboat for fishing or just to explore the lake. You must have a valid West Virginia state fishing license. Hikers have 23 miles of trails to explore, which lead through the forest and are often challenging. One trail is an exercise trail featuring exercise stations and suitable for walking and jogging. And for cyclists, there are more than 40 miles of trail, both through the forest and on the roads. The Allegheny Trail passes through the forest. It will lead you to Hanging Rock Tower for a view out over the valley below. In addition, the Greenbrier River Trail can be reached from the campground, offering a nice rails-to-trails option for hikers and cyclists. The campsites are a nice large size and set well apart from one another, offering even more of a secluded feel. One of the campsites is wheelchair accessible. There is a well that you can hand pump for drinking water. Sites are first come, first served. RV friendly.

117 Tea Creek Campground

Location: 17 miles northwest of Marlinton
Sites: 28 standard
Facilities: Vault toilets, fire rings, fire grills, picnic tables, picnic areas
Fee per night: $$
Management: USDA Forest Service / Monongahela National Forest / Marlinton Ranger District
Contact: (304) 799-4334; www.fs.usda.gov
Activities: Hiking, biking, fishing
Season: April to end of November
Finding the campground: Take US 219 headed north. Turn left onto SR 150, also called the Highland Scenic Highway. Watch for the Williams River Bridge Turnoff and "Campground Ahead" sign on the left-hand side, then turn left at the stop sign onto FR 86. At the bottom of the hill, turn left again to remain on FR 86. Follow it to the campground entrance located to the right.
GPS coordinates: 38.341512 / -80.230624
About the campground: This campground is conveniently located next to the Cranberry Wilderness Area and close to the Williams River. Near the campground mountain bikers and hikers can access the Tea Creek Trail System with more than 45 miles of trails to choose from that wind through the area from this campground, and that take you on and around Turkey Mountain and Tea Creek Mountain. One of the top picks for technical downhill mountain biking is Tea Creek Mountain, which has boulder fields that are a difficult challenge to ride over. Tea Creek, which the campground is named for, provides fishing, but there are a couple of things to be aware of before you do so. The section of the creek next to the campground is stocked with trout. Catch and release is in effect 2 miles below the campground and 2 miles farther downstream. To fish here, you will need a valid West Virginia state fishing license, a National Forest stamp, a Conservation stamp, and a trout stamp. Hand pumps provide fresh drinking water. Bear-proof trash cans are conveniently located in several spots in the campground. Sites are wooded and first come, first served; four of these sites are located next to the creek. RV friendly.

118 Cranberry Campground

Location: 14 miles northeast of Richwood
Sites: 30 standard
Facilities: Vault toilets, fire rings, picnic tables
Fee per night: $$
Management: USDA Forest Service / Monongahela National Forest / Gauley Ranger District
Contact: (304) 846-2695; www.fs.usda.gov
Activities: Hiking, biking, fishing
Season: Open mid-March to end of November
Finding the campground: Take US 39/55 headed east from Richwood. Turn left on FR 76 headed north. Follow it to the campground entrance.

GPS coordinates: 38.325557 / -80.441509

About the campground: Situated next to the Cranberry River, this somewhat primitive campground is popular with fishermen. You will need a valid West Virginia state fishing license, a National Forest stamp, a Conservation stamp, and a trout stamp to fish in either river. The river is stocked with trout in the spring and again in the early fall. Access excellent hiking trails in the Cranberry Backcountry and the Cranberry Wilderness Area, which cover more than 12,000 acres of forest. *Please note:* There is no biking allowed within the Wilderness Area, but you can use the forest roads that fall outside of the wilderness boundary. Glades Gate offers 16 miles of hiking. Some sites are located along the Cranberry River, some are open while others are wooded, and all are first come, first served. Hand pumps provide drinking water. Vault toilets are wheelchair accessible. RV friendly. Most sites are able to accommodate RVs up to 40 feet long.

119 Bishop Knob Campground

Location: 13 miles northwest of Richwood
Sites: 54 standard
Facilities: Vault toilets, fire rings, picnic tables
Fee per night: $$
Management: USDA Forest Service / Monongahela National Forest / Gauley Ranger District
Contact: (304) 846-2695; www.fs.usda.gov
Activities: Hiking, biking, fishing
Season: Open early April to end of November
Finding the campground: From Richwood take US 39/55 headed eastbound. Turn left onto CR 76 headed north to FR 81. When you come to a four-way intersection, take a left. This puts you on FR 101. Follow it to the campground entrance; you will see signs to guide you along the way.
GPS coordinates: 38.338518 / -80.488958

About the campground: A larger size but primitive campground, this is the westernmost camping spot in the midst of the Monongahela National Forest. The campground is composed of two loops and situated along a ridge with the Cranberry River on one side and the Williams River on the other. It is quiet and has a secluded feel and almost seems to be a secret, undiscovered location considering how many sites are offered here. Use it as a base for hiking and mountain biking, accessing the 2.5-mile Bishop Knob Trail just steps away. There is also the longer Cranberry Ridge Trail, which is 6 miles long, and Adkins Rockhouse Trail that is more than 2 miles long. With two nearby rivers, you can divide your fishing time between them. Trout is the fish of choice in both, and you will need a valid West Virginia state fishing license, a National Forest stamp, a Conservation stamp, and a trout stamp to fish in either river. Each loop has a hand pump to access fresh water. Vault toilets are wheelchair accessible. There are no reservable campsites: All are first come, first served, and nicely wooded. RV friendly up to 40 feet.

120 Big Rock Campground

Location: 7 miles north of Richwood
Sites: 5 standard
Facilities: Vault toilets, fire rings, picnic tables
Fee per night: $$
Management: USDA Forest Service / Monongahela National Forest / Gauley Ranger District
Contact: (304) 846-2695; www.fs.usda.gov
Activities: Fishing
Season: Open mid-March to end of November
Finding the campground: From Richwood head east on SR 39/55. Go north on FR 76. Follow it to the campground entrance.
GPS coordinates: 38.295954 / -80.523962
About the campground: Big name, small campground. Located next to the Cranberry River, this campground is one of the smallest in the Forest Service's offerings, not counting group-site-oriented campgrounds. You can fish in the Cranberry River with the following: a valid West Virginia state fishing license, a National Forest stamp, a Conservation stamp, and a trout stamp. *Please note:* Vault toilets are not accessible. Campsites are first come, first served. RV friendly for small- to medium-size vehicles.

121 Summit Lake Campground

Location: 10 miles east of Richwood
Sites: 33 standard
Facilities: Vault toilets, fire rings, picnic tables
Fee per night: $$
Management: USDA Forest Service / Monongahela National Forest / Gauley Ranger District
Contact: (304) 846-2695; www.fs.usda.gov
Activities: Hiking, fishing, boating, swimming
Season: April to end of November
Finding the campground: From Richwood head east on SR 39/55. Turn left at the Summit Lake Campground sign, which is CR 39/5. Follow the road to the campground entrance.
GPS coordinates: 38.248449 / -80.444778
About the campground: This campground is located next to 43-acre Summit Lake, which is stocked with trout and has panfish and bass. You can fish from the pier, which is accessible, and there is also a boat launch available. No gas-powered boats are allowed, but you can use an electric-powered or cartop boat. There are a couple of hiking trails located nearby: Summit Lake Trail is almost 2 miles long and goes around the lake and through the forest, and Pocahontas Trail is more than 20 miles long. Hand pumps provide fresh drinking water. Vault toilets are accessible to people with disabilities. Campsites are wooded, and all sites are first come, first served. RV friendly; can accommodate vehicles up to 53 feet in length.

122 Day Run Campground

Location: 22 miles west of Marlinton
Sites: 12 standard
Facilities: Vault toilets, fire rings, picnic tables
Fee per night: $$
Management: USDA Forest Service / Monongahela National Forest / Marlinton Ranger District
Contact: (304) 799-4334; www.fs.usda.gov
Activities: Fishing, hiking, biking
Season: Open mid-March to end of November
Finding the campground: Take US 219 north. Turn left on SR 150. When you see a sign that reads CAMPGROUND AHEAD, turn left at the sign. When you reach the bottom of the hill, turn right. Turn right at the intersection onto FR 216. Follow the road to the campground entrance.
GPS coordinates: 38.287075 / -80.215625
About the campground: Situated along the upper section of the Williams River near the Highland Scenic Highway. The river is stocked with trout, but to fish you must have the following: a valid West Virginia state fishing license, a National Forest stamp, a Conservation stamp, and a trout stamp. While there are no hiking and biking trails within the campground itself, there is the Tea Creek Trail System located about 4 miles away, providing 44 miles of hiking and mountain biking trails through the backcountry area, which cross streams and lead through forest. Trailheads can be located along the Highland Scenic Highway, FR 24, and Tea Creek Campground. Vault toilets are accessible to people with disabilities. For drinking water within the campground, there is a hand pump water spigot. All campsites are first come, first served, and reservations are not taken. There is a mix of open and wooded sites from which to choose. Close to the Cranberry Wilderness Area and Cranberry Glades Botanical Area, featuring bogs that cover the largest area in the state. RV friendly.

123 Watoga State Park

Location: 14 miles south of Marlinton
Sites: 38 standard, 50 standard electric
Facilities: Flush toilets, showers, fire grills, picnic tables, laundry facility, dish-washing station, dump station, swimming pool, boat rental, tennis court, basketball court, shuffleboard, croquet, badminton, volleyball, horseshoes, ping pong, picnic shelters, playground, arboretum, naturalist programs
Fee per night: $$$$
Management: West Virginia State Parks & Forests
Contact: (304) 799-4087; (800) 225-5982; www.watoga.com
Activities: Hiking, biking, swimming, fishing, boating, canoeing, kayaking, volleyball, basketball, tennis, badminton, shuffleboard, croquet, ping pong
Season: April through early December
Finding the campground: Take US 219 north to Route 20. Follow to the park entrance.

GPS coordinates: 38.116626 / -80.127767

About the campground: More than 10,100 acres of beautifully forested land with some campsites along a babbling stream. This state park is the state's largest. The Greenbrier River Trail is accessible from the campground, offering a biking option, in addition to the four trails within the park as well as paved roads where bikes are welcome. Altogether there are seventeen trails available offering 40 miles of hiking opportunities, ranging in length from 0.5 mile to 3 miles and in difficulty from easy to challenging. The Ann Bailey Trail leads to the Ann Bailey Lookout Tower and affords a great view of the valley below. It is so quiet up there you will feel as if time has been suspended. Cross-country skiing can be done on the roads during the winter along with four trails that are more suitable for this activity. None of the trails is maintained specifically for this sport, though. The swimming pool is spring fed and is heated by solar power. The pool and the game courts are available to campers for a small fee. During the season there are naturalist programs offered by park naturalists that include hikes, campfire activities, and nature activities. Brooks Memorial Arboretum is located on the park's grounds. At the lake there are paddleboat and rowboat rentals available. The lake covers 11 acres. Fishing is available with a valid West Virginia state fishing license, and you can fish for trout, bluegill, bass, and catfish. You can also fish, canoe, or kayak in the Greenbrier River, which runs alongside the park. There are two campgrounds from which to choose, Beaver Creek Campground and Riverside Campground. In the Riverside Campground there are fifty sites along the Greenbrier River; the Beaver Creek Campground is located closer to the park's entrance above the lake. Some sites are available for reservations with a minimum two-night stay. RV friendly. Senior discount available.

Watoga State Park Courtesy West Virginia Department of Commerce (www.wvcommerce .org)

124 Pocahontas Campground

Location: 14 miles south of Marlinton
Sites: 8 standard
Facilities: Vault toilets, fire rings, fire grills, picnic tables
Fee per night: $$
Management: USDA Forest Service / Monongahela National Forest / Marlinton Ranger District
Contact: (304) 799-4334; www.fs.usda.gov
Activities: Hiking, biking, fishing
Season: Open mid-March to end of November
Finding the campground: Take US 39 headed southeast. Turn right on SR 92 headed south. Follow it to the campground entrance.
GPS coordinates: 38.101642 / -79.967840
About the campground: This small campground in Monongahela National Forest has few campsites but does offer convenience of access to local hiking and biking trails. For mountain bikers this is an excellent access point to some very popular trails. Two trails begin right from the entrance of the campground, Two Lick Trail and Two Lick Bottom Trail. (It would be interesting to learn the history of how those names came about.) A couple of miles away from the campground, north on SR 92, is a picnic and recreation area called Rimel Area Trailhead and Picnic Area, from which you can access additional trails. Two seasonally stocked fishing spots are close by: Knapps Creek and the Greenbrier River. You must have the following for fishing here: a valid West Virginia state fishing license, a National Forest stamp, a Conservation stamp, and a trout stamp. A hand pump provides drinking water, and campsites are surrounded by beautiful pine trees. Sites are first come, first served. RV friendly.

New River / Greenbrier Valley Area

In the New River and Greenbrier Valley region in the southeastern section of the state, there are still plenty of mountains, but the terrain is different than in the south-central and southwestern section. If you are traveling east, you will begin to see hazy blue mountains in the distance. Over the state line into Virginia, the Blue Ridge

	Total Sites	Max. RV Length	Hookups	Fire Ring/Grill	Toilets	Showers	Drinking Water	Dump Station	Recreation	Fee ($)	Reservable
125 **Plum Orchard Lake Wildlife Management Area**	38			Y	F	N	Y	N	F, B, L	$$$	N
126 **Babcock State Park**	52	50	E	Y	F	Y	Y	Y	H, S, F, B, C, HB	$$$$	Y
127 **Little Beaver State Park**	46	40	E, W	Y	F	Y	Y	Y	H, F, B, C	$$$$	Y
128 **Lake Stephens Campground**	127		E, W, S	Y	P	Y	Y	N	H, S, F, B, C	$$$$	Y
129 **Twin Falls Resort State Park**	50		E	Y	F	Y	Y	Y	H, S, C	$$$$	Y
130 **Camp Creek State Park and State Forest**	38		E, W, S	Y	F, V, P	Y	Y	Y	H, F, C, HB	$$$–$$$$	Y
131 **Panther State Forest / Wildlife Management Area**	6		E	Y	P	N	Y	N	H, S, F	$$$	Y
132 **Berwind Lake Wildlife Management Area**	8		E, W	Y	V	N	Y	N	H, S, F, B, L	$$$	Y
133 **Pipestem Resort State Park**	82		E, W, S	Y	F	Y	Y	Y	H, S, F, B, C, HB	$$$$	Y
134 **Bluestone State Park**	76		E, W	Y	F	Y	Y	Y	H, F, B	$$$–$$$$	Y
135 **Bluestone Wildlife Management Area (WMA)**	330			Y	V	N	N	N	H, F, B, L, HB	$$$	Y
136 **Moncove Lake State Park**	48	40	E	Y	F	Y	Y	Y	H, S, F, B, L, C	$$$$	Y
137 **Greenbrier State Forest**	16		E	Y	F	Y	Y	N	H, S, C	$$$$	Y
138 **Blue Bend Recreation Area and Campground**	25			Y	F,V	Y	Y	N	H, S, F	$$$	Y
139 **Lake Sherwood Recreation Area and Campground**	104			Y	F,V	Y	Y	Y	H, S, F, B, L, C	$$$	Y

Max RV Length: Measured in feet
Hookups: W = Water, E = Electricity, S = Sewer
Fire Ring/Grill: Y = Yes, N = None
Toilets: F = Flush, P = Pit, V = Vault
Showers: Y = Yes, N = None
Drinking Water: Y = Yes, N = None
Dump Station: Y = Yes, N = None
Recreation: H = Hiking, S = Swimming, F = Fishing, B = Boating, L = Boat Launch, C = Cycling, HB = Horseback Riding, OHV = Off-Highway Vehicles
Fee: $ = 0–$5, $$ = $6–$10, $$$ = $11–$20, $$$$ = $21–$30+
Reservable: Y = Yes, N = No

New River/Greenbrier Valley Area

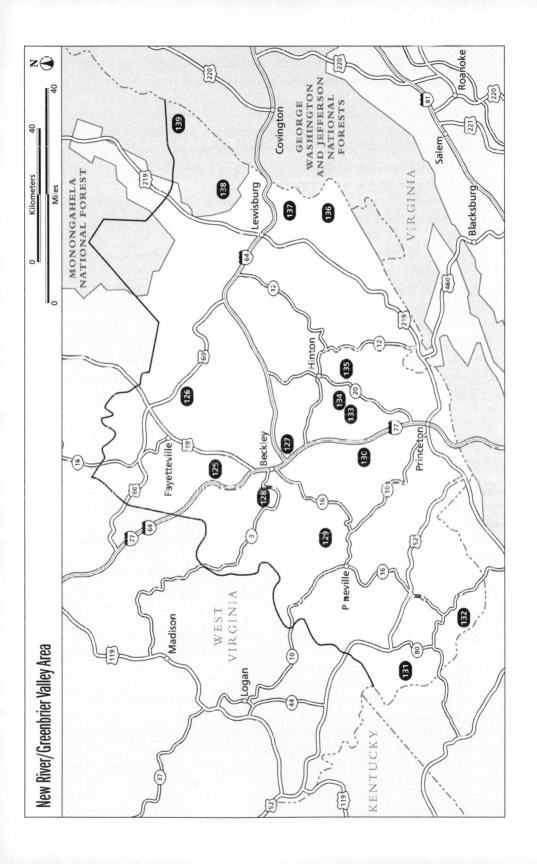

Mountains stretch to the west around the Roanoke area, spilling down into the Appalachian Valley on this western flank. The coloration is where the mountains got their name.

Here in this region you may notice that the mountains are more spread out, and it feels as if the vista widens considerably. There are pastures and wetlands. For example, if you travel east along I-65 toward Lewisburg on your way to Greenbrier State Forest, you will notice wetlands off the side of the highway, recognizable by the barren, stunted trees that jut up out of marshy water.

The Greenbrier River Trail begins in this region in Caldwell and travels north into Monongahela National Forest. It is a multiuse trail shared by cyclists, hikers, equestrians, and cross-country skiers.

In addition, the New River Gorge, New River, and the Gauley River provide tons of recreational opportunities. Canopy tours, zip lines, white-water rafting, rock climbing, hiking, biking, and many other outdoor offerings are there for the planning. The second biggest steel arch bridge in the world, also ranked the second highest in the country, spans the New River.

Located in this area is the Summit, or the Bechtel Family National Scout Reserve, a sprawling adventure center for the Boy Scouts of America. This is the location for the National Scout Jamboree; it also features a high-adventure base, a summer camp, and a leadership training center.

125 Plum Orchard Lake Wildlife Management Area

Location: 5 miles north of Pax
Sites: 38 tent only
Facilities: Flush toilets, fire grill, picnic tables, rowboat rentals, boat launch, rifle range
Fee per night: $$$
Management: West Virginia Division of Natural Resources
Contact: (304) 469-9905; https://wvtourism.com/company/plum-orchard-lake-wildlife -management-area/
Activities: Fishing, boating
Season: Open year-round
Finding the campground: From I-77 take either the Pax interchange, exit 54, or Mossy Interchange, exit 60, and follow Route 23 to the wildlife management area's entrance. (**Note:** The campground is not accessible from Route 19.)
GPS coordinates: 37.951512 / -81.232667
About the campground: The 40-foot-deep lake covers 202 acres located between Haystack Mountain and Packs Mountain, which provide a glorious backdrop to the lake. This wildlife management area covers more than 3,200 acres and is forested with a variety of mature oak and hickory trees. There are three boat launch ramps on the lake, and there are rowboat rentals available. Fish for bluegill, largemouth bass, catfish, and crappie. A fishing permit is required. Be aware that there is a restricted portion of the lake where only electric motors are allowed.

126 Babcock State Park

Location: 29 miles northeast of Beckley
Sites: 24 standard, 28 standard electric
Facilities: Flush toilets, showers, fire grills, picnic tables, dump station, laundry facility, gift shop, swimming pool, horseback-riding rentals, tennis court, volleyball court, basketball court, horseshoe pits, picnic shelters, playgrounds, naturalist programs, boat rentals
Fee per night: $$$$
Management: West Virginia State Parks & Forests
Contact: (304) 438-3004; (304) 438-3003 (reservations); (800) 225-5982; www.babcocksp.com
Activities: Hiking, biking, fishing, boating, canoeing, kayaking, swimming, tennis, horseback riding, cross-country skiing
Season: Mid-April through end of October (weather dependent)
Finding the campground: Take US 60 headed east. Take SR 41 south. Follow it through the town of Clifftop and to the campground entrance.
GPS coordinates: 38.005476 / -80.949327
About the campground: This state park covers more than 4,100 acres. Boley Lake is located within the park, spread across 19 acres and offering boating and fishing opportunities. You can rent a canoe, rowboat, or paddleboat from the marina. Fishing is also available in Glade Creek. Both the lake and the creek are stocked with trout. In addition, Boley Lake offers natives such as bass and bluegill. You must have a valid West Virginia state fishing license to fish in either the lake or the creek. Nine trails meander throughout the park. One, the Narrow Gauge Trail, has two swinging bridges. One interesting attraction is Glade Creek Grist Mill, a re-creation of a mill that once stood along the creek before the park came into existence. When the stream is running high enough for the mill to function and it is available, you can purchase freshly ground cornmeal. The nine trails total more than 20 miles, and distances range from 0.25 mile to 2.5 miles. Use caution: Some trails lead to overhangs and high cliffs. Bikes are allowed only on Narrow Gauge Trail, which has sections where you will need to dismount and carry your bike. Also, you can use the paved or graveled roads within the park. There are three trails that are good for cross-country skiing, but none is specifically maintained for that activity. When the campground is closed, the park roads are gated shut but provide a great skiing surface. There is also a swimming pool, and game courts are available for a small fee. Babcock Stables offers the opportunity to rent a horse and explore the park by horseback, and pony rides are available for kids. The trails, however, are not open to private horseback riding during the season while the stables are operating. A park naturalist provides programs that include tours, movies, sports, and campfire get-togethers. There are four accessible campsites at this location. About one-fourth of the campsites are reservable, and the rest are first come, first served. RV friendly up to 50 feet.

127 Little Beaver State Park

Location: 10 miles southeast of Beckley
Sites: 16 standard with water, 30 standard electric and water

Little Beaver State Park

Facilities: Flush toilets, showers, fire grills, picnic tables, playground, boat rental, camp store, laundry facility, picnic shelters, dump station

Fee per night: $$$$

Management: West Virginia State Parks & Forests

Contact: (304) 763-2494; (800) 225-5982; www.littlebeaverstatepark.com/camping

Activities: Hiking, biking, fishing, boating, geocaching

Season: March to November

Finding the campground: Take I-64 to CR 9 south toward Shady Spring (exit 129A). Take Grandview Road / CR 307. Follow it to the park entrance.

GPS coordinates: 37.755963 / -81.080308

About the campground: Newly opened in 2011, this park used to be day-use only. It is spread across 562 wooded acres featuring Little Beaver Lake. Visitors can now camp in addition to enjoying fishing or renting a paddleboat, rowboat, kayak, or stand-up paddleboard to explore its 18 acres. The lake offers trout, bass, crappie, channel cat, and bluegill. A valid West Virginia fishing license is required. There are eighteen trails from which to choose for hiking and biking. Stroll around the lake for an easy walk or select one of the very challenging trails, such as Crooked Rock Trail for hiking or Billy Goat's Gruff for mountain biking (the names give you a clue to their level of difficulty). Trails range in distance from 0.25 mile to 2.5 miles. The park is situated just south of Grandview National Park, which is part of the New River Gorge National River, a popular destination for white-water rafting. The closest main city, Beckley, has a unique offering called Tamarack right off I-64. Here West Virginia culture is showcased through the work of artisans, offering hand-made arts-and-crafts items and specialty foods. Twelve of the campsites are reservable, and the rest are first come, first served. RV friendly for vehicles up to 40 feet.

128 Lake Stephens Campground

Location: 9 miles west of Beckley
Sites: 27 standard, 100 RV-specific with water, electric, sewer
Facilities: Pit toilets, showers, fire rings, picnic tables, camp store, playground, picnic shelter, basketball courts, tennis courts, volleyball courts, skate park, paddleboat rentals, swimming beach, snack bar, marina
Fee per night: $$$$
Management: Raleigh County Recreation Authority
Contact: (304) 934-5323; (800) 786-8430; www.lakestephenswv.com/camping.aspx
Activities: Hiking, biking, swimming, boating, fishing
Season: Open May through end of October
Finding the campground: From I-64 and I-77 (parts of which require tolls in this area), take the exit for SR 3 headed west. Follow it to the park entrance.
GPS coordinates: 37.794547 / -81.300916
About the campground: The park sits alongside a 272-acre lake and is surrounded by forest. There is a marina on-site that offers rental docks for your boat. The park offers 20 miles of multi-use trails for hiking, biking, and horseback riding. There is a swimming beach for the lake, and a playground area in the RV park section. Rent a paddleboat at the concessionaire and explore the lake. You can also get snacks and drinks there, and if you want to spend time on the beach, there are shaded and sunny sites. In the tent campground area, you can have up to eight people and two tents on one site. If you have more people, you will need to get an additional site. RV friendly—there is a section specifically for RVs with pull-through sites. No tents are allowed in the RV park area. On the RV side you have flush toilets and showers (both of which are accessible to people with disabilities), a laundry facility, a playground, and a basketball court.

129 Twin Falls Resort State Park

Location: 23 miles southwest of Beckley
Sites: 25 standard, 25 standard electric
Facilities: Flush toilets, showers, fire grills, picnic tables, dump station, camp store, swimming pool, tennis court, game courts, playgrounds, picnic areas, picnic shelters, nature programs, gift shop, golf course, pro shop
Fee per night: $$$$
Management: West Virginia State Parks & Forests
Contact: (304) 294-4000; (800) 225-5982; www.twinfallsresort.com
Activities: Hiking, biking, swimming, golf, tennis
Season: Open year-round

Finding the campground: From I-64 and I-77 (parts of which require tolls in this area), take exit 42, Beckley and Robert C. Byrd Drive. Follow the road to the park entrance.

GPS coordinates: 37.636695 / -81.439710

About the campground: This state park is also a resort and covers close to 3,800 acres of beautiful mountains. For history buffs Pioneer Farm is a restored home, serving as a living history site that shows what similar homes and farms would have been like in the early 1800s. For hikers select from twelve different trails that wind through woods or to the two waterfalls, with some trails suitable for mountain bikers. As this is a resort, it would not be complete without an eighteen-hole golf course, which is open year-round, depending on the weather. It has a pro shop, where you can rent or purchase golf clubs, and you can also take lessons from a PGA Golf Pro. Nature programs are offered, from campfire activities to night hikes. You can use the swimming pool for a small fee, but **please note:** It is closed on Mondays and Wednesdays during the season. Campsites are spacious, and you have a choice between wooded and open sites. Half of the sites are available for advanced registration, the balance are first come, first served. RV friendly.

130 Camp Creek State Park and State Forest

Location: 29 miles south of Beckley, 20 miles north of Princeton

Sites: 12 rustic, tents only, 9 standard electric, 8 standard electric and water, 9 electric, water, and sewer

Facilities: Flush toilets, pit toilets, vault toilets, showers, fire grills, fire rings, picnic tables, wireless internet access, laundry facility, gift shop, amphitheater, picnic areas, playgrounds, basketball court, volleyball court, badminton court, horseshoe areas, dump station

Fee per night: $$$–$$$$

Management: West Virginia State Parks & Forests

Contact: (304) 425-9481; (800) 225-5982; www.campcreekstatepark.com

Activities: Hiking, biking, horseback riding, volleyball, badminton, basketball, horseshoes, fishing

Season: Open year-round (limited facilities November to April)

Finding the campground: Take I-77 (this section is part of West Virginia turnpike/toll road) to exit 20 / Camp Creek. Take US 19 south. Follow the signs to the park entrance.

GPS coordinates: 37.505312 / -81.133086

About the campground: Although the park is located close to a major interstate, it is tucked deep down in the woods so that you feel you're really secluded once you get there. With more than 5,500 acres of forest land and 500 park acres to explore, you will need to book a solid week of campsite time to do it all. (Be aware that hunting is allowed in the forest area during hunting season, so confirm with the park office what season it is when you arrive.) The park offers 40 miles of trails, with five trails devoted exclusively to hiking and eight trails that are multiuse, shared by hikers, mountain bikers, and equestrians. Select a trail that's 1 mile or the longest trail, which is 10 miles long, or combine a few and make your own trail. There are two waterfalls in this park: Mash Fork Falls and Campbell Falls. Mash Fork Falls Trail will give you a good workout with a steep climb that seems to go up and up. Trail posts are marked brown for the park and posts in the forest are marked green. In the forest area there are almost 35 miles for horseback riding. In addition, there are campsites accommodating horses available in the Double C campground, open May to December, that must be reserved in advance. There are only vault toilets in this section. There

Camp Creek State Park

is also a more primitive section that is tent only, the Blue Jay campground, which has pit toilets, a water fountain, and the regular site amenities such as fire rings, grills, and picnic tables. If you can't live without wireless access, opt for Mash Fork Campground, where you can get service for a small fee. Fishing is another recreational option, but you must have a West Virginia fishing license, which you can purchase at the park office. You can fish in one of several creeks, including Camp Creek and Bear Creek. RV friendly.

131 Panther State Forest / Wildlife Management Area

Location: 56 miles southeast of Williamson
Sites: 6 standard electric
Facilities: Pit toilets, fireplaces, picnic tables, well pump, picnic areas, picnic shelters, swimming pool, kiddie pool, volleyball court
Fee per night: $$$
Management: West Virginia Wildlife Management / West Virginia State Parks & Forests
Contact: (304) 938-2252; (800) 225-5982; www.pantherstateforest.com
Activities: Hiking, swimming, fishing, volleyball
Season: Open mid-April to October

Finding the campground: Take US 52 south and turn at the sign for Panther. Look for the Panther Post Office, then turn left at the sign. Follow this road to the park entrance.

GPS coordinates: 37.414511 / -81.880953

About the campground: This heavily wooded area, the southernmost forest in the state, covers more than 7,800 acres and is located in a rugged area near the border with Kentucky and Virginia, which are just to the south. Sites are more rustic than most, but the park does offer amenities, such as a swimming pool with a view of the mountains, making a gorgeous setting for swimming and relaxing. There is also a kiddie pool suitable for small children. Fishing is available in Panther Creek, which is stocked with trout during the spring. There are also hiking trails available that are mostly interconnecting with some that will take you to overlooks for breathtaking scenery. The campground has a hand pump you can use for obtaining water. RV friendly.

132 Berwind Lake Wildlife Management Area

Location: 54 miles southwest of Princeton

Sites: 6 standard, 2 standard electric and water

Facilities: Fire grills, vault toilets, picnic tables, picnic areas, picnic shelters, playground, swimming pool, boat rental, fishing pier, boat ramp

Fee per night: $$$

Management: West Virginia Wildlife Management / West Virginia State Parks & Forests

Contact: (304) 875-2577; (800) 225-5982; https://wvtourism.com/company/berwind-lake-wildlife-management-area/

Activities: Hiking, fishing, swimming, boating

Season: Open year-round

Finding the campground: Take I-77 south toward Princeton. Take exit 9, US 460 headed west. You will actually cross the state line into Virginia headed toward Tazewell before taking exit 2 for SR 16 north to go back into West Virginia. When you reach the town of War, on the outside of the city you will come to a bridge: Make a left turn onto the bridge. Follow this to the campground entrance.

GPS coordinates: 37.256014 / -81.685688

About the campground: This is now one of the smaller wildlife management areas in the state, covering just 93 acres. It was once more than 18,000 acres before a management lease expired and had not been renewed as of this writing. It is in an area with rugged terrain at the most southern tip of the state, thick with forest growth. Berwind Lake WMA features a lake covering 20 acres where you can fish and boat. Electric motorboats are permitted, but no gas-powered boats. Fish for bluegill, channel catfish, largemouth bass, and trout. The lake is stocked annually. There is a fishing pier, which is accessible. In addition, there's a path that goes around the lake from which to fish. You must have a valid West Virginia state fishing license. The swimming pool is available for a small admission fee and has bathhouses and a snack bar. *Please note:* It is closed on Mondays and Tuesdays. There are three trails available for hiking through the forested area. One of the campsites is accessible to people with disabilities. RV friendly.

133 Pipestem Resort State Park

Location: 14 miles north of Princeton, 12 miles south of Hinton
Sites: 32 standard, 19 standard electric, 31 standard electric, water, and sewer
Facilities: Flush toilets, showers, fire grills, picnic tables, dump station, camp store, playground, picnic shelters, Olympic-size swimming pool, horseback-ride rentals, aerial tramway, amphitheater, miniature golf, tennis courts, golf courses and pro shop, archery range, horseshoe pit, basketball courts, boat rental, bike rentals, gift shops, restaurant, snack bar, nature center
Fee per night: $$$$
Management: West Virginia State Parks & Forests
Contact: (304) 466-1800; (800) 225-5982; www.pipestemresort.com
Activities: Hiking, biking, swimming, fishing, boating, cross-country skiing, sledding, volleyball, basketball, horseshoes, golf, miniature golf, archery, concerts, nature programs, horseback riding
Season: Open year-round
Finding the campground: Take I-77 to exit 14 for SR 20 headed north. Follow it to the campground entrance.
GPS coordinates: 37.533866 / -80.994726
About the campground: This state park is a true resort, with lodges, restaurants, golf courses, and gift shops on-site. Located next to Bluestone Wildlife Management Area, it is next to the Bluestone River Gorge and offers more than 4,000 acres of mountainous splendor to behold. The park also offers an abundance of trail options—twenty total—for hiking, biking, cross-country skiing, and horseback riding. For horseback riding, there are horse stables that offer guided rides year-round. Look for the native Pipestem bush, which the park is named for. Back in the olden days, the hollow stems of this plant were used in making clay and corncob pipes. For help in identification of that and other plant and animal species, visit the Nature Center. Next to it is Harris Homestead, which has been reconstructed from the original early 1900s structure that included a house and barn. The park naturalist offers family-friendly activities that include nature and history learning programs, orienteering, bird walks, campfires, and crafts. The amphitheater offers concerts for a small fee during the season. Trails range in length and difficulty from less than 0.5 mile to more than 5 miles. Some trails are strictly for hikers, while others are multiuse and allow hikers, bikers, and equestrians. Trails interconnect in many spots, but be sure to have a trail map with you from the park office. You can rent a bike from the golf pro shop on-site. Take a short but strenuous hike up to Bolar Lookout Tower and take in the park from a 3,000-foot vantage point. Another way to see the area from above is by taking a ride on the aerial tramway, which goes across the Bluestone River Gorge and provides a stunning view. It is open May to October. During the colder months, make use of the seven trails suitable for cross-country skiing when there is snow on the ground. Or go sledding. You can rent equipment from the pro shop. There are two golf courses: One is an eighteen-hole course, the other is a par 3 course. Both courses also have driving ranges, and you can take lessons from a PGA Golf Pro. For water amenities Long Branch Lake covers 16 acres where you can fish for trout and smallmouth bass. Or rent a canoe or paddleboat to explore the water. Bluestone River is another fishing option, and the New River is nearby. You need a valid West Virginia state fishing license. If you get tired of cooking out, there is a restaurant located in McKeever Lodge, and the snack bar offers pizza and sandwiches. The swimming pool is open during the season, but *please note:* It is closed on Mondays and Wednesdays. There is also a heated

indoor pool. For both pools there is a small fee for admission. You also can elect to use one of the many game courts or practice your archery skills at the range. Go over to the stables and get a guided horseback tour or sign up for a hayride. This is one of those campgrounds where you just may not have enough time to do it all. About half the campsites are available for reservations, but you will need to reserve a minimum of two nights. The rest of the sites are first come, first served. Some sites are accessible to people with disabilities. RV friendly. Senior discounts available.

134 Bluestone State Park

Location: 22 miles southeast of Beckley
Sites: 44 rustic—tents or trailer, 10 standard, 15 standard with electric, 7 standard electric and water
Facilities: Flush toilets, fire rings, showers, laundry facility, picnic shelters, dump station, gift shop, swimming pool, game room

Bluestone State Park

Fee per night: $$$-$$$$
Management: West Virginia State Parks & Forests
Contact: (304) 466-2805; (800) 225-5982; www.bluestonesp.com
Activities: Hiking, fishing, boating, waterskiing
Season: Early May to late October
Finding the campground: Take I-64 (toll road) to SR 20, exit 139 south toward Sandstone / Hinton. Follow the road to the park entrance.
GPS coordinates: 37.617785 / -80.938614
About the campground: The campground is situated next to the beautiful Bluestone Lake, which covers 2,000 acres and is the state's second-largest body of water. There are several hiking trails from which to choose, including Big Pine Trail, a circuit path, and River View Trail, where you can see stream, lake, and waterfall all in one trek. You may want to choose to spend all your time on or in the water, either in the swimming pool or the lake itself. Bluestone Marina rents a range of boats, from fishing and pontoon boats to more recreational offerings such as paddleboats, rowboats, and canoes. For fishing enthusiasts, the lake offers largemouth bass, smallmouth bass, striped bass, and hybrid bass, as well as bluegill, crappie, and catfish. Or bring water skis and see how far across the lake you can make it. As for camping after a full day out on the water or on the trails, the more primitive campground, Old Mill, allows either tents or trailers. While there are shower facilities, they are cold water only. Meador campground allows tents and RVs and offers hot showers. The majority of sites are first come, first served, but eighteen of the sites are reservable. Because the campground areas are located in the flood storage basin for Bluestone Lake, water levels could potentially affect availability. Situated just north of Bluestone Wildlife Management Area. It is very easy to get a little lost on the back roads once you're off the main route, so take your time and make sure of your direction.

135 Bluestone Wildlife Management Area (WMA)

Location: Just south of Bluestone State Park
Sites: 330 primitive
Facilities: Fire grills, vault toilets, playground, picnic areas, shooting range, archery range, boat launches
Fee per night: $$$
Management: West Virginia Wildlife Management / West Virginia State Parks & Forests
Contact: (304) 466-3398; (800) 225-5982; www.bluestonewma.com
Activities: Hiking, fishing, boating, canoeing, kayaking, shooting, archery, horseback riding
Season: Open year-round
Finding the campground: Take I-64 (toll road) to SR 20, exit 139 south toward Sandstone / Hinton. Follow the road to the park entrance.
GPS coordinates: 37.541066 / -80.812486
About the campground: This wildlife management area covers an astounding 18,000 acres located next to Bluestone Lake, the second largest in the state. Bluestone State Park is adjacent to the wildlife management area just to the north. Nonreservable campsites are available first come, first served, and you can check in and pay at the check-in booth. Horses are permitted

on-site, and you can rent stable space. You can fish in the lake, Indian Creek, or on the New River with a valid West Virginia state fishing license. The creek is stocked with trout. The lake offers large-mouth and smallmouth bass, striped bass, catfish, muskie, and panfish. Bring a canoe, kayak, or other boat, as there are six launch ramps but no rentals available within the wildlife management area. Choose from multiple hiking and horseback-riding trails covering 22 miles for exploring this beautiful area. Campsites are spread across seven different campgrounds that are scattered across the park. There are sites next to the lake as well as beside the New River. RV friendly. Senior discounts available.

136 Moncove Lake State Park

Location: 15 miles south of White Sulphur Springs
Sites: 14 standard, 34 standard electric
Facilities: Flush toilets, showers, fire grills, picnic tables, dump station, swimming pool, boat rentals, boat ramp, playgrounds, game courts, picnic areas, picnic shelters
Fee per night: $$$$
Management: West Virginia State Parks & Forests
Contact: (304) 772-3450; (800) 225-5982; www.moncovelakestatepark.com
Activities: Hiking, biking, fishing, swimming, boating, bird watching
Season: Mid-April to October
Finding the campground: Take I-64 east toward Lewisburg. Take US 219 south toward Union. Take SR 3 to Gap Mills, then take a left headed northbound on CR 8. Follow it to the campground entrance.
GPS coordinates: 37.621771 / -80.352964
About the campground: This park is spread across almost 900 acres and includes a Wildlife Management Area, and also features 144-acre Moncove Lake. The lake provides a great opportunity for casting a line for catfish, trout, largemouth bass, and bluegill and is also stocked with walleye. Fishing in the lake requires a valid West Virginia state fishing license. You can also rent a rowboat or paddleboat to explore the lake. Motorboats are permitted, but the motor must meet the requirement of less than five horsepower. A boat ramp is provided. There is no swimming allowed in the lake, but there is a swimming pool on-site, and *please note:* It is closed on Mondays and Wednesdays. There are five trails from which to choose to explore the park, ranging up to 2 miles in length and up to moderately difficult terrain. You can also access the Allegheny Trail, which is located nearby and runs along Peter's Mountain, where it meets up with the Appalachian Trail, offering miles and miles of additional hiking. Follow the Allegheny Trail up to Hanging Rock Tower for a view from the top of Peter's Mountain. The Greenbrier River Trail is also nearby and is very popular among cycling enthusiasts. This area is big for birding due to the ridge formations of the Appalachian Mountains, which create a byway for migrating birds. Peter's Mountain has been the location of numerous hawk sightings, particularly in September and October during their fall migration, as well as sightings of a host of migrating birds that are unusual and not indigenous to the area. All campsites are first come, first served. Located near Greenbrier State Forest. RV friendly up to 40 feet. Senior discount available.

137 Greenbrier State Forest

Location: 15 miles southeast of Lewisburg
Sites: 16 standard with electric
Facilities: Flush toilets, showers, fire pit/grill, picnic area, picnic shelters, playground, archery range, muzzleloader range, disc golf, volleyball, swimming pool
Fee per night: $$$$
Management: West Virginia State Parks & Forests
Contact: (304) 536-1944; (800) 225-5982; www.greenbriersf.com
Activities: Hiking, biking, swimming, volleyball, disc golf, archery, shooting, horseshoes
Season: Mid-April to end of November
Finding the campground: Take I-65 east toward Lexington to exit 175 toward US 60 / White Sulphur Springs. Turn left onto Harts Run Road. Turn right onto US 60. Turn right onto CR 60 and follow it to the park entrance.
GPS coordinates: 37.753378 / -80.352790
About the campground: This park in the southeast region of the state is right down the road from the Virginia state line to its east. It is just south of White Sulphur Springs, where a National Historic Landmark and one of the most luxurious resorts, the Greenbrier Resort, is located. Within the park there is a heated swimming pool available. There are several picnic areas, with some that are accessible. There are 13 miles of trails leading visitors throughout the forest and also forest management roads suitable for hiking and biking enthusiasts. Trails range from a 1-mile fitness trail to an almost 8-mile strenuous hike option. Since many of the trails cross one another, you can create your own trail options to shorten or lengthen distance. Also, the Greenbrier River Trail begins near the park, offering more than 70 miles of biking, hiking, and in the winter, cross-country skiing. If you like to fish, head over to Greenbrier River for smallmouth bass or select a stream or lake for trout, walleye, crappie, catfish, smallmouth and largemouth bass, and bluegill. You will need a valid West Virginia fishing license. RV friendly.

138 Blue Bend Recreation Area and Campground

Location: 12 miles northeast of White Sulphur Springs
Sites: 21 standard, 4 walk-to sites
Facilities: Flush toilets, vault toilets, showers, fire grates, picnic tables, picnic areas
Fee per night: $$$
Management: USDA Forest Service / Monongahela National Forest / White Sulphur Ranger District
Contact: (304) 536-2144; (877) 444-6777; www.fs.usda.gov
Activities: Hiking, swimming, fishing
Season: Early March to end of November
Finding the campground: Take I-64 headed east. Turn left onto SR 92 going north. Take a left on CR 16/2 headed west. Follow it to the recreation area and campground entrance.
GPS coordinates: 37.920410 / -80.270895
About the campground: Situated next to Anthony Creek, which you can swim in and fish for trout that are stocked during the first part of the year and again in the fall. The Greenbrier River is

nearby and offers both trout and bass. To fish you should have a valid West Virginia state fishing license, a Conservation stamp, and National Forest stamp, and if you fish for trout, you will need a trout stamp as well. For hikes you can take the Beaver's Tale Interpretive Trail, which is a very short distance. Or venture out on the Blue Bend Loop Trail, which is 5 miles in length and leads to scenic overlooks. It connects to Anthony Creek Trail, which follows the creek, adding another almost 4 miles to your hike. Fresh drinking water is supplied through hand pumps during spring and fall, and vault toilets are all that is open. Running water is available during the summer and flush toilets are available. Campsites are wooded and reservable. RV friendly and can accommodate larger vehicles.

139   Lake Sherwood Recreation Area and Campground

Location: 27 miles northeast of White Sulphur Springs
Sites: 104 standard
Facilities: Flush toilets, vault toilets, showers, fire grills, picnic tables, picnic shelters, playground, picnic area, dump station, boat ramp, fishing pier, swimming beaches, volleyball courts, amphitheater, boat rental
Fee per night: $$$
Management: USDA Forest Service / Monongahela National Forest / White Sulphur Ranger District
Contact: (304) 536-2144; (877) 444-6777; www.fs.usda.gov
Activities: Hiking, biking, swimming, fishing, boating, volleyball
Season: Early March to end of November
Finding the campground: Take I-64 headed east. Turn left onto SR 92 going north. Take a right on SR 14 headed east. Follow it to the recreation area and campground entrance.
GPS coordinates: 38.006346 / -80.010872
About the campground: This campground is located in the farthest southern reach in Monongahela National Forest. Lake Sherwood has the distinction of being the largest lake within the forest area and is beautifully surrounded by mountains and lush pine trees. The campground provides plenty of family-friendly amenities. There is a boat ramp, so head out and explore the 165-acre lake. You can rent a boat or a canoe from the on-site concessionaire. Only electric motors are permitted on the lake. If you like to fish, the lake offers plenty of variety: bullhead, bluegill, tiger muskie, channel catfish, and largemouth bass. You will need a valid West Virginia state fishing license. For hiking there are several trails from which to choose. One is more than 3 miles in length, goes around the lake, and is also suitable for mountain bikes. Longer hiking trails include Lake Sherwood-Allegheny Mountain Loop and Meadow Creek Trail. With two swimming beaches to choose from, you should not feel too crowded during the warmer months. One of the beaches is located on an island and reachable by a footbridge. There are no lifeguards, so use caution. Showers and flush toilets depend on running water, which is available only during the summer season. During the off-season, in spring and fall, there are vault toilets and hand pumps that supply fresh drinking water. The campground is divided into several loops with some sites overlooking the lake. RV friendly.

Camping Etiquette

You are on vacation, yes, but there are some things to know to make sure you are a good neighbor. Just think: A potentially bad neighbor could be reading this right now and taking notes, and you will never realize what I have saved you from. So, any of the following may not pertain to you, but surely it applies to someone because these things have a way of cropping up in people's relatively small list of campground complaints. You rarely hear of anyone complaining about the scenery: It is your neighbors that can detract from the experience.

One of my favorite camping etiquette situations was while camping at one of the state parks. (I won't mention the name, because it is not the park's fault and I would not want anyone unfairly disparaged.) It's funny in hindsight. Arriving at the park after a long drive and still in "go" mode, I usually need at least a full evening to decompress and move into camping, slow-your-pace mode. Unfortunately, a campsite neighbor's idea of relaxing was having his radio going, and it was loud enough to drown out any sounds of wildlife or the nearby stream. The gentleman in question was also apparently having a few happy-hour cocktails while he cooked and did his camp thing. It wasn't until some hours had gone by, and my nerves were really frazzled, that the music was finally turned off. Probably around the "quiet" hour of well past dark. So finally, the sounds of nature.

Until I am awakened from a fitful slumber (it also takes me a night to get used to sleeping soundly in my tent) by someone groaning and what sounds like thrashing inside of his tent. I am feeling very nervous at this point and thinking this gentleman must be quite in his cups, and if he comes anywhere near my tent, I will explain his unconscious body to the park ranger in the morning. The scratching and groaning goes on until he finally locates his tent's zipper and the loud "rip" of its being opened probably can be heard throughout the otherwise silent campground. I hear him crashing through the area just outside of his tent, heading away from it. I am ready to pounce if need be, but I soon learn his intention. Another zipper sound, then the sound of a human "stream" and very loud moans of relief.

The moral of the story? There are so many, where do we begin?

First, campgrounds all have their own policies about alcohol possession and consumption. When in doubt, ask. For example, in West Virginia's state parks, disturbances, disorderly conduct, and public drunkenness are against the rules. And, it is just being a good camp neighbor to not drink to excess or to the point where you are unable to locate your tent's zipper in the wee hours of the night. Plus, it saves you from having a little water accident in your sleeping area.

Also, you may enjoy your music, but that does not necessarily mean your one hundred new neighbors necessarily do. People camp for many reasons, but some of the reasons most often cited are "getting away from it all," "enjoying the sounds of nature," and "the peace and quiet." This does not mean you have to observe

Bluestone State Park

no music or television—just be mindful of the neighbors. Or if you are a music lover, treat yourself to a stay at one of the campgrounds that has an amphitheater where you can catch a concert. Check with the campground and see what is in the lineup. All campgrounds have rules governing quiet hours, usually between the hours of 10 p.m. and 7 a.m., and of course excessive noise is considered "prohibited" at all times.

Other good etiquette guidelines include cleaning up after yourself by picking up any trash that is dropped, disposing of your trash quickly so wild animals are not unnecessarily drawn into the camp area, and storing food appropriately for the same reason.

I am a proponent of "Leave No Trace," an outdoor awareness movement that has seven principles or ethical guidelines to minimize impact for anyone venturing outside. The Leave No Trace organization encourages passing along these seven principles:

- Plan ahead and prepare.
- Travel and camp on durable surfaces.
- Dispose of waste properly.
- Leave what you find.

- Minimize campfire impacts.
- Respect wildlife.
- Be considerate of other visitors.

The member-driven Leave No Trace Center for Outdoor Ethics teaches people how to enjoy the outdoors responsibly. Learn more about Leave No Trace and further details at www.LNT.org.

Camping with Kids

Camping is fun, but you may have to convince the kids of that first, especially if they are used to being hooked into electronics all day and night. If you are traveling by RV, this may not be a problem, but many parents prefer their kids enjoy at least some of the outdoor experience.

For some kids, you may need to do a little sales pitch to get them excited for the trip. Talk about the amenities at the campground where you are going, or have them help select the campground. One caveat: If your camping vacation depends on a specific amenity such as a swimming pool, call the park before you make your final plans so you do not have a disappointed child on your hands.

If possible, pack bikes. Even if you have no plans to go ride on a trail, most parks provide paved or graveled roads for kids to ride around the vicinity of your campsite and farther out around the campground. Bring bike helmets for the kids, because there are different laws on the books, so better to be safe than sorry.

Many campgrounds include at least a playground. If there is a stream area, kids can enjoy exploring, but I recommend you keep a close eye on kids around any water. Wet rocks can make for some slippery surfaces, and kids do not realize this until they go down. Also, some waterways may look deceptively slow on the surface but have very swift currents running just beneath that can quickly take the legs out even from under adults, let alone kids.

Include the kids in the camp chores such as gathering wood, preparing food, and cleaning up. These chores, for some reason, do not seem as "chore" like when done in the outdoors, so maybe Mom and/or Dad can get a little break.

Speaking of camp foods, I think s'mores were invented to lure kids into camping trips by their parents. With treats like that promised for the campground, it just may be your winning pitch. Other foods to consider include making popcorn over the campfire or wrapping baking potatoes in foil and placing them near the hot embers. You can also grill hot dogs on a stick. You never know what will excite a child, but for some it may be the thought of choosing their own cooking stick.

Younger kids: Everyone has to go through their "first" camping experience, and for anyone, the earlier the better. Little kids are naturals for camping, because most of them love to go outside and play. The idea of camping in a tent will be considered a huge adventure. As bold and courageous as the little folks may be, though, when the lights go out above, it is a good idea to let them have some sort of light source for

Water recreational opportunities at Douthat State Park

comfort. Dark is really dark in the majority of campgrounds, something not experienced in city areas if that is where you are traveling from. This quality of darkness makes for great stargazing but may test the fear threshold for children. I remember for my son's first camping trip, I let him hold the lantern. I can still picture him clutching it in front of him as we sat in a group and talked. Be careful giving kids flashlights without the instruction of "keep it pointed at the ground," or no doubt you will experience being blinded when the beam is accidentally pointed in your face.

Older kids: It is the birthright of many older kids to complain about family trips in general, especially one where they will be away from friends, home-style amenities, and potentially electronics and phones. Many areas will have weak, if any, phone service, as cell towers are often far away from remote areas. If the children are bringing some type of handheld electronic devices, pack spare batteries, or instead of enjoying the sounds of nature, you will experience the joys of their nagging you to drive to the nearest store selling batteries.

Safety Tips

Even if you are traveling with your entire immediate family, it is always a good idea to let someone know where you are going. This is why I have listed as in-depth

Mountain mist

information as possible regarding who manages each campground. Especially under the Forest Service listings, you will note that the management area has several names, including the forest where the campground is located, the district that manages that region, and any concessionaire-type management entities that may handle things for the district. This is so, in case of emergency, you can be reached more quickly, or if you are calling for help, you can help pinpoint which area you are in. A lot of these locations can be quite remote, so the more information you have and can give to others, the better. Just in case.

I recommend you travel with some type of first-aid kit to treat cuts and other minor medical issues that can crop up. You can purchase a kit that is already put together from a sporting goods store, and even many store pharmacies will carry them. Or put your own kit together and be sure to include items for treating scrapes, cuts, headaches, allergic reactions, etc.

Ticks are more than a nuisance as are mosquitoes. Both carry nasty things, with deer ticks responsible for transmitting Lyme disease and mosquitoes transmitting West Nile virus. The best thing you can do to protect yourself is have a good defense in place: long shirts, pants, and everything tucked in to make it more difficult for ticks, especially, to gain entrance. Ticks especially seem to like scalp areas where they can hide in your hair, as well as other, shall we say, "more delicate" areas.

You can also use some sort of insect repellent that fends off ticks and mosquitoes. Just follow the instructions.

When you are around streams, rivers, waterfalls, etc., exercise caution. Rocks can be very slippery with algae, or just because they are wet. Of course, the water is tempting and looks inviting, and the rocks can look deceptively safe—until your feet go out from under you.

About the Author

Desiree Smith-Daughety is also the author of *OPM: Using Other People's Money to Get Rich*, a book geared toward entrepreneurs. Smith-Daughety is a freelance writer specializing in business, lifestyle, and health topics, with articles appearing in *Up.St. ART Annapolis* magazine, *What's Up? Annapolis* magazine, and others. Additionally, she owns a career-coaching company (intrepidcareerservices.com). For fun and adventure, she loves to camp, hike, bike, and kayak. The outdoors inspires her writing, as demonstrated by her personal writing website, dlarasmith.com. She can be reached at desireesmith@verizon.net.